THE CHRONICLES OF

WHOLESOME ENTERTAINMENT OR GATEWAY TO PAGANISM?

To contact the authors, please write or call:

Dr. Douglas D. Stauffer
P.O. Box 1611, Millbrook, AL 36054
1-866-344-1611
e-mail: dougstauffer@rightlydivided.com.

Dr. Larry Spargimino
P.O. Box 100, Bethany, OK 73008
1-800-652-1144
e-mail: larry@swrc.com.

Printed in the United States of America

ISBN 1-933641-11-8

THE CHRONICLES OF

WHOLESOME ENTERTAINMENT OR GATEWAY TO PAGANISM?

Trading Biblical Absolutes for Pagan Myths

Dr. Douglas Stauffer, Ph.D.
Dr. Larry Spargimino, Ph.D.

Contents

Introduction

In this volume the authors will examine the life, works, and influence of C. S. Lewis (1898–1963). This is no mere academic exercise. For years Lewis has been held in high esteem in the college and seminary classrooms. Now, however, he is coming into the hearts of a another generation of unsuspecting people worldwide by virtue of the new movie, *The Lion, The Witch and the Wardrobe*, and its scheduled sequels.[1]

While most evangelicals are overjoyed at Lewis' growing popularity, we have some concerns regarding what Lewis really believed and taught. Issues that have *not* been adequately addressed. As a practical matter, we should always examine what an author stood for prior to endorsing his works and helping to expand his influence.

According to many people who knew Lewis personally, he would be very disturbed if he knew that American evangelicals now claim him as one of their own. Lewis was quite un-evangelical in many respects. Lewis' best biographer and longtime friend, George Sayer, mentioned in his biography of Lewis that:

> … after I had been taught by him for three years, it never entered my mind that he could one day become an author whose books would sell at the rate of about two million copies a year. Since **he never spoke of religion** while I was his pupil, or until we had become friends 15 years later, **it would seem incredible that he would become the means of bringing many back to the Christian faith.**[2]

---

1 Walden and Disney studios are already developing the first Narnia sequel, *Prince Caspian*.

2 Quoted by Ted Olsen, "Apologetics: C.S. Lewis," *Christianity Today* (1/1/2000). Bold type supplied by authors for emphasis throughout this book.

Every discerning Christian should be quite disturbed to find out about Lewis' total lack of interest in evangelizing the lost. James Houston, an Oxford University lecturer for twenty-three years, said that Lewis "had no cultural connections with Evangelicals. . . . **His friends were all Anglo-Catholic or Catholic.** . . . Lewis, of course, has been adopted by the Evangelicals in America in a way that would have made him very uncomfortable. He didn't associate with them; he didn't think of himself as one of them."[3]

It is comments like this that raise many questions in our minds. Are these comments true? They certainly would seem to be, coming, as they do from those who knew Lewis quite well. Our purpose was to find out whether these statements were true or false. Hence, this book, which is an effort to investigate the individual who has now become somewhat of an icon among American evangelicals, as well as others.

We believe that we have scriptural warrant for such an investigation. The Bible commands us to "prove all things; hold fast that which is good. Abstain from all appearance of evil."[4]

"But Wasn't Lewis a Great Apologist?"

Assuredly, there are some commendable statements in Lewis' writings. A classic statement that will warm the heart of every Christian is found in his immensely popular book *Mere Christianity,* where Lewis challenges those who claim that Jesus was merely a "good man." Lewis writes:

> We are faced with a frightening alternative. The man we are talking about either was (and is) just what He said or else a lunatic, or something worse. Now it seems to me obvious that He was neither a lunatic nor a fiend: and consequently, how-ever strange or terrifying or unlikely it may seem, I have to accept the view that He was and is God. God has landed on this enemy-occupied world in human form.[5]

---

3   James Houston, "Reminiscences of the Oxford Lewis," in *We Remember C. S. Lewis: Essays and Memoirs,* David Graham, editor, (Nashville: Broadman and Holman, 2001), p. 136.

4   1 Thessalonians 5:21–22.

5   C. S. Lewis, *Mere Christianity* (Harper, SanFrancisco, 1952), p 53.

We must surely agree with Lewis. Anyone who would claim, as did Jesus, that He is the Son of God and that a person's relationship to God depends on that person's relationship to Himself, must be accepted as God or rejected as an outright madman. Yet, Lewis also gives some surprisingly bad counsel, in the same volume, regarding how a person becomes a Christian.

In chapter five of *Mere Christianity*, entitled "The Practical Conclusion," Lewis writes

> In Christ a new kind of man appeared: and the new kind of life which began in Him is to be put into us. How is this done?"
>
> Now, please remember how we acquired the old, ordinary kind of life. We derived it from others, from our father and mother and all of our ancestors, without our consent—and a very curious process, involving pleasure, pain, and danger. A process you would never have guessed. Most of us spend a good many years in childhood trying to guess it: and some children, when they are first told, do not believe it—and I am not sure that I blame them, for it is very odd. **Now the God who arranged that process is the same God who arranges how the new kind of life—the Christ life—is to be spread.** We must be prepared for it being odd too. He did not consult us when He invented sex: He has not consulted us either when He invented this.
>
> **There are three things that spread the Christ-life to us: baptism,** belief and that mysterious action which different Christians call by different names—**Holy Communion, the Mass, the Lord's Supper.** At least, those are the three ordinary methods. And I am not saying anything about which of these three things is the most essential.[6]

Lewis first defines this "Christ-life" and then goes on to name three things that confer this new life upon an individual. It is inconceivable that Lewis would be hailed by evangelicals after including baptism and the Mass, along with believing, as the means to becoming a Christian!

---

6 Ibid., pp. 60–61.

Throughout this volume we will give many lengthy quotes to defuse the charge that we are somehow taking Lewis out of context. We do not want to portray ourselves as somehow speaking with some official unction that makes our testimony compelling. We are simply presenting information that we have discovered—and which others can also read—that is being ignored by mainstream evangelicalism.

A Better Way for Reaching the Lost?

Most people are aware of the evangelistic claims made by the producers and promoters of the most recent Hollywood productions, such as Mel Gibson's *Passion* movie. This Hollywood extravaganza helped Christians justify looking to Hollywood and its costly moviemaking apparatus for mass evangelization rather than remaining dependent upon God and His Word.

No doubt some people will be annoyed by what they perceive to be an audacious challenge set forth in this book. Can all of the spiritual gurus proclaiming the apologetic and evangelistic potential of fantasy and Hollywood moviemaking be wrong? Hasn't the twenty-first century church finally found the cure-all for evangelizing the lost while also relieving the individual Christian of the inconveniences and challenges of personal witnessing?

Karen Long writing for the *Times Picayune* characterized the present Hollywood-driven thrust quite well. "The new movie [*The Lion, the Witch and the Wardrobe*] arrives at a culturally pregnant moment. Detractors are hoping it tanks. Some believers are praying that the bliss Lewis found in Christianity—he was the past century's most famous convert from atheist to Anglican—**begets a new come-to-Jesus momentum.**"[7]

There is no doubt that some good can come from any situation, but the *ends* should never be used to justify the *means* of getting results when our methods fall outside biblical bounds. To do so would be to fall into the pit of crass pragmatism. Long continues the article, further revealing the gross hypocrisy of the situation. "The divisions are so pitched that the movie soundtrack comes in two versions: rock-tinged music for the secularist and

---

7   Karen R. Long, "With 'Narnia,' C. S. Lewis Becomes Part of the Culture Wars," *Times-Picayune*. www. Nola.com/movies/t-p/index.ssf?/base/entertainment-0/1134109941218830.xml

Christian-influenced tunes for the believer."[8]

Hollywood[9] has certainly hired some high-dollar, well-qualified publicists to dupe those who should know better. Should Christians be that desperate that they are grasping for every new-fangled evangelistic gimmick that comes from the West Coast?

Hollywood consistently ignored the Christian market when the Christian market had enough sense not to support its perverse immorality. Hollywood has always supported and promoted profanity, nudity, drunkenness, violence, and every kind of sexual sin. Along with these moral deficiencies it has always presented a perverted picture of Christ and His gospel. At every turn it has ridiculed the Bible and the true believer. Now all of a sudden it has become the great purveyor of truth in the eyes of many and the Christian community comes crawling with filthy lucre in hand to fund the next evangelistic project!

The *Los Angeles Times* quoted Paul Lauer, whose Motive Entertainment orchestrated the *Passion* campaign: "While the Hollywood-church bond was strained at times, it ebbed and flowed over the years. The commercial success of "The Passion" increased studio openness to the church-based audience. . . ."[10]

For Shame! As Christians have continued to move away from a Bible–believing, God-honoring position, they have increasingly lost their sense of spiritual discernment. The degenerating world condition mirrors the severe drought of spiritually discerning Christians. "But the natural man receiveth not the things of the Spirit of God: for they are foolishness unto him: neither can he know them, because they are **spiritually discerned. But he that is spiritual judgeth all things**, yet he himself is judged of no man."[11]

Truly spiritual Christians judge all things!

---

8   Ibid.

9   Hollywood is meant to be a generic term for the movie making industry.

10   Elaine Dutka, "'The Lion, the Witch,' the Faithful," *Los Angeles Times*, (10/5/05). http://pewforum.org/news/display.php?NewsID=5458

11   1 Corinthians 2:14–15.

A Call To Parents and Pastors

Parents concerned with the influences upon their children should examine everything by the Word of God. In this case, that would mean that we should scrutinize Lewis' life, his work, his associations, and his influences in the light of truth. It is no sin to be discerning, nor does it show a lack of love. The apostle wrote to the Philippians and said: "And this I pray, that your love may abound yet more and more in knowledge and in all judgment."[12]

"Love," "knowledge," and "judgment" are not enemies but companions. With this in mind we must determine which is more important—truth or popular opinion. We must determine to know the truth and decide that truth is more important than being popular or accepted. Then we are in a position to take a firm stand. Otherwise, the Lord's admonition will duly apply to us: "And the Lord commended the unjust steward, because he had done wisely: for **the children of this world are in their generation wiser than the children of light.**"[13]

The following irreligiously-written commentary clearly conveys the world's lack of respect for those who let their guard down. The gross hypocrisy of going to movies arm-in-arm with those with whom we have nothing in common should be alarming.

> The reality is that if the books are being so ruthlessly scoured for hints of heresy by conservative Christian factions, one can only imagine how much more so will be the movie.... One can only hope (dare I say pray?) that all those non-churchgoing, non-Bible believing, liberal thinking, tobacco-smoking and alcohol-drinking and left-wing-voting "lost souls" out there are more tolerant and less nit-picking than their more sanctified movie-going counterparts.[14]

---

12 Philippians 1:9.

13 Luke 16:8.

14 Phoebe Kate Foster, "When We're Old Enough to Read Fairy Tales Again," Part 3 of 3. www.pop matters.com/books/features/051209-narnia-3.shtml.

The world recognizes the hypocrisy of yoking together with the world. Why don't Christians display this type of spiritual discernment? Such mockery of Christians who valiantly stand for the truth should concern every true believer. Should Christians be mocking those who stand for the truth? Will the authors of this present volume be getting e-mails and hate mail from professing Christians who, by their attitude, identify with Phoebe Kate Foster?

The real question: Does this issue really matter? It is hard to see how anyone could say it doesn't. The Narnia movie is getting widespread attention, even in churches. When a Hollywood production begins having widespread effects upon what is preached from the pulpit, Christians must ask themselves "Why? What does such popularity reveal about the state of the church?" Berit Kjos writes:

> With eager anticipation, churches across America are getting ready for the great event of the year. Many encourage parents to read *The Lion, the Witch and the Wardrobe* to their children. Some hold seminars to train parents and grandparents in constructive Narnia dialogue. Pastors are using the book instead of the Bible for Sunday morning inspiration. Church leaders are planning to bus their congregations to reserved theaters where members will enjoy a collective experience. And this feel-good consensus is effectively silencing most of the voices that disagree.[15]

Regardless of how many voices have been silenced, we have resolved to biblically investigate this matter leaving no stone unturned. Lewis is far from the typical soul winner in the average evangelistic church. In fact, Lewis never experienced what has become affectionately coined "the real world" having spent most of his life on college campuses as a student and then as a professor.

In 1918 Lewis traveled to Oxford to attend school, graduating in 1925

---

15   Berit Kjos, "Narnia—Part 2: A Four-legged Creator of Many Worlds," December 2005. http://crossroad.to/articles2/05/Narnia-2.htm

with first-class honors in Greek and Latin Literature, Philosophy and Ancient History, and English Literature. He remained at Oxford for twenty-nine years. From 1954 until his death, he was professor of Medieval and Renaissance English at Cambridge University. In 1955, in addition to his teaching duties at the university, Lewis began to publish books. His first major work, *The Pilgrim's Regress* (1933), was about his own spiritual journey to what he termed as the Christian faith.[16]

The man who is influencing countless numbers spent most of his adult life at Oxford and Cambridge universities following his turbulent childhood. His early life is a good place to begin our study of this most enigmatic individual.

---

16   C. S. Lewis, *The Pilgrim's Regress: An Allegorical Apology for Christianity, Reason and Romanticism* (London: Geoffrey Bless Ltd., 1992).

Chapter 1

C. S. Lewis: The Man and His Work

Childhood

Clive Staples Lewis (known as "Jack") was born on November 29, 1898, in Belfast, Ireland (now Northern Ireland) and passed away on November 22, 1963.

According to most biographers, Lewis had a very turbulent childhood. Lewis' mother, Florence Hamilton Lewis (1862–1908), died of cancer when Lewis was nine years old. "With my mother's death," he wrote, "all that was tranquil and reliable disappeared from my life." His father, Albert Lewis (1863–1929) never fully recovered from the grief of his wife's death "and his erratic and sometimes cruel subsequent behavior alienated his sons."

Lewis had one brother, Major Warren Hamilton Lewis (1895–1973). Known as "Warnie," Warnie Lewis is reported to have returned to belief in Christianity five months before C. S.'s conversion to Christianity. He too was a frequent participant in weekly meetings of the Inklings—a tiny counterculture consisting of Lewis and his intellectual friends who discussed everything from metaphysics to current events. Warnie's forty-year battle with alcoholism was a source of great concern to his brother.

One other individual who was important in Lewis' early circle of friends and acquaintances was Arthur Greeves (1895–1966) whom Lewis described by saying "after my brother, my oldest and most intimate friend." Lewis wrote Greeves some three hundred letters throughout his life.[17]

---

17 "A Gallery: Family and Friends of C.S. Lewis," *Christianity Today* (7/1/85). www.ctlibrary.com/3365

Lewis' early favorite literature included E. Nesbit's works *The Railway Children, Five Children and It, The Phoenix and the Carpet, The Story of the Amulet, et. al*—all occult fantasies. Of these, Lewis wrote that his favorite was *The Story of the Amulet*: "It first opened my eyes to antiquity, the 'dark backward and abysm of time.' I can still reread it with delight."[18] What was *The Story of the Amulet* like? Here is a short section from one page of the book that greatly influenced Lewis' childhood and adult writing, and continued to be a source of delight throughout his adult life:

"Oh what a dream!" cried the learned gentleman. "Dear children, if you love me—and I think you do, in dreams and out of them—**prepare the mystic circle and consult the Amulet!**"... They crouched in a circle on the floor... **Jane said the Name of Power.** And instantly the light went out, and all the sounds went out too, so that there was a silence and a darkness, both deeper than any darkness or silence that you have ever even dreamed of imagining.... Then out of the vast darkness and silence came a light and a voice.... And the light was the light that no man may look on and live, and voice was the sweetest and most terrible voice in the world.[19]

Lewis wrote that he could still find pleasure in reading Nesbit even after having professed Christ some twenty-five years earlier. The title—*The Story of the Amulet*—denotes an unusual connection. An *amulet* is supposed to bring good luck according to many believers in astrology.[20] For C. S. Lewis, fairy tales were very powerful. He wrote that he delighted in fairy tales so intensely that he even began to hallucinate, or so he thought.

Curiously enough it is at this time, not in earlier childhood, that I chiefly remember delighting in fairy tales. **I fell deeply under the spell of**

---

18   Lewis, C. S., *Surprised by Joy: The Shape of my Early Life, Revised Edition*, (Orlando, FL: Harcourt Brace & Co.: 1995), p. 14.

19   E. Nesbit, *The Story of the Amulet* (New York, NY: Penguin Books, 1996), p. 287.

20   www.calastrology.com/goodluckpieces.html

> **Dwarfs**—the old bright-hooded, snowy-bearded dwarfs we had in those days before Arthur Rackham sublimed, or Walt Disney vulgarized, the earthman. I visualized them so intensely that **I came to the very frontiers of hallucination**; once, walking in the garden, I was for a second not quite sure that a little man had not run past me into the shrubbery. I was faintly alarmed, but it was not like my night fears. [21]

The year his mother died, Lewis was sent to boarding school in Hertford-shire, England. He immediately hated it. In his biography he wrote that he developed a "great taste" for all fiction about the ancient world. He described his desire for it as insatiable.

> I also developed a great taste for all the fiction I could get about the an-cient world: *Quo Vadis, Darkness and Dawn, The Gladiators, Ben Hur.* . . . Early Christians came into many of these stories, but they were not what I was after . . . the attraction, as I now see, was erotic, and erotic in rather a morbid way. . . . **The interest, when the fit was upon me, was ravenous, like a lust.**[22]

Lewis mentions *Quo Vadis* as one of his favorites. The front cover of this book says that it was the "winner of the Nobel Prize for literature in modern translation by W. S. Kuniczak." Here are two short excerpts to give the reader some idea as to the influences in Lewis' impressionable early life and his ac-ceptance of the unorthodox later in life. One of the books that influenced him contained very negative impressions of Christians, calling them "the enemies of life and all humanity" because of their "self-denying dogma."

> Try to forget your problems. Ah, what the devil! We've conquered the whole world so we've a right to amuse ourselves! You, Marcus, are a very beautiful young man, and I imagine that's partly to blame for my fondness

---

21   Lewis, *Surprised By Joy*, pp. 54–55.

22   Ibid., p. 35.

of you. Ah, by Diana of Ephesus! . . . If it weren't for that **absurd Christianity,** Ligia would be waiting in your house right now. Try all you want
to prove they aren't **the enemies of life and all humanity,** but you'll be
wasting your time. . . . If I were in your place, I'd soon hate their deadly,
self-denying dogma and look for pleasures where they are, right here
on earth among us. You're a beautiful young man, I repeat, and Rome is
full of easy divorcees.[23]

Is it any wonder that Lewis turned to atheism with these types of influences
during an impressionable period in his life? These materials encourage a
life of amusements and self-pleasure while despising the life of a dedicated,
consecrated, holy Christian. They are also indicative of the present world
in which we live. Here is another excerpt that also had an impact on the
young Lewis.

. . . Marcus, you still cling to life as if it held some hidden promises and
meanings. I think if you were to die today, you'd be unpleasantly surprised
that it's time to go, while I'd accept death as something necessary and
natural, knowing there are no pleasures in this world that I haven't tasted.
. . . **All I care about is that I manage to amuse myself until the end.** . . .
Your Christians, on the other hand, fill the world with gloom, playing
the same role in life as rain does in nature. . . . "And who's to blame for
that if it's not your Christians? **What can you expect from people who
pick a cross, the most despised object in the empire, for their symbol?**
. . . **What can such a teaching give the world?** . . . Stick your tongue out
at any Christian you find in your house."[24]

These are the early childhood and teenage influences that helped develop
the psyche of the man who would be proclaimed by evangelical readers

---

23   Henryk Sienkiewicz—translated by W.S. Kuniczak, *Quo Vadis* (New York: Hippocrene, 2002),
     p. 276.

24   Ibid., p. 276–277.

of *Christianity Today* as "the most influential writer in their lives."[25] His imagination became fixed upon fantasy in preference to what he considered a faulty reality. His life was steeped in fantasy when he wrote, "for in a sense the central story of my life is about nothing else (except fantasy)." [26] *Christianity Today* relates that Lewis studied under a private tutor by the name of William Kirkpatrick. "Ironically, though Kirkpatrick was an atheist, he was partly responsible for shaping the critical faculties of the 20th century's greatest Christian apologist." [27]

After advancing to preparatory school at Wyvern, Lewis drifted off into atheism. He proclaimed the fostering of imagination a more reliable instrument for knowing God or becoming a god.

Overview of Lewis' Works

C. S. Lewis penned over fifty books, some of them compiled posthumously. He wrote seventeen biblical, theological, and philosophically-related works, fourteen works of literary criticism, twenty of a more imaginative literary nature (including seven children's books, four science fiction thrillers, and four books of poetry), and three compilations of his letters.

Lewis' first two books of atheistical poetry were published under a pseudonym—Clive Hamilton (his first name and his mother's maiden name). At least fifteen of his books were released after his death. Here is a brief breakdown of three of his most popular theological works.

Mere Christianity

This well-known volume was published in 1952 as a collection of five series of radio talks that Lewis gave on late-night BBC radio during WW II. The talks had already been published in three slim volumes: *Broadcast Talks* (1942),

---

25   J. I. Packer, "Still Surprised by Lewis: Why This Nonevangelical Oxford Don has Become our Patron Saint," *Christianity Today* (9/7/98).
www.ctlibrary.com/ct/1998/september7/8ta054.html

26   Lewis, *Surprised by Joy*, p. 17.

27   "Myth Matters," *Christianity Today* (4/17/01).
http://www.christianitytoday.com/ct/2001/006/1.32.html

Christian Behaviour (1943), and *Beyond Personality* (1944).[28]

According to *religionfacts.com* the title, *Mere Christianity*, "is taken from the writings of Richard Baxter (1615–1691), an author who sought to articulate the fundamentals of the Christian faith on which all denominations could agree." [29]

Because William and Emilie Griffin studied and wrote extensively about C. S. Lewis, including a biography on Lewis entitled *C. S. Lewis: The Authentic Voice*, we will focus on their writings in this section. Both William and Emilie are members of the Catholic Commission on Intellectual and Cultural Affairs. Emilie Griffin likens her spiritual conversion to the Catholic church to that of Lewis' conversion.

> Some twists in his story echoed my own latent spirituality. When, for example, Lewis did not believe in God, he was angry at God for not existing. He was equally angry at God for making a world. So in ways reminiscent of Lewis, I too accepted Jesus Christ and his Church. . . . I also had begun to write a book about conversion in which Lewis figured quite prominently.[30]

Emilie Griffin also wrote that "*Mere Christianity* has brought many people to the Christian faith and contributed to ecumenical dialogue, moving easily across Christian denominations by focusing on the basic teachings that most Christians believe." [31]

While Griffin's review is rosy, the book doesn't merit such an outlook. The concept of "mere Christianity" means agreeing on a small common denominator of Christian truth while tolerating great areas of disagreement.

---

28 William Griffin, "Recommended Resources: C. S. Lewis," *Christianity Today*. www.ctlibrary.com/3373, July 1, 1985.

29 http://religionfacts.com/Christianity/people/lewis/works.htm#works

30 Emilie Griffin, "Lewis and Me: Through the Years with C. S. Lewis," 2005. http://www.explorefaith.org/lewis/influence.html.

31 Emilie Griffin, "Who Is C. S. Lewis?" http://www.explorefaith.org/lewis/bio.html

In 1993 *Christianity Today* explained why C. S. Lewis is so popular among evangelicals. Among the reasons given for this popularity—Lewis' concern to avoid "ecclesiastical separatism."[32] How does this square with the apostolic injunction to "come out from among them, and be ye separate"? [33]

The Screwtape Letters

Lewis admits to taking his readers into forbidden territory in this one: readers go on a tour of the Devil's mind. Lewis' book describes the Devil in the manner of medieval drama as he teaches a "junior devil" the "tricks of the trade." William Griffin explains: "In fact, under Lewis' imaginative hands, Screwtape, one of the Devil's minions, is a sort of fussy professor at a technical college, a downscale establishment up the hill from Oxford proper. He's tutor to a young graduate named Wormwood, who, for his final collegiate exercise, has been sent to London and assigned to tempt one soul."[34] *Screwtape* landed Lewis on the cover of *Time* magazine. Lewis unwisely used *The Screwtape Letters* to present supernatural characters that were devilish-minded and even devil-possessed.

One excerpt from the book should reveal Lewis' perspective and theological tendencies. The Devil informs his devil-in-training that it would be good if the sacraments would take on lesser importance, inferring Lewis' belief in their importance. "Provided that meetings, pamphlets, policies, movements, causes, and crusades, **matter more to him than prayers and sacraments** and charity, he is ours."[35] Of course, since this book is written from the Devil's perspective, one would surmise that the Devil is fearful of the sacraments and really is the one who wants to discourage one's participation in these enterprises.

Richard Sandor, M.D., memorized the entire book word for word. He explains his understanding of the theme of the book—to cause Christians to

---

32   *Christianity Today*, 10/25/93. http://rapidnet.com/~jbeard/bdm/exposes/lewis/general.htm

33   2 Corinthians 6:17.

34   William Griffin, "Recommended Resources."

35   Lewis, *The Screwtape Letters*, p. 34–35.

lose their salvation and end up in Hell. His brief synopsis of *The Screwtape Letters* is as follows:

> For those who don't know the book, the setup is this: Screwtape himself is a senior devil in the "overarch of Our Father Below." The letters are directed to his nephew Wormwood, a Junior Tempter on Earth, working on one of us—whom they call a "patient." **The letters themselves follow Wormwood's efforts to tempt the patient, who has (to Screwtape's "grave displeasure") by the second letter, become a Christian. The goal of damnation is to "secure his soul forever"**—to turn him against God (to Screwtape, "the Enemy" and "our Oppressor") so that on entering Eternity, the man will become "a brimful living chalice of despair and horror and astonishment which you can raise to your lips as often as you please." It turns out that to the devils, we humans are "primarily food." [36]

Letters to Malcolm, Chiefly on Prayer

This work was published the year after Lewis' death. On January 5, 1953, Lewis wrote to the Roman Catholic priest Don Giovanni Calabria that he was attempting to write a book on prayer for those who "have been recently converted to the Christian faith and so far are without any sustained regular habit of prayer."[37]

Who was Father Giovanni Calabria? According to one Lewis specialist, he was a "gift" to Lewis.

> In this midst of all this [a time of depression following the completion of *The Lion, the Witch and the Wardrobe*, which Lewis described as a time in which he was chiefly occupied with "dog's stools and human vomit"], the arrival of Don Giovanni Calabria in his life (if only through letters) was a gift . . . a single bright spot in a dark prospect. Don Giovanni had written to Lewis in praise of *The Screwtape Letters*—then the only book

---

36 http://www.explore faith.org/lewis/screwtape.html.

37 William Griffin, "Recommended Resources."

of Lewis' translated into Italian (Don Giovanni knew no English)—and **rightly discerned in Lewis a person who shared his deep concern for the reunification of the Christian churches. . . . In 1988 Pope John Paul II came to Verona to proclaim Giovanni Calabria's beatification.** [38]

The Problem of Pain

Lewis wrote several other works. In *The Problem of Pain* (1940) he addresses the oft-discussed issue of suffering. He wondered if God is good and all-powerful, why doesn't He remove all pain and suffering? Others have followed the same line of reasoning: if God is loving, the fact that pain and suffering do exist must mean that He does not have the power to remove pain and suffering. Others have reasoned that if God is all powerful, the existence of pain and suffering must mean that while God could remove suffering He simply doesn't want to, and therefore He really cannot be loving.

Lewis attempts to solve the difficulty by appealing to free will. God is both all-powerful and all-loving, but because man is truly free, evil will exist. Human freedom is far better, according to Lewis, in a world of pain and suffering than a lack of freedom in a world where there is no pain and suffering because human freedom makes real love possible. Love that is coerced and that is inevitable is not really love.

Lewis again picked up this theme with *A Grief Observed* (1961). This time, however, it is Lewis who is suffering. The book chronicles his suffering over the illness and death of his wife, Joy Davidman, from cancer. It was dramatized in the film *Shadowlands*, starring Anthony Hopkins as Lewis and Debra Winger as Joy.

Lewis' Space Trilogy

Out of the Silent Planet (1938) and *Perelandra* (1943) form what has been dubbed Lewis' "space trilogy." They tell of the attempt to populate Malacandra (Mars) and Perelandra (Venus) with humankind whom the evil, atheist

---

38 Alan Jacobs, *The Narnian: The Life and Imagination of C. S. Lewis* (New York: HarperCollins, 2005), pp. 248–250.

professor Edward Weston, considers to be the most advanced species in the universe.

> Ransom [the main character] manages to escape and discovers the beautiful, colorful terrain of Malacandra. He meets its friendly inhabitants, including the hrossa (otter-like creatures who create song and poetry), the seroni (spindly-limbed creatures with giant heads who turn out to be philosophers) and the pfifltriggi (bespectacled badger-like creatures who are goldsmiths).
>
> The book [*Out of the Silent Planet*] culminates in a trial scene of Ransom and his former captors before Oyarsa, the great ruler of Malacandra. Dr. Weston, blind to any sense of splendor or awe, treats the Malacandrans assembled there as idiots, and makes a fool out of himself. In the course of the trial we learn of Weston's diabolical agenda to take over planet after planet, and that Oyarsa could have annihilated him at any time. We discover that Earth is known as Thulcandra—the silent planet. Because its Oyarsa chose to strike out on his own in an attempt to seize the omnipotence of Maleldil (the ruler and maker of all worlds), the inhabitants of our planet are deaf to the "Music of the Spheres" and our telescopes are blind to the glory of the universe. [39]

Lewis' Motive For Writing

According to C.S. Lewis, Narnia was not a Christian allegory by design. He did not plan to write a series that would teach Christian truth and make such truth plain to young readers. However, he certainly intended to bring to life the paganism so prevalent in his works. Lewis' evangelical advocates do not seem to realize that they are in fact promoting the idea that Christianity and paganism can somehow be melded together.

According to *Christianity Today* "not only was Lewis hesitant to call his books Christian allegory, but the stories borrow just as much from pagan

---

39   http://www.relgionfacts.com/Christianity/people/lewis/works.htm#works

mythology as they do from the Bible."[40] The authors would agree with this and wonder if Lewis' books would be better categorized as pagan allegories, rather than Christian ones. Lewis wrote:

> Let me now apply this to my own fairy tales. Some people seem to think that I began by asking myself how I could say something about Christianity to children; then fixed on the fairy tale as an instrument; then collected information about child-psychology and decided what age group I'd write for; then drew up a list of basic Christian truths and hammered out "allegories" to embody them. This is all pure moonshine. I couldn't write in that way at all. Everything began with images, a faun carrying an umbrella, a queen on a sledge, a magnificent lion. **At first there wasn't even anything Christian about them; that element pushed itself in of its own accord.** [41]

Lewis reveals that "everything began with images, a faun carrying an umbrella, a queen on a sledge, a magnificent lion." This helps to explain the presence of mythical creatures. According to the online encyclopedia, *wikipedia.org*:

> Narnia is a fantasy world created by the Anglo-Irish author C. S. Lewis as a location for his *Chronicles of Narnia*, a series of seven fantasy novels for children. In Narnia, animals can talk, mythical beasts abound, and magic is common. . . . The name "Narnia" refers to not only the Narnia world, but especially to the land of Narnia within it, which its creator, Aslan the great lion, filled with talking animals and mythical creatures.

The same online encyclopedia lists the mythological creatures found in Narnia: "Boggles, Centaurs, Cruels, Dragons, Dryads, Efreets, Fauns, Ghouls, Gnomes, Hags, Hamadryads, Horrors, Incubi." Incubi is plural for incubus.

---

40   Josh Hurst, "Into the Wardrobe and Straight to Hollywood," *Christianity Today* (11/07/05). wherein he cites David Van Biema.
www.christianitytoday.com/movies/special/narnia-news.html.

41   C. S. Lewis, *Of Other Worlds: Essays and Stories* (Florida: Harcourt, 1994), p. 36.

What is an incubus? Going back to *wikipedia.org,* we read: "Incubus (demon) . . . In Western medieval legend, an incubus (plural *incubi*; from Latin *incubare,* 'to lie upon') is a demon in male form supposed to lie upon sleepers, especially on women in order to have sexual intercourse with them. . . ."

We find it hard to believe that C. S. Lewis, a scholarly expert in medieval lore and fluent in Latin, did not know the significance of the mythological creatures inhabiting Narnia—a place of his own creation.

Who Owns the Lewis Copyright?

After Lewis died in 1963, Warren Lewis began receiving the royalties from his brother's writings until his death in 1973. At that time David and Douglas Gresham acquired the rights to their stepfather's literary works. Eight years later, the Greshams sold the Lewis copyright to C. S. Lewis Pte. Ltd. (Private Limited), a company set up in Singapore to manage the publication of Lewis' works and collect the royalties.

There are many questions that could be raised about the Lewis copyright. This much we do know. The royalty money goes to Liechtenstein, located in the Swiss Alps. In 1998, C. S. Lewis Pte. Ltd. began employing Douglas Gresham. Gresham claimed that he did not know who owned the company "and did not care, as long as he was paid." In 1999, the owner of the copyright hired Simon Adley to market Lewis' works. [42]

Insights From Douglas Gresham, Stepson

The Lewis estate is in the hands of Lewis' stepson, Douglas Gresham. Gresham recently turned sixty and has written a book about his stepfather entitled *Jack's Life.* He also served as co-producer and consultant to *The Lion, the Witch and the Wardrobe* movie. Gresham's writings and thoughts reveal confusion in some of the very same areas as his stepfather. Could Gresham's attitude be characteristic of the sad outcome of harboring such beliefs? Is all this Narnia hype dangerous to one's spiritual health?

---

42   Marvin Olasky, "Off With His Head," *WORLD Magazine* (6/16/01), Vol. 16, No. 2. http://www.worldmag.com/displayarticle.cfm?id=5075.

Gresham demeans books that analyze and expound the various doctrines of Scripture, calling them complex and obscure. According to a lengthy interview with Mark Moring of *Christianity Today*, Gresham believes that these types of books simply "complicate the issues." He continues by saying that "God sent down all his rules and regulations; they were ignored. He sent the prophets; they were ignored. Jesus came down himself to tell us how to live real human lives, and he was ignored." [43]

Gresham has the same misconceptions evident in C. S. Lewis and his writings. Christ did not become a man simply to teach us how to live our lives. For God to become a man in order to set a perfect example for depraved sinners doesn't help anyone, since His example would be one that nobody could emulate. First and foremost, Christ took upon Himself the form of human flesh in order to take away the sins of the world and to make a perfect propitiatory sacrifice that would satisfy the divine justice of God.

As Gresham discusses a strategy that would give the Narnian Chronicles a wider audience, another of his spiritual misconceptions surfaces. In order to justify dumbing down Christ's message Gresham believes that Jesus' message needs to be *secularized* so that it will have a more worldly feel to it.

> **Did [Jesus] take his message only to the Pharisees and Priests or did he "secularise" it, try to make it available to a wider audience,** by teaching the sinners and ordinary folk in the streets and fields? In today's world the surest way to prevent secularists and their children from reading [the Narnian Chronicles] is to keep it in the "Christian" or "religious" section of the bookstores or to firmly link Narnia with modern Evangelical Christianity. [44]

Gresham may have a point concerning the loss of sales if the Narnia Chronicles were simply placed in the religious section of the bookstores. However,

---

43 Mark Moring, "The Man Behind the Wardrobe" (10/31/05). http://christianitytoday.com/movies/interviews/douglasgresham.html

44 Corrie Cutrer, "Mere Marketing?" *Christianity Today* (7/31/01). http://www.christianitytoday.com/ct/2001/010/8,.19.html

he misspeaks when He implies that Christ would have spoken in some type of ecclesiastical tone if He were speaking only to the religious leadership.

There never was a need for Jesus to *secularize* His message because Jesus never spoke in some type of monastic or other-worldly manner. He spoke plainly, except when He was using parables with the religious leaders due to their hypocrisy, but even the parables were drawn from common life situations. Jesus spoke in a common, ordinary way but He never resorted to "gutter language" nor using "street slang." Nor did His ordinary language present *un*truths about God, man, and the plight of man.

Not only is Gresham confused about the purpose of Christ's coming to earth, but he is also confused about the Christian life.

In October 2005 Gresham was interviewed by Mark Moring of *Christianity Today*. During the interview Gresham was asked about Lewis' lack of Christian character. Moring asked: "Americans have latched on to C. S. Lewis, and yet here's a guy who was a chain smoker, who liked his pints, who told ribald [dirty] jokes, and in general, wouldn't fit what we think of as the 'typical evangelical.' And yet we've all wrapped our arms around him. Why is that?" [45]

Evidently, this question alone about Lewis' lack of spirituality seemed to irritate Gresham. As much as we should be saddened by what the question communicates concerning Lewis' lifestyle, which is documented elsewhere as well, Gresham's answer should be a wake-up call to all of those who are dazed by all of this Lewis hype. Twice in one paragraph *Christianity Today* had to bleep out Gresham's response while he belittles those who think it important to have certain moral standards as a Christian. Gresham answered:

> One of the reasons is that through the—if you can excuse the expression—the **bulls---** that has come to be taken so seriously in American Christianity, through all of that, they can still see the essential truth that Jack represented. The problem with evangelical Christianity in America today, a large majority of you have sacrificed the essential for the sake of the

---

45   Mark Moring, "The Man Behind the Wardrobe."

> trivial. **You concentrate on the trivialities—not smoking, not drinking, not using bad language, not dressing inappropriately in church, and so on. Jesus doesn't give two hoots for that sort of bulls---. If you go out and DO Christianity, you can smoke if you want, you can drink if you want—though not to excess, in either case.**[46]

We certainly agree that these things—smoking, drinking, language, and dress—should not be the things we major on in lieu of the weightier matters—judgment, mercy, and faith.[47] However, Christians overtaken by these faults will not be a very effective witness for the Lord in a world that is becoming increasingly pagan. Gresham admits that doing these things to excess is wrong, yet the very things that he admits to be unacceptable in excess characterized C. S. Lewis' lifestyle and behavior. The Bible tells Christians to be different—in fact, *peculiar.* "Who gave himself for us, that he might redeem us from all iniquity, and purify unto himself **a peculiar people, zealous of good works.**"[48]

No Christian can be conformed to this divinely-sanctioned standard if he is like the world. And he will not present the kind of Christian witness mandated by Scripture. Astoundingly, within the same interview Gresham claimed that Lewis was "the finest man and the best Christian I've ever known."[49] Gresham's standards are certainly not biblically based.

Gresham relates the following story about Lewis to prove that C. S. Lewis was such a fine Christian. Hopefully, no one would be so naïve as to think that Gresham's standards reveal an acceptable threshold of godliness.

> A guy approached Jack on the street one day and asked him if he could spare a few shillings. And Jack immediately dove into his pocket and brought out all his change and handed it over to this beggar. And the chap he was with—I think it was Tolkien—said, "Jack, you shouldn't have given that

---

46 Ibid.

47 Matthew 23:23.

48 Titus 2:14.

49 Mark Moring, "The Man Behind the Wardrobe."

fellow all that money, he'll just spend it on drink." Jack said, **"Well, if I had kept it, I would have only spent it on drink."** . . . I don't really know of any major vice that Jack took to his grave.[50]

Most people would disagree with Gresham's assessment that Lewis was without vice upon his death since he was a heavy drinker and smoker. As the interview with *Christianity Today* progressed, Gresham was asked the following question: "Christians are concerned that this film retains the apparent Christian imagery of . . ." Gresham again seemed agitated by the question about possible Christian elements in the film. He cut the question off before it was finished with this revealing answer: "You have to bear in mind that **Hinduism** has a dying god who dies for his people, then comes back. **Norse mythology** has the dying god. **Greek mythology** has the dying god. This myth is not new and it's not unique to Christianity."[51]

Gresham likens Aslan's dying and coming back to life in the movie to Hinduism, Norse mythology. as well as Greek mythology. He makes the point that this movie could just as easily appease the pagan and Christian alike. In fact, the likeness to a Stonehenge sacrifice in *The Lion, the Witch, and the Wardrobe* is sure to appease the pagan while being overlooked by the unsuspecting Christian who assumes that any sacrificial death and resurrection scene must be Christian. Is this really the message that Christians should convey? Is this really the influence that Christian parents want their impressionable children exposed to?

Another interviewer asked Gresham if he were concerned about "the whole Christian camp out there" that can't be pleased by anything Disney does. Gresham responded that those who have seen the movie know that the Christian issue is "such a nonissue. . . And if you want to read certain things into it, they're certainly there. And if you don't, you don't. I really hope that everybody's going to enjoy the movie." [52]

50   Ibid.

51   Mark Moring, "Narnia Comes To Life," *Christianity Today* (11/1/05). http://www.christianitytoday.com/movies/interviews/douglasgresham2.html

52   http://Preview.gospelcom.net/interviews/narnia.html

Well, he shouldn't worry. Everybody—pagans, atheists and many Christians—will enjoy the movie. The death and resurrection scenes are drained of any offending "Christian" elements. Hollywood has never been, or ever wanted to be, distinctively Christian. They will use their $200 million budget to put pictures and images into the hearts and minds of this generation that will make this and future generations carnally at ease in their unregenerate condition.

As we continue to consider the various Gresham interviews, his glaring hypocrisy and dangerous deception becomes apparent. Once the professional advertising agencies got involved, Gresham considered his answers from the financial point of view before answering his questions. They want the churches to openly support the movie revealing that their allegiance is to mammon ($). Gresham's position seems clear in the following interview with the Australian magazine, *The Age*: ". . . that is what people are always getting wrong—it's not a Christian film and the Narnia books aren't Christian novels." [53]

Here it is from the stepson of the author—the Narnia books are *not* Christian novels. Here it is from the co-producer—the *Lion* movie is not a Christian film. That morsel of information should satisfy all of those concerned about the "potentially damaging" Christian influence on all of these impressionable children that need to avoid Christianity at all costs!

Is the Holy Spirit In Charge?

Sounding eerily similar to the *Passion* promoters looking for a tantalizing promo for gullible Christians, one month prior to the release of the film Gresham stated: "Being a Christian, I am fully aware that **the Holy Spirit is in charge of these things.**"[54]

Like Gresham, Mel Gibson seemed to have all of the right terminology to promote his movie venture in the Christian community, too. In fact, Mel

---

53   Damian Thomas, "At Home In Narnia (12/4/05).
      www.theage.com.au/news/books/at-home-in-narnia/2005/12/03/1133422143366.html

54   Jeff Giles, "Next Stop: Narnia" *Newsweek* (11/7/05).
      http://msnbc.msn.com/id/9863780/site/site/newsweek/print/1/displaymode/1098/

Gibson, set the precedent for "Christian movie advertising."

Although Gibson repeatedly admitted that it was Ann Catherine Emmerich's book, *The Dolorous Passion* that inspired him to make the movie, he too claimed that the Holy Ghost was in charge. In an interview with Focus on the Family in August of 2003 after a screening of the movie, Gibson said that "This is God's movie. . . . The Holy Ghost was running the show. I was just directing traffic." According to the article, "Gibson hopes the film leads everyone who sees it to a saving faith in Christ." He said that many on the movie set in Italy "came to faith during the making of the film."[55]

Gibson seems to have been coached to say all the right things—"the movie was Holy Ghost led . . . saving faith in Christ," etc. However, has everyone who has the correct terminology personally experienced the saving power of Christ in their lives? Did Mel Gibson use these phrases in the same context as a Bible-believing, born-again Christian? To be sure, Gibson claimed sincerity and stated:

> But I really feel my career was leading me to make this [movie]. The Holy Ghost was working through me on this film, and I was just directing traffic. I hope the film has the power to evangelize. . . . Everyone who worked on this movie was changed. There were agnostics and Muslims on set converting to Christianity.[56]

We don't want to be "technical," but a basic question is: "How does Mel Gibson define Christianity?" Doesn't he really mean that they were converted to Roman Catholicism? Does converting to Roman Catholicism really bring a person to saving faith in Christ? How could it when Roman Catholic theology teaches that the Catholic Church, not Jesus Christ, is the repository of grace? The Protestant Reformation revolved around the issue of works salvation or *sola fide*—faith alone. Did Gibson see the light of salvation by grace through faith or was he simply well coached? Did he

---

55 *Focus on the Family Magazine* –Christian Living
    http://www.family.org/fofmag/cl/a0029428.cfm

56 http://www.pluggedinonline.com/movies/movies/a0001657.cfm

dupe his gullible Christian audience who was desperately looking for some entertainment with a religious setting?

Both Gibson and Disney hired the same advertising agencies experienced in researching Christian terminology and making entertainers sound like they are "from the inside." Because of this deceptive trend, Christians should be wary of anyone who sounds Christian at times but fails to consistently portray a solid Christian testimony.

Can we really take media hype promoting so-called Christian productions at face value? After C. S. Lewis spent his entire life denying that his writings were Christian allegories, an unpublished letter supposedly written by Lewis was released just prior to the movie opening. It refutes everything Lewis ever said denying the alleged allegorical meanings of his works. This letter was supposedly written to a fan in 1961 stating that "the whole Narnian story is about Christ . . . supposing there really was a world like Narnia . . . and supposing Christ wanted to go into that world and save it (as He did ours) what might have happened?"[57] The letter continues: "The stories are my answer. Since Narnia is a world of talking beasts, I thought he would become a talking beast there as he became a man here. I pictured him becoming a lion there because a) the lion is supposed to be the king of beasts; b) Christ is called 'the Lion of Judah' in the Bible."[58]

Whether or not the letter is genuine doesn't prove much. There is enough in the *Chronicles of Narnia*, and in Lewis' writings and associations, to show that if he intended to write a Christian allegory, he failed miserably.

The Lion, the Witch and the Wardrobe has done well at the box office, and its sequels will bring in millions too. However, the utter confusion created by so-called Christian movies that are devoid of doctrinal content and biblical integrity is tragic. How great this confusion is can be seen in the following quote from the book *Showtime for the Sheep? The Church and the Passion of the Christ*, by T. A. McMahon:

---

57 Christopher Morgan, "Narnia's lion really is Jesus" (12/4/05).
    www.timesonline.co.uk/article/0,,1-523-1903338-523,00.html

58 Ibid.

Not too long ago, the *National Catholic Reporter* ran a contest asking artists from around the world to submit slides of their works that best portrayed "Jesus for the third millennium." More than 1,000 entries from 19 countries were received. The winner, titled "Jesus of the People," featured a dark-skinned, effeminate character in dreadlocks, complete with a yin-yang symbol and Indian feathers. Although it had its enthusiasts, most were not pleased. One critic wrote, "It is nothing but a politically correct modern blasphemous statement reflecting the artists' and the so-called judge's spiritual depravity." Another, commenting on the "universality" of the winning image, felt he could do better: "My Jesus will be a narcoleptic vegetarian astronaut clown mime who lives in a Sri Lankan tree with three lesbian popes and sings the boogie-woogie in Navajo. And I'll probably win."

The latter critics' sarcasm highlights the utter absurdity in all of this, while the former critic describes the blasphemous nature of such an endeavor.[59]

Lewis' Drinking and Smoking

The December 2005 edition of *Christianity Today* (CT) featured C. S. Lewis on the cover, and almost every article was devoted to him, including the cover story entitled "C. S. Lewis Superstar." The connection with the blasphemous movie *Jesus Christ Superstar* is unavoidable. The lead article in CT commented on how a "British intellectual with a checkered pedigree became a rock star for evangelicals." Just how checkered was his life? The CT article reveals the sad state of Christianity by comparing his popularity and lifestyle with that of Elvis Presley.

Just prior to his death, Lewis drank and smoked heavily. In *C. S. Lewis: A Biography* we read: "If we ignore the kind of man Lewis was, in our anxiety to dismiss him as a fraud or canonize him a plaster saint, we miss the unmistakable and remarkable evidence of something like sanctification which occurred in him towards the end of his days. . . . He went on being

---

59 Tom McMahon, *Showtime for the Sheep*, Bend, OR: The Berean Call, 2004. pp. 77–78.

a red-faced Ulsterman, **he continued to smoke and drink heavily. . . ."**[60] When Lewis wrote for children "he was a man who admitted that he didn't much care for the company of children. . . . Lewis loved the fellowship of other men, particularly around lively conversation, a few pints of ale, and a good pipe."[61]

According to *Newsweek*, the year that Lewis wrote *The Lion* he was leading a multiplicity of lives.

> In 1949, the year he finished writing "The Lion, The Witch and the Wardrobe," C. S. Lewis was leading at least four different lives. His reputation as a Christian apologist had already been launched with several books and a series of BBC radio speeches. He was a charismatic Oxford professor, an expert in Milton and Spenser. He was a generous host **who presided over long, drunken nights of bawdy talks and badinage.** And he was the head of a household that, even by today's standards, would be considered unconventional. His domestic partner for nearly three decades was a woman 25 years his senior, whom he called "my mother," but who was not, in fact, his mother.[62]

All of this helps us to understand Lewis' use of Bacchus—the god of wine and orgiastic religion—in *The Lion*. In one scene the faun began to talk to Lucy about the forest prior to the spell of the White Witch. Unashamedly, Lewis introduces the vile pagan god Bacchus and his orgies as a desirable thing that was part of Narnia's revered past. In *The Lion*, we read:

> He had wonderful tales to tell of life in the forest . . . old Silenus on his fat donkey would come to visit them, and sometimes **Bacchus himself,**

---

60   A. N. Wilson, *C. S. Lewis: A Biography* (New York: W. W. Norton & Co., 2002) p. 292.

61   Jay Tolson, "God's Storyteller: The curious life and prodigious influence of C. S. Lewis, the man behind 'The Chronicles of Narnia.'" *U.S. News & World Report* (12/12/05), p. 46. http://www.usnews.com/usnews/news/articles/051212/12lewis.htm

62   Lisa Miller, "A Man and His Myths: The Creator of Narnia was a Scholar, a Drinker—and a Believer." *Newsweek* (11/7/05). http://sojo.net/index.cfm?action=news.display_article+mode=s+NewsID=5020

and then streams would run with wine instead of water and the whole forest would give itself up to jollification for weeks on end. "Not that it isn't always winter now." [63]

Answers.com describes Bacchus in this manner: "The god of wine and of an orgiastic religion celebrating the power and fertility of nature."[64] We will further delve into Bacchus when we investigate the direct pagan elements in Lewis' writings.

What did publishers do with Lewis' references to his secular proclivities? According to a 1990 *London Times* article, there was a concerted effort by Lewis' publishers to delete all references to drinking and smoking from his books. "[Lewis] acolytes on both sides of the Atlantic engage in violent feuds, like warring religious sects, and Lewis' reputation is jealously guarded. Some American publishers have sought to expunge references to alcohol and tobacco from his books, so as to obscure the fact that he was a drinker and a heavy smoker."[65]

Lewis' Relationship with Women

"Strange and unorthodox" best describes the two main female relationships in Lewis' life. For thirty years Lewis lived with Janie Moore, a woman twenty-five years his senior. The relationship began with her while Lewis was a student at Oxford. Some of his biographers claim that the relationship was simply one of friendship, but Lewis admitted to his brother, Arthur, that he loved Mrs. Moore.

Much of the documentary evidence of this relationship was destroyed by Mrs. Moore herself when she thought she was dying. At that time, she burned all of Lewis' correspondence to her. However, those who knew them well attested to the love affair that existed between the two of them. Alan Jacobs writes:

---

63   Lewis, *The Lion, the Witch, and the Wardrobe*, pp. 15–17.

64   http://www.answers.com/main/ntquery?method=4&dsid=2222&dekey=Dionysus&gwp=8& curtab=2222_l&link text=Dionysus

65   John Carey, "A Bully Bewitched," *The London Times* (11/11/90).

I once heard a longtime friend of Lewis' give a lecture, at the end of which a member of the audience flatly asked whether Lewis and Mrs. Moore had a sexual relationship. The lecturer's face assumed a pained look, and he hesitated—but then the elegant voice of his wife piped up from the back of the room: "Oh, of course, they did, dear—go ahead and say it!"[66]

In April of 1950 Janie Moore was confined to a nursing home in Oxford. That same year, Joy Davidman Gresham, after having read two of Lewis' books, wrote to him from New York. Her writing impressed Lewis and an "intense correspondence followed" with this married woman. Two years later, Mrs. Gresham crossed the Atlantic to visit her spiritual mentor in England. Soon thereafter, she moved to London with her two young children. Phoebe Kate Foster relates the story:

> When they first became acquainted, initially through correspondence and later in person when she spent four months in London, Joy was married, apparently unhappily, to another man. A few months after she visited Lewis in England, Joy's husband William Gresham (who had not accompanied her on the London trip) sued for divorce on the grounds of desertion, and Joy left the States with their two sons to move to England.[67]

In 1956, Lewis married Joy Gresham. Here is the story, as related by Gary Lenaire: "She met Lewis in England, returned to the States and was divorced from her husband, then traveled back to England to marry Lewis. According to two of Lewis' friends, Gresham's husband divorced her on the grounds of desertion."[68]

Lewis helped Joy Davidman financially by underwriting the boys' board-

---

66   Alan Jacobs, *The Narnian: The Life and Imagination of C. S. Lewis* (New York, NY: Harper Collins, 2005), p. 94

67   Phoebe Kate Foster, "When We're Old Enough To Read Fairy Tales Again," Part 2 of 3. http://www.popmatters.com/books/features/051209-narnia-2.shtml

68   Gary Lenaire, "The Other Side of Narnia: Why Fundamentalists Hate C. S. Lewis." http://www.realityspoken.com/cslewis.htm

ing school education. He also paid the rent on her house, which was not far from his own. According to Olsen, love was not their primary motivator for marriage. It was her inability to renew her permit to live and work in England unless she married an Englishman. They were married first in a civil ceremony and then in an "ecclesiastical" one.[69]

George Sayer, one of Lewis' students at Oxford in the 1930s, asserted that Lewis and Joy Davidman had not had physical relations and sought to refute A. N. Wilson, one of Lewis' other biographers. Sayer's comments are quite revealing concerning the "ecclesiastical" ceremony that took place when Davidman was supposedly on her death bed.

> Wilson also quotes a statement made by Father Bide, who performed the ceremony of the Christian marriage, in the hospital in 1956: **"Joy desperately wanted to solemnize her marriage before God, and to claim the grace of the sacrament before she died."** But this does not mean, as he supposes, that smitten with guilt because of her adultery, she had virtuously and correctly not been receiving the sacrament of the Eucharist. It means rather that **she desired another sacrament, that of matrimony,** and therefore offers no support for Wilson's theory.[70]

No matter what the motive for a second religious ceremony, their concept of marriage was certainly unbiblical, in that they referred to the "sacrament" of marriage. The Eucharist was also referred to as a "sacrament." The definition of a sacrament is that it is a rite that conveys sanctifying grace. *The American Heritage Dictionary of the English Language* offers this definition:

> a. In the Eastern, Roman Catholic, and some other Western Christian churches, any of the traditional seven rites that were instituted by Jesus and recorded in the New Testament and that confer sanctifying grace.

---

69 Ted Olsen, "Apolgetics: C. S. Lewis," *Christianity Today*, (1/1/2000).

70 George Sayer, "C. S. Lewis and Adultery." *We Remember C.S. Lewis: Essays and Memoirs*, David Graham, ed. (Nashville: Broadman & Holman, 2001), p. 102

b. In most other Western Christian churches, the two rites, Baptism and the Eucharist, that were instituted by Jesus to confer sanctifying grace.[71]

Lewis and "Turkish Delight"

Due to the nature of Lewis' lifestyle, his casual comments are often quite perplexing. Here is one example. A personal letter from Lewis to Sheldon Vanauken is reproduced in *A Severe Mercy* in which he suggests that upon his next visit to England the two of them "must have some good, long talks together and perhaps we shall both get high."[72] Gary Lenaire observes: "In light of this [comment by Lewis], it is interesting that in *The Lion, the Witch and the Wardrobe*, Lewis' fantasy children's tale, a hero named Edmund meets a magical witch who conjures up for him a box of Turkish Delight, which Edmund devours and begs for more. Turkish Delight is a name for hashish."[73]

A simple search of "Turkish Delight" and "hashish" on the Internet will show that it is a type of marijuana candy. One website that provides the sordid history of marijuana revealed this interesting tidbit concerning the hashish candy exported from Egypt to Europe: "Turkish Delight: square pieces of hashish containing sugar and gelatin; a particular favorite of the students at Cambridge University in England."[74]

Note, the connection is made between this hashish candy and the university where Lewis taught. Some Lewis supporters would insist that everyone ignore this seemingly remarkable association between Turkish Delight, Cambridge, and Lewis. Instead, they would claim that Turkish Delight is simply a delectable candy to be enjoyed as any other.[75]

---

71 *The American Heritage Dictionary of the English Language,* Fourth Edition, (Houghton Mifflin Co., 2000).

72 Sheldon Vanauken, *A Severe Mercy* (New York, NY: HarperCollins, 1987), p. 191.

73 Gary Lenaire.

74 http://www.hoboes.com/html/Politics/Prohibition/Notes/Marijuana12000.html

75 http://www.tulumba.com — search for Turkish Delight

Yet further suspicions arise when one scrutinizes the effects upon the young boy who partakes of this highly addictive substance. Chapter four of *The Lion, the Witch and the Wardrobe* is entitled "Turkish Delight." It offers a vivid description of someone who has an overwhelming urge for any addictive substance.

> The Queen let another drop fall from her bottle onto the snow, and instantly there appeared a round box, tied with green silk ribbon, which, when opened, turned out to contain several pounds of the best Turkish Delight. . . . He was quite warm now, and very comfortable . . . the more he ate the more he wanted to eat . . . anyone that once tasted it would want more and more of it, and would even, if they were allowed, go on eating it till they killed themselves. . . .[76]

To entice a young boy to betray his family, the Queen claimed that her house had "whole rooms full of Turkish Delight. . . ."[77] This Turkish Delight sounds strangely similar to known addictive substances. Edmund no longer cared about the consequences associated with this "addiction"—he simply wanted more. The Queen offered him the opportunity of becoming her Prince who would "wear a crown and eat Turkish Delight all day long. . . ."[78] The young man "sells his soul to the Devil" so to speak, simply for "one more high." ". . . When he heard that the Lady he had made friends with was a dangerous witch he felt even more uncomfortable. But he still wanted to taste that Turkish Delight again more than he wanted anything else."[79]

It would be irresponsible to simply ignore the very real similarities between this description of a candy in a children's book and the devastating effects on those fully addicted to drugs. Edmund was totally obsessed with this addictive substance. Should it surprise the Lewis faithful if the Turkish Delight carried more than one meaning, since so much of Lewis' materials

---

76 C. S. Lewis, *The Lion, the Witch and the Wardrobe*, pp. 36–38.

77 Ibid.

78 Ibid., p. 39.

79 Ibid., p. 42.

are often invested with dual meanings? Do we really believe that Lewis was simply unaware of the fact that Turkish Delight was the name for a hashish candy at Cambridge?

Lewis and the Occult

The world is increasingly turning toward the occult. Those with a heart toward myth and magic are more likely to become blind to the wonders of God and to the utter evil of sin than those who have fixed their minds on God's truth. The Bible warns against having a divided mind: "A double minded man is unstable in all his ways."[80] Is the lack of conviction in the pulpit symptomatic of an age engrossed in occultic fantasy?

Satan is subtle. His deceptive schemes do not generally hit the unsuspecting Christian head-on. He is much more apt to entice the unwary through mystical fantasy worlds and induce them through forbidden attractions by convincing them that God really does not mind so long as they don't go too far. Contrast such parameters with the biblical paradigm spoken by Jesus: "Blessed are they which do hunger and thirst after righteousness: for they shall be filled."[81]

Christians are to "hunger and thirst after righteousness," yet Lewis' autobiography reveals that he not only dabbled in the occult, but that he relished the experience. In his book *Surprised by Joy*, Lewis makes a surprising admission.

> The vagueness, the merely speculative character, of all this Occultism began to spread—yes, and to **spread deliciously**—to the stern truths of the creed. The whole thing became a matter of speculation: I was soon (in the famous words) "altering 'I believe' to 'one does feel.'" And oh, the relief of it! . . . From the tyrannous noon of revelation **I passed into the cool evening of Higher Thought, where there was nothing to be obeyed, and nothing to be believed except what was either comforting or exciting.**[82]

---

80 James 1:8.

81 Matthew 5:6.

82 Lewis, *Surprised by Joy*, p. 60.

As one writer put it, Lewis had an ". . . irresistible attraction to the shadow world of occult fantasy—a mingling of darkness with light evident in writings apart from his apologetics."[83]

Since Lewis' checkered background would assuredly come through in his writings, a simple cursory investigation seems less than adequate. His mingling of two opposing forces makes it necessary to always keep the author's perspective in mind when reading his writings. Lewis wrote of his obsessions repeatedly. In fact, he describes his attraction to the occult in an early life biography much the same way that an honest and forthright alcoholic might describe his addiction to alcohol.

> And that started in me something with which, on and off, I have had plenty of trouble since the desire for the preternatural, simply as such, **the passion for the Occult. Not everyone has this disease; those who have will know what I mean.** I once tried to describe it in a novel. **It is a spiritual lust; and like the lust of the body it has the fatal power of making everything else in the world seem uninteresting while it lasts.**[84]

It is inconceivable after reading Lewis' own well-conceived and highly informed statements about the occult how parents simply "convince" themselves that movies and books that include this type of "entertainment" are simply innocent and nothing to be feared and avoided. Lewis continues with a warning that our current rebellious generation must certainly heed or suffer the consequences.

> There is a kind of gravitation of the mind whereby good rushes to good and evil to evil. This mingled repulsion and desire drew toward them everything else in me that was bad. The idea that if there were **Occult knowledge** it was known to very few and scorned by the many became an added attraction. . . . [It] **appealed to the rebel in me.**[85]

---

83 http://www.rapidnet.com/~jbeard/bdm/exposes/lewis/general.htm

84 Lewis, *Surprised by Joy*, p. 58.

85 Ibid., p. 174.

Lewis' Attitude Toward Death

Lewis died at his home, "The Kilns," in Headington Quarry, near Oxford, on November 22, 1963, after a brief illness. On his gravestone is a line from Shakespeare's *King Lear*—one of his mother's favorites: "Men must endure their going hence."[86] Shakespeare's quotation on the tombstone was on his father's calendar the day that his mother died.[87] Even his tombstone reflects his lifelong pursuit of academia.

What did the apostle Paul write about death? "For me to live is Christ, and to die is again. But if I live in the flesh, this is the fruit of my labour; yet what I shall choose I wot not. For I am in a strait betwixt two, having a desire to depart, and to be with Christ which is far better. . . ."[88]

Lewis did not seem to have this peaceful assurance within his heart. His outlook on death seems not to be fortified with a well-grounded assurance of salvation, and a certainty of a home in heaven. In *C. S. Lewis, A Biography* we read:

> Like many (most?) religious people, Lewis was profoundly afraid of death.
> His dread of it, when in the midst of life, had been almost pathological
> and obsessive. Physical extinction was a perpetual nightmare to him and,
> whatever his theological convictions and hopes, he was unable, before
> his wife's death, to reconcile himself to the transition which death must
> inevitably entail.[89]

Lewis' Conversion

It is certainly not the intention of the authors of this study to claim that Lewis was, or was not, a Christian. Christians are far from perfect. Sanctification is a life-long process as we grow in grace.

---

86 Emile Griffin, "Lewis and Me: Through the Years with C. S. Lewis," 2005.
    http://www.explorefaith.org/lewis/influence.html

87 "Did You Know?" *Christianity Today* (7/1/85). http://www.ctlibrary.com/6276

88 Philippians 1:21–23.

89 Roger Lancelyn Green, p. 293.

However, it is also true that Christians must know something about their spiritual leaders and what they stand for. Because of Lewis' increasing popularity, he has certainly become a spiritual leader. So, what about Lewis' conversion experience?

The front flap of his autobiography presents what is, at best, an ambiguous conversion scenario: "He is, most persuasively, a modern man who thought his way to God."[90] We have to ask: "Do people 'think their way to God'"? If they do, how do we explain the following Scriptures?

> But the natural man receiveth not the things of the Spirit of God: for they are foolishness unto him: neither can he know them, because they are spiritually discerned.[91]

> No man can come to me, except the Father which hath sent me draw him. [92]

> At that time Jesus answered and said, I thank thee, O Father, Lord of heaven and earth, because thou hast hid these things from the wise and prudent, and hast revealed them unto babes.[93]

> And the servant of the Lord must not strive; but be gentle unto all men, apt to teach, patient, In meekness instructing those that oppose themselves; if God peradventure will give them repentance to the acknowledging of the truth. . . .[94]

Lewis relates his conversion to monotheism (the belief in one God) in his autobiography, *Surprised by Joy*. In the last chapter of that book he briefly discusses his conversion to "Christianity." Yet, strictly speaking, even that

---

90   C. S. Lewis, *Surprised by Joy,* front flap.

91   1 Corinthians 2:14.

92   John 6:44.

93   Matthew 11:25.

94   2 Timothy 2:24–25.

conversion, let alone his conversion to monotheism, is not to true Christianity. It is simply a new found belief that Jesus Christ is the Son of God.

In his biography Lewis writes that the Gospels could not be myths because they did not have the "mythical taste." He goes on to reveal his conversion to believing in monotheism. "And no person was like the Person it depicted; as real, as recognizable . . . a god. But if a god—we are no longer polytheists—then not a god, but God. Here and here only in all time the myth must have become fact; the Word, flesh; God, Man."[95] Lewis speaks of this as his "last transition" and that it was "less certainly than any [of the other transitions] which went before it . . . "[96]

One's belief in monotheism is insufficient for salvation. Even the devils believe that much; however, they do not trust in Christ which is the only thing sufficient to bring about a true conversion.

Thou believest that there is one God; thou doest well: the devils also believe, and tremble.[97]

Saying, Let us alone; what have we to do with thee, thou Jesus of Nazareth? Art thou come to destroy us? I know thee who **thou art, the Holy One of God.**[98]

The evil spirits that came into direct contact with the Saviour during His earthly ministry believed that He was "the holy one of God." Evil spirits knew exactly who Jesus was. Acts 19 tells about the seven sons of Sceva who tried to cast out evil spirits: "And the evil spirit answered and said, **Jesus *I know*,** and Paul I know; but who are ye? And the man in whom the evil spirit was leaped on them, and overcame them, and prevailed against them, so that they fled out of that house naked and wounded."[99]

---

95 Lewis, *Surprised by Joy,* p. 228.

96 Ibid.

97 James 2:19.

98 Mark 1:24.

99 Acts 19:15–16.

No Bible student would ever claim that a knowledge of Jesus and the fact that He is "the holy one of God" is sufficient to spare the lost from their ultimate doom. Lewis' "conversion to Christianity" is tantamount to an acceptance of the doctrine of the incarnation, but is the *knowledge* of the identity of Jesus equivalent to trusting in Jesus alone for salvation?

We will certainly admit that an individual may be saved who doesn't use the precise terminology that one may consider to be theologically correct. In the case of both children and adults, a person may have a definite salvation experience without knowing how to biblically define and explain that experience. One is not saved by being able to theologically articulate what salvation is, but by faith in Christ. We are saved by faith. It is Christ who saves us through faith, and if that faith is genuine that person is a Christian in the fullest sense of the word. Yet, Lewis' description of salvation is, to say the least, somewhat troubling.

A recent report entitled "Survey: two thirds of evangelicals doubt Jesus' words regarding salvation thru him alone" makes the salvation question quite crucial. We quote a large section of the report.

For years, most evangelical Christians have been taught and accepted the words of Jesus in John 14:6 where He states, "I am the Way, the Truth, and the Life, and no man cometh unto the Father but by Me." But now a new *Newsweek/Beliefnet* poll is showing a shocking number of people who call themselves evangelical and born-again have come to reject those words.

The question in the poll read: "Can a good person who isn't of your religious faith go to heaven or attain salvation, or not?"

According to the poll results of more than 1,000 adults 18 years of age and older, 68 percent of evangelical Christians believe "good" people of other faiths can also go to heaven. Nationally, 79 percent of those surveyed said the same thing, with an "astounding" 91 percent agreement among Catholics, notes Beliefnet. Beliefnet spokesman Steven Waldman calls the results "pretty amazing."

"Evangelicals are among the most churchgoing and religiously attentive people in the United States," Waldman writes, "and one of the ideas they're most likely to hear from the minister at church on a given Sunday is that the path to salvation is through Jesus."

In light of that, how—he asks—could so many Americans toss aside such a central element of theology?

Waldman believes the best explanation is found in the *Newsweek* cover story that grew out of the survey. The conclusion it draws is that Americans have become so focused on a very personal style of worship—that is, forging a direct relationship with God—that spiritual experience has begun to supplant dogma, or teaching based on the authority of the Bible.[100]

During the recounting of his spiritual journey Lewis wrote in the preface to *Mere Christianity*:

> You will not learn from me whether you ought to become an Anglican, Methodist, a Presbyterian, or a Roman Catholic. . . . Ever since I became a Christian I have thought that the best, perhaps the only, service I could do for my unbelieving neighbors was to explain and defend **the belief that has been common to nearly all Christians at all times.** . . . Our divisions should never be discussed except in the presence of those who have already come to believe that there is one God and that Jesus Christ is His only Son.[101]

For this reason, he admits that he sent his book, *Mere Christianity,* to an Anglican, Methodist, Presbyterian, and a Roman Catholic asking for their input and criticisms prior to publishing. He wrote that the book "did at least succeed in presenting an agreed, or common, or central, or 'mere' Christianity. . . . If I have not directly helped **the cause of reunion,** I have perhaps made it clear why we ought to be reunited."[102] Lewis admits and actually seems to boast that his purpose was to unite the various differing offshoots

---

100 http://headlines.agape press.org/archive/8/232005g.asp (8/25/05)

101 Lewis, *Mere Christianity*, Preface, VIII–IX.

102 Ibid., Preface, XI.

of Catholicism—we would assume with Rome.

Lewis was a prolific writer who was able to convey his thoughts clearly, yet there seems to be much confusion and uncertainty concerning the account of his conversion to "Christianity." The evening before Lewis' reported conversion, he had a long talk with J.R.R. Tolkien and Hugo Dyson. That discussion was the catalyst that brought about his conversion to the belief that Jesus was the Son of God the next day. The account of that discussion is published in Arthur Greeves' *They Stand Together: The Letters of C. S. Lewis to Arthur Greeves (1914–1963)*. Again reporting from Lewis' biography:

> I know very well when, but hardly how, the final step was taken. I was driven to Whipsnade one sunny morning. When we set out I did not believe that Jesus Christ is the Son of God, and when we reached the zoo I did. Yet I had not exactly spent the journey in thought.[103] [NOTE: the "we" is Warnie and C. S. Lewis—they were riding together on a motorcycle.]

Lewis' conversion account—telling of a reluctant man who came "kicking, struggling and resentful"—strikes us as odd. Here are Lewis' own words.

> You must picture me alone in that room in Magdalen, night after night, feeling, whenever my mind lifted even for a second from my work, the steady, **unrelenting approach of Him whom I so earnestly desired not to meet**. That which I greatly feared had come upon me. In the Trinity Term of 1929 I gave in, and admitted that God was God, and knelt and prayed: perhaps, that night, **the most dejected and reluctant convert in all England.** I did not then see what is now the most shining and obvious thing; the Divine humility which will accept a convert even on such terms. The Prodigal Son at least walked home on his own feet. But who can duly adore that Love which will open the high gates to a **prodigal who is brought in kicking, struggling, resentful, and darting his eyes in every direction for a chance of escape?** [104]

103 Lewis, *Surprised by Joy*, p. 229.

104 Ibid, pp. 221.

Does God save people against their will and without a heartfelt submission to Christ? Is it possible to be saved believing with the *mind* certain facts about God and Christ, while resisting with the *heart* the will of God? Moreover, how many "gospels" are there? Galatians 1 shows Paul's concern for the spiritual condition of his readers when he wrote: "I marvel that ye are so soon removed from him that called you into the grace of Christ unto another gospel: Which is not another; but there be some that trouble you, and would pervert the gospel of Christ."[105] By his own testimony, Lewis had moved on an intellectual level from idealism (no idea of a personal God) to pantheism (believing in an impersonal God resident in everything), and then to theism (belief in the existence of a personal God).

Interestingly, we read of Lewis surrendering, kneeling, and praying at some point in his spiritual pilgrimage, and yet it is said that this is something that happened in 1929 and not in 1931, when he claims his actual conversion took place. The following is a perceptive commentary on Lewis:

> Soon Lewis recognized that most of his friends, like his favorite authors—MacDonald, Chesterton, Johnson, Spenser, and Milton—held to this Christianity. In 1929 these roads met, and Lewis surrendered, admitting "God was God, and knelt and prayed." Within two years the reluctant convert also moved from theism to Christianity and joined the Church of England.[106]

George Sayer pointed out that Lewis revealed that he loved the Greek Orthodox liturgy. His book makes reference to a holiday where Sayer, C. S. Lewis and Lewis' wife, Joy, went off to Greece. Lewis attended some liturgies and a wedding.

> At Rhodes, which he told me was "simply the Earthly Paradise," they went to the Greek Orthodox cathedrals for part of the Easter service. Jack [C.

---

105 Galatians 1:6–7.

106 Ted Olsen.

S. Lewis] was moved by it. . . . Thereafter whenever the subject came up between us, he said that he preferred the Orthodox liturgy to either the Catholic or Protestant liturgies. He was also impressed by Greek Orthodox priests, whose faces, he thought, looked more spiritual than those of most Catholic or Protestant clergy.[107]

Lewis commented about the Orthodox service in his biography:

What pleased me most about a Greek Orthodox mass I once attended was that there seemed to be no prescribed behaviour for the congregation. Some stood, some knelt, some sat, some walked; one crawled about the floor like a caterpillar. And the beauty of it was that nobody took the slightest notice of what anyone else was doing. I wish we Anglicans would follow their example.[108]

Summary of C. S. Lewis' Lifestyle and Beliefs

Perhaps the best summary of Lewis' beliefs comes from *Christianity Today,* a publication that hardly can be called "right wing" or "fundamentalist." It is inclined to view him in the most favorable light possible, yet notice what is reported.

Clive Staples Lewis was anything but a classic evangelical, socially or theologically. **He smoked cigarettes and a pipe, and he regularly visited pubs to drink beer with his friends.** Though he shared basic Christian beliefs with evangelicals, **he didn't subscribe to biblical inerrancy or penal substitution. He believed in purgatory and baptismal regeneration.** How did someone with such a checkered pedigree come to be a theological Elvis Presley, adored by evangelicals?[109]

107 *Jack,* p. 378.

108 *Letter To Malcolm,* p. 10.

109 "C. S. Lewis Superstar," *Christianity Today* (11/23/05).

One cannot read C. S. Lewis and doubt that he had major problems with many of the fundamental doctrines of the Christian faith. As we will see in this book, He is known for:

1. Turning to the Catholic Church before his death.
2. Believing in the efficacy of prayers for the dead.
3. Believing in purgatorial purification.
4. Confessing his sins regularly to a priest.
5. Attributing salvation to the sacraments.
6. Receiving the Catholic sacrament of last rites on July 16, 1963.
7. Believing that there is salvation in pagan religions.
8. Denying the biblical teaching of an eternal, fiery Hell.
9. Denying the substitutionary blood atonement of Jesus Christ and its complete and final efficacy for the salvation of those who put their faith in Him.
10. Rejecting the doctrine of the bodily resurrection.
11. Preferring ecumenism to doctrinal teaching.
12. Publicly using profanity.
13. Frequently becoming inebriated with his students.
14. Supporting theistic evolution.
15. Rejecting the Bible as the full and final Word of God.

Lewis viewed salvation as a process rather than an act and considered "transformation" (a New Age buzz word) as a process of redemption. He did not believe in Christ's once-and-for-all sacrificial death.[110] Instead he was influenced by the Roman Catholic idea of grace plus works.

Lewis erroneously understood God as accepting those who are sincere even though they are wrong. He also taught that one can be saved by works, even evil works, so long as they are done wholeheartedly.[111] Yet the Bible is clear: "Neither is there salvation in any other: for there is none other name

---

110   See Hebrews 9:25–28; 10:11–14.

111   See Lewis' *The Last Battle*, pp. 204–205.

under heaven given among men, whereby we must be saved."[112] Shockingly, J. I. Packer, in an article commemorating the hundredth anniversary of Lewis' birth, called him "our patron saint." Packer remarked that Lewis "has come to be the Aquinas, the Augustine, and the Aesop of contemporary Evangelicalism" although he "theologically had undecidedly un-Evangelical elements."[113]

J. I. Packer is an ecumenical, neo-evangelical. The reference to Aquinas, Augustine, Aesop, and patron saints sounds more like a review from the Vatican than an evangelical commentary. Peter Chattaway, in *Canadian Christianity*, offers an excellent analysis of J. I. Packer's assessment of Lewis:

> According to the far-from-Evangelical *Christianity Today* magazine, September 7, 1998, **Lewis "has come to be the Aquinas, the Augustine, and the Aesop of contemporary Evangelicalism** (an interesting choice of "heroes," considering that Aquinas was a Roman Catholic apologist, Augustine was a persecutor of true Christians and an early "Catholic" in doctrine, and Aesop, although he taught many moral truths with his stories, was a heathen).[114]

Regretfully, some people will be personally offended by these claims and by the other information in this book. But the truth will sometimes offend those unconcerned about peddlers of erroneous beliefs. We are to speak the truth in love[115] which is not condemned by the Bible, nor yet criminalized in America. Why should we be thought radical because we are opposed to the encroaching of paganism into the churches?

---

112 Acts 4:12.

113 "Still Surprised by Lewis: Why this nonevangelical Oxford don has become our patron saint," *Christianity Today* (9/7/98).

114 Peter T. Chattaway, "Comment: The Paganism of *Narnia*" http://www.canadianchristianity.com/cgi-bin/na.cgi?nationalupdates/051124narnia

115 "But **speaking the truth in love**, may grow up into him in all things, which is the head, even Christ" (Eph. 4:15).

Chapter 2

How Does Pagan Fantasy Fit In?

Christianity Today featured an interview entitled "C. S. Lewis, the Sneaky pagan." The subtitle read: "The author of *A Field Guide to Narnia* says Lewis wove pre-Christian ideas into a story for a post-Christian culture."[116] In the face of such statements how anxious should Christian parents be to have their children read Lewis or view movies from his works?

Scripture admonishes parents to raise their children "in the nurture and admonition of the Lord."[117] Parents have a responsibility to God regarding their children. In fact, *their* children are not really *theirs* at all, but the Lord's. Consequently, the Bible informs us regarding our duties. So we have to ask, "Does the fantasy of Narnia help or hinder parents in fulfilling their duties?" "Are the Narnia stories Christian allegories similar to John Bunyan's classic *Pilgrim's Progress?*"

As we have pointed out, C. S. Lewis steadfastly claimed that he did not write his Narnia tales to teach Christian truth or principles. Another *Christianity Today* article reports that:

> Lewis often said [that] the Narnia novels are not allegories; the characters and incidents do not function simply as pictures whose sole purpose is to illustrate Christian virtues or vices (as they do in [Bunyan's] *Pilgrim's Prog-*

---

116 http://www.christianitytoday.com/ct/2004/126/12.0.html

117 Ephesians 6:4.

ress). Rather, they possess their own separate life and integrity (many have read the Chronicles without being aware of their Christian message). [118]

There is a big difference between Lewis' tales and those of Bunyan. John Bunyan, "The Tinker of Bedford," was not writing to create an art form in which the characters and events "possess their own separate life and integrity" but to illustrate basic Bible truths using characters that were distinctly Christian in nature.

Bunyan also did not create half-man/half-animal creatures whose existence is derived from pagan literature. No one who conscientiously read Bunyan's allegories could miss the particular message of Scripture—something that could never be said of C. S. Lewis. Nobody could claim that Bunyan's Christian allegories conveyed conflicting messages by merging paganism with an abstract type of Christianity.

Helping God Out?

Evidently, Lewis supporters think fantasy and myth are valuable means of conveying truth. According to *Christianity Today,* Christ "came not to put an end to myth but to take all that is most essential in the myth into himself and make it real." [119]

In his *Christianity Today* article Louis Markos concludes by stating: "In Aslan, Christ is made tangible, knowable, real." [120] David Cloud comments on this and states: "As if we can know Jesus Christ best through a fable that is vaguely and inaccurately based on biblical themes and intermingled with paganism." [121]

The honest observer cannot honestly equate the thought process that goes into imagining Jesus' parable about a man that *built his house upon the*

---

118 Louis Markos. "Myth Matters" *Christianity Today* (4/23/01), Vol. 45, No. 6, p. 32. www.christianitytoday.com/ct/2001/006/1.32.html

119 Ibid.

120 Ibid.

121 "C. S. Lewis and Evangelicals Today," FBS, updated and enlarged (12/20/05).

sand and *the sower who went forth to sow* with Lewis' heathen mythology, magic, curses, gods, fairies, demons, ogres, and monsters. Some, enamored with Lewis' success, have attempted to make this very association.

The Bible's first mention of magicians is found in Egypt with Joseph and Pharaoh in Genesis 41. The next mention of them is when Moses stands before Pharaoh and the magicians replicate the miracles of God. "Then Pharaoh also called the wise men and the sorcerers: now **the magicians of Egypt, they also did in like manner with their enchantments.**"[122] The hardening of hearts is the end result of all of the enchantments done by the magicians. "And the magicians of Egypt did so with their enchantments: **and Pharaoh's heart was hardened,** neither did he hearken unto them; as the LORD had said."[123]

Magic hardens the heart and fantasy blurs the real world with the unreal. As such, fantasy can prove highly deceptive, especially when the deception is couched in the truth and the truth is blended in with the deception. Most movie-going Christians—and certainly the general population at large—are oblivious to the fact that the serpent in the Garden of Eden was the first to blend partial truths with an enticing lie. Remember, a half truth is a whole lie.

Are we wrong for being disturbed by our Saviour being presented as an animal sacrificed on an altar which resembles the pagan sacrifices at Stonehenge? Berit Kjos put it this way:

> Christian Narnia fans may have forgotten a major lesson in Genesis 3: By blending partial truths with an enticing lie, the serpent presented Eve with a catastrophic deception. Yes, there are allusions to truth in the Narnia stories. But there are many more contrary messages, and the over-all context is pagan, not Christian. Keep in mind, what looks like truth makes the deception more palatable!

---

122 Exodus 7:11.

123 Exodus 7:22.

Whether Lewis intended it or not, the main "Christian" justification for filling minds with Narnian suggestions is that a four-footed mammal helps us to understand Jesus and respond emotionally to His sacrifice. Yet, this **animal representation** of our indescribably holy Lord is more vivid to our imagination than any Old Testament idol ever was! Paul's letter to the Romans makes it abundantly clear that God doesn't want to be pictured in this way. [124]

Read the Scripture alluded to in the previous quotation: "Professing themselves to be wise, they became fools, **And changed the glory of the incorruptible God into an image made like to corruptible man, and to birds, and four footed beasts,** and creeping things."[125]

Many Christians are raving about *The Chronicles of Narnia.* Supposedly, they help to convey the message of redemption. Yet, when the truth is couched in fantasy there is the very real possibility that the truth may be mistaken for myth and vice-versa. Without a prior knowledge of the Bible, the allegory is useless to serve its perceived purpose and, in fact, may frequently convey the wrong message and actually counteract truth.

It's quite common for Lewis supporters to commend Lewis and his use of animals. Angela Dobson has a web article entitled "Aslan, Jesus and C. S. Lewis."[126] The subtitle is: "Clive Staples Lewis' use of Christianity in the Chronicles of Narnia." On page 2 we read that Aslan, the creator of Narnia, is really Jesus and that "Lewis expresses the connection between Aslan and Jesus with clarity."

In *The Voyage of the Dawn Trader,* the children see a lamb, who turns into Aslan before their eyes. Again, Angela Dobson believes that Lewis is conveying the message that Jesus is the Lamb of God. She also expresses what she thinks concerning Lewis' use of mythological creatures to express himself. "C. S. Lewis wanted his readers to understand a little more of God without **the discouragement of Sunday school preaching.** He wanted them to share

---

124   Berit Kjos, part2, p. 2.

125   Romans 1:22–23.

126   www.geocities.com/angela11nh/thesis.htm

the same love and desire that he had for Christ, the deep connection with God. He felt it more important than the rules of the church." [127]

In other words, we are to set aside the Word of God, and the local church, defined in the Bible as "the pillar and ground of the truth"[128] for Lewis' books which make up for the alleged "deficiencies" in God's methods.

But is the Bible really incomplete and does it need to be supplanted, added to, updated and improved? The Bible indicates otherwise when it says, *"All Scripture is given by inspiration of God, and is profitable for doctrine, for reproof, for correction, for instruction in righteousness; That the man of God may be perfect, thoroughly furnished unto all good works."* [129] Scripture is sufficient and it is "profitable." God did not give the His Word simply to hear Himself speak. He gave it to us for our good. With the Bible we have everything we need to love and serve our glorious Saviour, the Lord Jesus Christ.

Dare we suggest that something is missing in Scripture and that Narnia somehow fulfills or supplies that necessary missing element, much like the *Passion* movie supposedly fulfilled our "need" to visualize Christ's physical sufferings?

Some will say: "But Jesus used parables"

Supporters of Lewis argue that the Bible uses allegory and that Jesus used make-believe stories—parables—to teach spiritual truth. If Jesus used parables, doesn't that make a little bit of fantasy acceptable?

Not at all! In the parables, Jesus used people, items, and experiences common to His day. There is a sower, leaven, a mustard tree, wheat and tares. Jesus never referred to or incorporated stories of magic or magical spells in His teachings. There are no witches in the parables or mythological creatures, nor do we find Jesus using talking animals. But what do we find in *The Lion, The Witch and the Wardrobe*?

---

127   Ibid.

128   1 Timothy 3:15.

129   2 Timothy 3:16–17.

Stepping through the wardrobe, Lucy Pevensie—and, soon afterward, her sister and two brothers—discover an enchanted world locked in an epic struggle between good and evil. It is a world populated by every manner of fantastic creature, from **fauns, centaurs, hags and witches to a host of talking animals,** none more literally awe-inspiring than a lion called Aslan, Lord King of Narnia. [130]

Today's digitally-produced magic makes all of this make-believe seem all too real. Where does this movie transport the minds of our children? What kind of enticements does it feed to their human nature and emotional appetites? Which suggestions will leave lasting impressions in their hearts and minds? Those are questions parents, and others, should soberly consider. Might it lead some of them into the world of the occult?

Children and Fantasy

We do not live in a moral vacuum. For this reason alone, any discussion of entertainment, literature, and recreation must consider the moral and spiritual climate of the age. What are the times in which we live? In his commentary on Jude, Noah W. Hutchings writes:

The importance of Jude's warning [in Jude 6–7] is that spiritual apostasy always brings with it degeneration in all forms and in every stratum: political corruption, economic degeneration, defilement of knowledge and education, increase in crime with violence spreading even into the home, and a corresponding increase in adultery, divorce, prostitution, and as Paul declared in Romans 1, sexual debauchery of every type imagined by men and angels. This is descriptive of conditions today. And as Jude declared, it began with ungodly men creeping, unnoticed, into our churches, bringing with them their apostate doctrines, denying God and the Lord Jesus Christ who bought us with His precious blood. [131]

130 Jay Tolson, p. 46.

131 Noah W. Hutchings, *The Whole Realm of Rebellion* (Oklahoma City: Bible Belt, 2005), p. 31.

Children, as well as adults, are increasingly confused by the shifting values and moral cross-currents that come at them from school, church, and society. They are grappling with basic life issues such as: sexual identity and "same-sex marriage," the value of human life as compared to plant and animal life, and many other perplexing issues. The fantasy novels of Lewis and others like J.R.R. Tolkien do nothing but heighten and intensify this confusion. Rather than learning about these issues from the Word of God, children are further confused by the mixed and conflicting signals coming from so-called "Christian entertainment." If there was ever a time for people to stand for the pure Word of God it is now.

While many Lewis supporters are defending the books on the basis that they show the struggle between good and evil, this struggle can be shown in varying ways and has been expressed in a number of religions. On the surface, that would make any religion a positive influence where they have a good moral lesson to be learned. However, it is very dangerous when any spiritual message lacks a distinctly biblical basis, especially when it contains cultural and mystical baggage. It confuses and confounds an already mixed-up generation.

Children are easily influenced in the wrong direction through inexperience combined with a lack of general discernment. The exciting and powerful Aslan challenges the Saviour for the heart of the youthful reader and viewer. This danger is exacerbated when atrocious philosophies are intertwined with a truly exciting plot and story via the vehicle of powerful and dramatic cinematographic imagery. Parents need to diligently seek God's counsel before exposing their children to the *Chronicles of Narnia*.

Don't let C. S. Lewis be your guide, or better yet, do not let him be your children's guide into a progressive paganization of society. Those who knew Lewis best pointed out he had no children of his own, nor was he particularly devoted to them. *Christianity Today* reports, "The strange thing about the Narnia books is that Lewis never had children. According to his biographers, he was never particularly fond of them, either."[132]

---

132   "C. S. Lewis Superstar," *Christianity Today* (11/23/05).

Children do not always like the reality of life and frequently fail to effectively differentiate between the real world and the make-believe one. George Sayer, perhaps Lewis' finest biographer, ends his chapter on Narnia by telling how his "little stepdaughter, after she had read all of the Narnia stories, cried bitterly, saying, 'I don't want to go on living in this world. I want to live in Narnia with Aslan.'"[133] This young lady's reaction is not unique nor even unusual concerning the effect of fantasy upon impressionable children.

Her reaction is eerily similar to the letters received by J. K. Rowling, which she received from children who had read her *Harry Potter* books. Children would write to the head schoolmaster of Hogwarts asking to be allowed to attend Rowling's make-believe school. In an interview Rowling related: "I get letters from children addressed to Professor Dumbledore... begging to be let into Hogwarts, and some of them are really sad."[134]

Yet despite these problems with fantasy, evangelicals are plunging ahead in a feverish rush to praise magic and mythology, allowing their impressionable children to be exposed to these influences. In the book *Narnia Beckons*, Ted and James Baehr speak about "deeper magic." C. S. Lewis made it clear, they argue, "that it is wrong to use magic, especially for personal gain, but even when people do such an evil thing, there is a deeper magic (or law) written into the creation by the Creator to right the wrongs."[135] Using Romans 8:21[136] as their basis, they explain:

Throughout the centuries, with this principle in mind, the church has redeemed and reinvested ancient ceremonies, holidays and devices with Christian meaning and content. Thus, both C. S. Lewis and Tolkien reinvested the word *magic* with redemptive meaning. In *The Chronicles*

---

133 Sayer, *Still Surprised*

134 See Douglas D. Stauffer, *Harry Potter: Innocent Entertainment or Darkness Disguised* (Millbrook, AL: McCowen Mills Publishers, 2001), DVD.

135 Ted and James Baehr, *Narnia Beckons: C. S. Lewis' The Lion, the Witch, and the Wardrobe and Beyond* (Nashville: Broadman and Holman, 2005), pp. 4–5.

136 "Because the creature itself also shall be delivered from the bondage of corruption into the glorious liberty of the children of God."

of Narnia, Lewis uses *magic* as a synonym for laws that God has written into the universe.[137]

But why would anyone want to "reinvest" a word that has decidedly evil connotations with "redemptive meaning"? What, we ask, is accomplished by such a verbal sleight of hand? With words being redefined and history being rewritten by revisionists, we doubt if such a confusing ploy can serve any redeeming purpose.

Rather than being convinced by the above line of reasoning, we find that our case is strengthened for rejecting these false and dangerous teachings. *The American Heritage Dictionary of the English Language,* New College Edition, gives a lengthy and revealing definition of "magic":

> (1) The art that purports to control or forecast natural events, effects, or forces by invoking the supernatural. (2) The practice of using charms, spells, or rituals to attempt to produce supernatural effects or to control events in nature ... *synonyms:* magic, black magic, sorcery, voodoo, witchcraft, necromancy, alchemy. *Magic* is the most inclusive of these related nouns; it pertains to all supposedly supernatural powers that affects natural events, but is often used broadly in the sense of that which seems to transcend rational explanation.

If "magic" "is used broadly in the sense of that which seems to transcend rational explanation," why can't the word then be applied to any invisible irrational force—such as occultic and demonic powers? Do we really want to risk exposing children and adults to a film that sends the wrong message about these irrational forces?

While Lewis supporters may scoff at such comments, we must not forget the nature of the times in which we live. We see astrological tables in the newspapers, *Harry Potter* books and movies being taught to children, books on magic and witchcraft in public libraries, with no Christian books

---

137   Ted and James Baehr, p. 5.

allowed, and we strenuously disagree with those who want to sanitize "magic." Christians simply must not be party to the effort to indoctrinate children into paganism—whether through ignorance or willful submission.

There are many problems with *The Chronicles of Narnia* and its fantasy cast. The blurring of human and animal identity can only confuse young minds. But why would Lewis supporters see nothing wrong with this? They state, "We are all, as Lewis reminds us in *Mere Christianity,* filled with a longing for the original holiness of Eden. We all, too, he adds, long for paradise in the future. Narnia reminds us that an essential part of that longing is a healing of the old wound between man and beast."[138]

But by what strange theological ramblings can we believe that "a longing for the original holiness in Eden" will lead us to some merging of man and beast? Was Eden populated with mythological creatures found in ancient pagan literature?

This blending of human and animal in Lewis' mythological creatures was intended to convey a message, we are told. "Throughout the *Chronicles,* creatures with an animal body and human head prove good; creatures with a human body and animal head embody bad."[139] That really makes things plain, doesn't it?

We are not being facetious. Supposedly, the message of the Bible is made plain by the use of symbolical and allegorical language. But we, quite frankly, find that Lewis' symbolical and allegorical language fails miserably to make anything in the Bible plain. We'll let someone who thinks Lewis speaks plainly through symbols show us what he means.

> When the witch confronts Aslan, she reminds him of the "Deep Magic," that "every traitor belongs to me as my lawful prey and that for every treachery I have a right to kill." This seems to be an oblique reference to Romans 6:23, "The wages of sin is death." The word *lawful* is appropriately chosen, as the magic is written on the stone table, which represents the

---

138 Ibid., p. 96.

139 Ibid., p. 134.

requirements of the Old Testament law. It is also written (in American editions before 1994) on "the World Ash Tree," **another blending of Norse and Christian elements.** While the stone table (which according to the white witch has been used for sacrifice before) represents a symbol of death, the Norse regarded the World Ash Tree, or Yggdrasill, as a symbol of life. Dew from this tree provided nourishment for two humans while the rest of the world was undergoing the long winter. **Symbolically, then the Old Testament law provided nourishment during the time before the sacrifice of Christ.**[140]

The "blending of Norse and Christian elements" does not make the Bible "plain." Moreover, the juxtaposition of "dew" from this tree providing "nourishment," and the claim that the Old Testament law provided nourishment during the time before the sacrifice of Christ is simply defective theology. The Bible states that the law was our *schoolmaster.* "Wherefore the law was our schoolmaster to bring us unto Christ, that we might be justified by faith. But after that faith is come, we are no longer under a schoolmaster."[141]

The purpose of the schoolmaster was to bring us unto Christ. The Bible does not teach that the law is (or was) our *sustainer* in any way.

The Old Testament was also specific about how to handle magic, etc. God warned Israel not to associate with anyone who used divination, observed times (the zodiac, astrology), etc. These were an abomination to the Lord. There is no reason to think that their status has been changed today.

> There shall not be found among you any one that maketh his son or his daughter to pass through the fire, or that useth divination, or an observer of times, or an enchanter, or a witch, Or a charmer, or a consulter with familiar spirits, or a wizard, or a necromancer. For all that do these things are an abomination unto the LORD: and because of these abominations the LORD thy God doth drive them out from before thee.[142]

---

140   Ibid., pp. 134-135.

141   Galatians 3:24-25.

142   Deuteronomy 18:10–12.

In an article entitled "C. S. Lewis—Who He Was & What He Wrote," Tony Zakula expresses the warning that every parent must seriously consider before turning their children's mind loose in this New Age world.

> A child reading the book, is, as advertised, "stepping into another world"—a world of fantasy. Lewis, like Disney, was a New Ager. He built entire surrealistic worlds for our children to escape into—escape from reality and from real life. These worlds invariably contain creatures of every sort endearing our children, **performing heroic feats, and displaying often greater powers than our Savior displayed when He was on earth.** . . . Who will our children most readily identify as having awesome power—Lewis' characters, Disney characters, some time-space traveling hero, or the almighty Jesus? Is it any wonder that we have a very difficult time convincing our children to give their all to Someone so far down the totem pole of their experience?[143]

Every parent should seriously consider this wise counsel. The world today is a very dark place with everything pointing away from living righteous and godly. Our children are being bombarded with anti-Christian influences from every side. We must be very discriminating about the influences that effect our children.

So Why Would Anyone Be Critical of C. S. Lewis?

We think the answer to this question is obvious. Yet, with so many claims being made about how Lewis' writings have helped so many people, here are five reasons in nutshell form:

* His lack of a clear spiritual salvation testimony, his outright heresies, his worldly behavior and lifestyle.
* His associations with witchcraft and pagan mythology, and his

---

143 Tony Zakula, "C. S. Lewis—Who He Was & What He Wrote." www..keepersofthefaith.com/BookReviews/BookReviewDisplay.asp?key=4

endorsement of such associations.

◆ The danger of presenting the miracle working power of God as synonymous with magic.[144].

◆ The nature of the times in which we live and the proliferation of evil into the home and church.

◆ The biblical mandate to reprove evil. "And have no fellowship with the unfruitful works of darkness, but rather reprove them."[145]

Many Christians, including those who hope to use the Disney films as an evangelistic tool, tend to excuse the pagan elements in Lewis' books as just so much window dressing. They consider it "fairy-tale bait" that he set to lure unbelievers into his Christian world. But there is much more to Lewis' use of pagan myth than that. [146]

If Lewis' works can be used to "lure unbelievers into his Christian world," why doesn't the opposite hold true concerning the lure of the mythological world? Can Christians and non-Christians be lured into the world of the occult through the very same works? It should be obvious who is served through this yoking together of two opposing influences. God is displeased and Satan is euphoric over the confusion.

Lewis had many pagan influences, including that of J.R.R. Tolkien, who was a contemporary of his. Both were exporters of Medieval lore. Tolkien contrasts myth with simple fiction stating that fiction involves "invented facts," whereas myth "works with the truth" dressing it up in fancy disguises.

> . . . the power of Tolkien lies in the way that he succeeds through myth, in making the unseen **hand of providence felt by the reader** . . . in his mythical creations, or sub-creations as he would call them, he shows how the unseen hand of **God is felt more forcefully in myth** than it is ever

---

144   See Mark 3:28–30.

145   Ephesians 5:11.

146   Peter T. Chattaway, "Comment: The Paganism of *Narnia*."
      www.canadianchristianity.com/cgi-bin/na.cgi?nationalupdates/051124narnia

felt in fiction. Paradoxically, fiction works with facts, albeit **invented facts,** whereas **myth works with truth, albeit truth dressed in fancy disguises.**[147]

Tolkien's explanation of the difference between fiction and myth reveals the danger of using myth to present spiritual truths. Do they cease to be true? Can impressionable minds become confused where to draw the line? The answer is most assuredly yes on both accounts.

A further reason for being critical of Lewis is his amazing popularity with the public at large, and the Christian viewing audience. Lewis has always been highly esteemed in theological seminaries, schools, and academies, but now he has moved from academia into the living room. Lewis' annual book sales remain over two million (half of which comes from *The Chronicles of Narnia* series). With millions of copies of his writings in print, his influence is inestimable. Since 1950, the Narnia books have sold 95 million copies worldwide and have been translated into 41 languages.[148]

C. S. Lewis was a prolific author of more than seventy titles, including works of science fiction, fantasy, poetry, letters, autobiography, and Christian apologetics. In fact, he is the best-selling Christian author of all time. His creatures perform the heroic feats which endear them to our children in lieu of those who should be their real heroes, like David, Paul, John, and the Lord Jesus Christ. When the Bible competes with fantasy, who wins? Or, the more appropriate question might be: Are there any winners in such a contest?

As always, the real issue in evaluating the value of an individual's work hinges on his or her view of Scripture. What did C. S. Lewis think of the Bible, and does his view strengthen our faith in God's Word? To this question we now turn.

---

147 *The Letters of J.R.R. Tolkien,* Humphrey Carpenter, ed. (Boston: Houghton Mifflin Company, 1981), p. 201.

148 Lisa Miller, "A Man And His Myths."

Chapter 3

The Bible According to C. S. Lewis

C. S. Lewis wrote, "I have the deepest respect for Pagan myths, still more for myths in the Holy Scriptures."[149] Was Lewis putting pagan myths and Scripture on the same plane, and if so is this indicative of his tendency to elevate myth and depreciate the unique authority of the Bible? In a chapter entitled "Scripture" in his *Reflections on the Psalms*, Lewis wrote that although Jesus' teachings were perfect, yet the accuracy of the transmission of these teachings was somehow less than perfect.

> We may observe that the teaching of OUR Lord Himself, in which there is no imperfection, is not given us in that cut-and-dried, fool-proof, systematic fashion we might have expected or desired. He wrote no book.[150]

In another essay, Lewis goes so far as to say that Jesus was "wrong." He claimed that our Lord's ignorance was an embarrassment to the disciples.

> It is clear from the New Testament that they **all expected the Second Coming in their own lifetime.** And, worse still, they had a reason, and one which you will find very embarrassing. **Their Master** told them so. **He shared, and indeed created, their delusion.** He said in so many words, "this generation shall not pass till all these things be done." **And he was wrong.** He clearly knew no more about the end of the world than anyone

---

149   C. S. Lewis, *The Problem of Pain* (New York: Harper Collins edition, 1996), p. 66.

150   Lewis, *Reflections on the Psalms*, p. 112.

else. **It is certainly the most embarrassing verse in the Bible.** Yet, how teasing also, that within fourteen words of it should come the statement, "But of that day and that hour knoweth no man, no, not the angels which are in heaven, neither the Son, but the Father." **The one exhibition of error and the one confession of ignorance grow side by side.** That they stood thus in the mouth of Jesus himself, and were not merely placed thus by the reporter, we surely need not doubt. . . . The facts, then are these: that **Jesus professed himself (in some sense) ignorant, and within a moment showed that he really was so.**[151]

Here are several points regarding Lewis' beliefs reflected in the previous quote:

1. The disciples were wrong about the Second Coming.
2. Jesus contributed to their error.
3. This constitutes an embarrassment for Christians today.
4. Our Lord's "error" was joined with His ignorance.
5. The Bible testifies against Jesus.

This last point is particularly damaging to Lewis. First, he affirms that these words were really the words of Jesus—"That they stood thus in the mouth of Jesus himself, and were not merely placed thus by the reporter, we surely need not doubt." Lewis then says that he believes Matthew (the reporter) writing in Matthew 24. For Lewis, Matthew basically testifies against his Lord because Jesus really spoke these words! How sacrilegious! Christians who tolerate an individual with such beliefs as being teacher for them and their children is simply symptomatic of the apostasy and confusion in the churches today. A simple heartfelt trust in the Saviour would certainly clear up the confusion.

It is important to observe that while Jesus did profess *ignorance*—He

---

151   C. S. Lewis, "The World's Last Night," *The World's Last Night and Other Essays* (Orlando: Harcourt, Inc., 1987), pp. 97–99.

did not know the day nor the hour[152]—a profession of ignorance is not the same thing as being "wrong." If Jesus were "wrong" as Lewis asserts, then Jesus was guilty of leading His disciples astray—which is exactly what Lewis believed. If this is true, then on what grounds do we believe anything that Jesus said? Maybe He was "wrong" too in the Sermon on the Mount, or in dozens of other passages dear to Bible-believing Christians. Would you want C. S. Lewis teaching in Sunday school if you knew that he would intentionally teach such things to your children openly on Sunday morning? If not, then why is okay for him to have access to them at other times through his written works?

When Jesus said "This generation shall not pass, till all these things be fulfilled,"[153] He was referring to the cataclysmic judgments of the Tribulation period and was speaking of the nearness of the end to the signs that He was predicting. The generation that sees all of the signs that He foretold would not end until the prophecy is completely fulfilled. It is that generation to whom He referred, not the one that was standing before Him.

During His earthly ministry Jesus knew a lot of things. He knew about the Samaritan woman's past.[154] He knew that Peter was going to catch a fish with a coin in its mouth.[155] He also knew that Lazarus was dead.[156] It may be that Lewis believed in the heretical "Kenosis Theory," the view that Jesus emptied Himself of His deity. This theory, quite popular in England in Lewis' day—holds that the words of Philippians 2:7—"But made himself of no reputation"—should be translated "But he emptied himself." Yet a little study and reflection will show that Jesus "made himself of no reputation" not by ceasing to be what He was but by taking upon Himself something that He was *not* prior to the Incarnation—humanity.

Throughout the earthly ministry of our Lord, Christ exhibited the

---

152 Matthew 24:36, Mark 13:32.

153 Matthew 24:34.

154 John 4:7ff.

155 Matthew 17:27.

156 John 11:11-13.

prerogatives of deity. He claimed that only God could forgive sin, but did Himself forgive sin and proved it through a miracle.[157] Jesus taught authoritatively because His authority was primary and not acquired, as in the case of the scribes.[158] Moreover, Jesus exhibited divine capacities beyond which any mere mortal was completely incapable. Though "alone on the land" he saw His disciples "toiling in rowing"[159] and stilled the angry wind and waves.[160]

Whatever Jesus needed to know and do in fulfillment of His messianic ministry He knew and did. Certain limitations resulting from His human nature can be seen in the Gospels, but we are nowhere told that He was "wrong," or that He taught "error" and contributed to any "delusion" on the part of the disciples or anyone else. It is heretical to teach otherwise. Jesus *lived* as God manifest in the flesh with certain imposed limitations. He hungered,[161] thirsted,[162] and tired as a man. Jesus *died* on the cross in fulfillment of His messianic ministry, but He certainly did not die as a sinner.

In the earthly ministry of Jesus we do NOT see deity irrevocably lost, but rather deity deliberately restrained. Since there can be no remission of sin apart from the shedding of blood[163] and since "it behooved him to be made like unto his brethren,"[164] Jesus was truly man, yet without sin.[165]

Lewis had no more respect for the Old Testament than did he for the New. He felt free to liken his storytelling to that of the book of Job. "The Book of Job," wrote Lewis, **"appears to me unhistorical because** it begins about a man quite unconnected with all history or even legend, with no genealogy, living in a country of which the Bible elsewhere has hardly anything

---

157   Mark 2:5-12.

158   Mark 1:22.

159   Mark 6:47–48.

160   Mark 6:51.

161   Matthew 21:18.

162   John 19:28.

163   Hebrews 9:22.

164   Hebrews 2:17.

165   Hebrews 4:15.

to say; because, in fact, **the author quite obviously writes as a story-teller not as a chronicler.**" [166]

It would seem an obvious point to say that Lewis did not believe, nor respect the Word of God. What do we mean when we say that the Bible is the Word of God? In the words of J. Gresham Machen, a Christian scholar who was a contemporary of C. S. Lewis:

> When we say that the Bible is the Word of God, we mean something very definite indeed. We mean that the Bible is true. We mean that the writers of the Bible, in addition to all their providential qualifications for their task, received an immediate and supernatural guidance and impulsion of the Spirit of God which kept them from the errors that are found in other books, and made the resulting book, the Bible, to be completely true in what it says regarding matters of fact, and completely authoritative in its commands. That is the great doctrine of the full or plenary inspiration of the Holy Scripture. [167]

We believe the full inspiration and preservation of the Bible is the only adequate view of Scripture in today's world of confusing "isms" and shifting moral values. C. S. Lewis, however, came nowhere near this basic belief in the Bible as the Word of God. Rather, he found it to be fraught with contradictions and marred by the marks and characteristics of fallible human authors.

On May 7, 1959—some four years before his death—Lewis commented on Wheaton College's views regarding the inspiration of the Bible. Each of the six numbered points below expresses Lewis' high degree of skepticism regarding the inspiration and authority of the Bible. His comments sound eerily similar to those made by non-believers. In each case we, the authors, respond to his criticisms of the Bible. Lewis wrote:

---

166   Lewis, *Reflections on the Psalms*, (Harvest Books, 1964), p. 110.

167   J. Gresham Machen, *The Christian View of Man* (London: Banner of Truth Trust, 1965, originally published in 1937, p. 14.

Whatever view we hold on the divine authority of Scripture (we) must make room for the following facts:

1. **The distinction which St. Paul makes in 1 Cor. vii between ["not I, but the Lord"] and ["I speak, not the Lord"].**

   The authors' answer to Lewis' statement: Lewis is here making a classic blunder that has been repeated by skeptics who have argued for centuries that there are degrees of inspiration in the Bible. Paul, allegedly, believed that some of what he wrote had a higher degree of authority because he was simply repeating what the Lord said, but that other teachings in Scripture—"I speak, not the Lord"—have a lower degree of authority because Paul, and not the Lord, was giving the teaching.

   However, Lewis is reading more into the passage[168] than is really there. In the former the apostle is citing the command of the Lord Jesus Christ given during His earthly ministry. In the latter, Paul is *not* quoting a direct command of the Lord *because Jesus never directly addressed the issue that Paul was then addressing*—namely the case of a marriage where one partner is a pagan and the other is a believer.

   Paul ministered in a pagan environment; Jesus did not. Should a person who has become a Christian after being married stay in the marriage? Paul's answer is "yes." Jesus never taught on this issue during His earthly ministry, hence the apostle's statement that he is speaking, not the Lord. Paul's admission is simply his particular style of writing and certainly not intended to lessen the importance of this particular passage of Scripture! All of Paul's canonical writings are the words of God.

2. **The apparent inconsistencies between the genealogies in Matt i and Luke ii: with the accounts of the death of Judas in Matt xxvii 5 and Acts i. 18-19.**

   Authors' answer: Once again, Lewis is finding fault with the Bible and using what he perceives to be "inconsistencies"—a nice word for "errors"—to soften any claim to the full inspiration and preservation

---

168   1 Corinthians 7:10 and 12.

of the Bible.

These so-called inconsistencies arise from the different purposes of Matthew and Luke and are definitely not errors. Matthew, who evidently was targeting a Jewish audience and seeking to prove that Jesus Christ is Israel's Messiah, begins with Abraham, the father of the Jewish people, while Luke traces the line in reverse order and goes back to Adam, showing Jesus' relationship to the entire human race. Matthew was interested in tracing the legal descent of the house of David and essentially restricts himself to heirs to the throne. Any "contradiction" is conceived by men that simply do not believe the book.

Regarding the death of Judas, there is no conflict. Although the accounts are not identical, they are not contradictory but rather complementary. In fact, if all the parallel passages in the Bible—both Old and New Testaments—were identical, one would be inclined to suspect some kind of deliberate attempt on the part of the human authors to make everything "fit"—sort of a conspiracy to make the Bible sound like the Word of God. The fact that there are differences (which have often led skeptics to claim there are "errors") suggests that the writers were simply reporting facts from their perspective. Matthew 27:5 reports that Judas hung himself; but the body finally fell, as recorded in Acts 1:18, either because of decay or because someone cut the rope. Either the force of the fall, or the decomposed state of the body, could have caused it to break open in the middle.

3. **St. Luke's own account of how he obtained his matter (i.1-4).**

Authors' answer: There is nothing in the biblical doctrine of divine inspiration which requires that the inspired writer's source of information be a direct revelation from God. The doctrine simply teaches that God superintended the message of the writer so that what he wrote—whether from direct inspiration or otherwise—he was guarded from error. Luke carefully investigated everything concerning the ministry of Jesus that was handed down by eyewitnesses and recorded only that which was true.

4. **The universally admitted unhistoricity (I do not say, of course, falsity)**

of at least some narratives in Scripture (the parables), which may well extend also to Jonah and Job.

Authors' answer: Parabolic and symbolic portions of Scripture are usually identified as such. When Jesus said, "The kingdom of heaven is *like* . . ." we know that He was speaking a parable. Some spoken and written discourse may contain symbols. However, both the books of Jonah and Job, as well as the creation account of Genesis and the fall of man, report events that are told in straightforward historical discourse. If Lewis believes that they are "unhistorical," it is because of a preconceived bias on his part and his comments should be given no greater consideration than any other misconceived pronouncement by any other person who has such a low regard for Scripture.

5. **If every good and perfect gift comes from the Father of Lights then all true and edifying writings, whether in Scripture or not, must be in some sense inspired.**

    Authors' answer: Lewis has revealed one of his core beliefs. He had a high view of "true and edifying writings," whether scriptural or not, and a low view of Scripture.

    We take strong exception to this, and to Lewis' statement in point 5. A gift can be *good and perfect* without being divinely inspired, and normative in the sense that Scripture is inspired and normative. No doubt, God has blessed pagans with a measure of wisdom and knowledge. He makes the sun to shine and the rain to fall on the righteous as well as on the unrighteous. This is "common grace."[169] But "common grace" did not produce the inspired Scripture. Non-canonical writings can in no way be inspired in the same sense as canonical writings. To maintain that they are in any sense opens a door to all kinds of error and heresy.

6. **John xi 49–52. Inspiration may operate in a wicked man without his knowing it, and he can then utter the untruth he intends (propriety of making an innocent man a political scapegoat) as well as the truth he does not intend (the divine sacrifice).**

---

169   See Matthew 5:45.

Authors' comments: This is simply an extension of what Lewis has said under point 5. The same critique that is offered under that point can be applied here.

Lewis then draws the following conclusions based on his six points, which serve to further reveal his confusion and scriptural infidelity. Lewis writes:

> It seems to me that 2 and 4 rule out the view that every statement in Scripture must be historical truth. And 1, 3, 5, and 6 rule out the view that inspiration is a single thing in the sense that, if present at all, it is always present in the same mode and the same degree. Therefore, I think, rule out the view that any one passage taken in isolation can be assumed to be inerrant in exactly the same sense as any other: e.g., that the numbers of O.T. armies (which in view of the size of the country, if true, involve continuous miracle) are statistically correct because the story of the Resurrection is historically correct. That the over-all operation of Scripture is to convey God's Word to the reader (he also needs his inspiration) who reads it in the right spirit, I fully believe. That it also gives true answer to all the questions (often religiously irrelevant) which he might ask, I don't. The very kind of truth we are often demanding was, in my opinion, not even envisaged by the ancients. [170]

Lewis doubts that the Bible "gives true answer to all the questions (often religiously irrelevant)" that people ask. But what is "religiously irrelevant"? Is the creation of the universe out of nothing "religiously irrelevant"? Are historical and archaeological facts "religiously irrelevant"? Lewis might say "yes"; but if we can't trust God's Word in what we can see and verify, how can we trust it in matters that we can't see and verify, such as the Rapture, the Millennial Kingdom, the necessity of the new birth, and dozens of other topics?

We also wonder about the validity of his statement concerning what was

---

170   Michael J. Christensen, *C. S. Lewis on Scripture* (Abingdon, 1979), Appendix A.   www.
cresourcei.org/lewisbib.html

"envisaged by the ancients." Did the writers of the Bible have to understand everything about which they wrote? Couldn't they have addressed issues by the inspiration of the Holy Spirit, which were beyond their understanding? It is certainly true, for example, that they did not have to understand how God created all things out of nothing for it be a valid teaching of the Bible.

Lewis maintained what could rightly be called a "neo-orthodox" view of Scripture, and would have been very comfortable with Karl Barth and Emil Brunner on biblical authority. Lewis argued, for example, that the Bible is not the Word of God, but rather that Scripture "carries the word of God." This sounds very much like the neo-orthodox claim that the Bible is not the Word of God but that it somehow "becomes" the word of God in some kind of an "existential encounter" with the recipient of revelation. Along these lines is a noteworthy statement found in Lewis' *Reflections on the Psalms* in which Lewis wrote:

> Naïveté, error, contradiction, even (as in the cursing Psalms) wickedness are not removed. **The total result is not "the Word of God" in the sense that every passage, in itself, gives impeccable science or history.** It carries the Word of God.... [171]

Within the same Lewis book, John Robbins points out that: "Lewis claimed that certain parts of the Psalms are characterized with 'fatal confusion' and are in part 'devilish,' 'diabolical,' 'contemptible,' 'petty' and 'vulgar.'" [172]

These statements simply cannot be glossed over or ignored. Lewis has placed himself as judge over the Bible. This same faithless expression has spread through the seminaries at near epidemic proportions. With Lewis' perspective, will Christians allow Scripture to mold their lives or will they become the judge of Scripture? What chance of transformation is there if the Scripture we don't like becomes "contemptible" and "petty"? This is not

171 Lewis, *Reflections on the Psalms*, p. 111-112.

172 John W. Robbins, "Did C.S. Lewis Go To Heaven?," Trinity Foundation (12/22/05), p. 61. www.trinityfoundation.org/journal.php?id=103

submission to the Word of God! Evidently, Lewis believed that the Bible must be judged by human reason and not the other way around.

Yet, the apostle writes that gentiles walk "in the vanity of their mind, having the understanding darkened, being alienated from the life of God through the ignorance that is in them, because of the blindness of their heart."[173] Does Lewis exclude himself and other intellectuals from this and other indictments of the natural mind? If he does, there is very little hope of transformation for those with a similar mindset.

Lewis believed that certain parts of the Bible are more inspired by God than others, and that certain parts of Scripture are totally pagan and unworthy of our serious attention.

As a literary critic C. S. Lewis brought his critical skills to his study of the Bible. Sprague writes:

> I think what Lewis would say in defense of his definition for inspiration is that "not all Scripture is inspired for the same purpose or in the same way." . . . Again we are faced with his beliefs that Job, Jonah and Esther were non-historical and that the early stories of Genesis are mythical. But he would argue that their non-historical elements and mythology say nothing about their spiritual truth. Lewis would continue to argue that the writers were moved, guided, unctioned—whatever word you want—"by the divine pressure" of God.[174]

Lewis sought to justify his view of Scripture by his understanding of myth which, in his view, may have historically verifiable elements, but not necessarily so. One author writes that Lewis viewed myth "as a story that could be and might be true, but does not need to be historically or scientifically true because it is meant to communicate something bigger than history

---

173 Ephesians 4:18.

174 Duncan Sprague, "The Unfundamental C.S. Lewis: Key Components of Lewis' View of Scripture," (12/19/05), pp. 8–9.
www.leaderu.com/marshill/mhr02/lewis1.html

or science."[175] It is spiritual infidelity to claim that the Old Testament stories—Jonah, Esther, or even the creation account—may not be historical at all but simply communicate something significant to man.

This kind of thinking, unfortunately, has become increasingly popular in evangelical circles. Many evangelicals, often embarrassed by a "talking snake" or a worldwide deluge, seek to maintain their "academic credibility" with the unbelieving world by arguing that the meaning of the story, and not necessarily its historicity, "is the main thing." They hope to maintain a credible image with their faithless peers by claiming that the Scripture contains "factual errors," but the overall message is reliable.

However, there is absolutely no indication that the creation account is at all allegorical. In fact, all the marks of a true historical account are to be found in the text. We are never told that Genesis 1–3 is parabolic, and we never read, "The creation of the world is *like* . . ." Both the Lord Jesus Christ[176] and the apostle Paul[177] regarded those chapters as historical. The point that Paul makes in the Romans 5 passage is that just as sin was imputed to the race in Adam, so also is righteousness imputed to the sinner through the faith of Jesus Christ. If the imputation of the one is not real, i.e., if Adam never existed, then one cannot logically believe that the imputation of the other is real either.

So much for "the Bible according to C. S. Lewis." Let's change our perspective and look at "C. S. Lewis according to the Bible."

C. S. Lewis According to the Bible

With the plethora of uncertain sounds emanating from pulpits and "Christian" ministries, churches have never been less prepared to combat the false and dangerous teachings that are continuing to multiply.

Significantly, the apostasy of which the Bible speaks comes from within the ranks of professing Christendom. "Apostasy" means to fall away from

---

175   Ibid., p. 8.

176   See Luke 17:26.

177   See Rom 5:12ff.

something, hence "apostasy" cannot happen to those who have never made a profession of faith, or to those who have never been part of the visible church. Paul warned the Ephesian elders, "For I know this, that after my departing shall grievous wolves enter in among you, not sparing the flock. **Also of your own selves shall men arise, speaking perverse things,** to draw away disciples after them."[178]

The Bible assures us that the very thing that men imagine to be right in their own hearts is never a good measure of what is right or true. In every age God warns about deception and man's natural proclivities to be lead away from God's truth.

> And the LORD smelled a sweet savour; and the LORD said in his heart, I will not again curse the ground any more for man's sake; **for the imagination of man's heart is evil from his youth**; neither will I again smite any more every thing living, as I have done.[179]

> **The heart is deceitful above all things**, and desperately wicked: who can know it?[180]

> **Woe unto them that call evil good,** and good evil; that put darkness for light, and light for darkness; that put bitter for sweet, and sweet for bitter![181]

> Not everyone that saith unto me, Lord, Lord, shall enter into the kingdom of heaven; but he that doeth the will of my Father which is in heaven. Many will say to me in that day, Lord, **Lord, have we not prophesied in thy name? And in thy name have cast out devils? And in thy name done many wonderful works? And then will I profess unto them, I never knew you:** depart from me, ye that work iniquity.[182]

---

178   Acts 20:29–30.

179   Genesis 8:21.

180   Jeremiah 17:9.

181   Isaiah 5:20.

182   Matthew 7:21–23.

See then that ye walk circumspectly, not as fools, but as wise, Redeeming the time, **because the days are evil.**[183]

On the basis of Scripture we can affirm that what the Bible says, God says. It is truly God's Word and God's words. The Bible has the same authority as God Almighty. It is to be obeyed with the same earnestness, diligence, and reverence because the words of Scripture are the very words of God.

The book of Romans is instructive in this regard: "For **the scripture saith unto Pharaoh,** Even for this same purpose have I raised thee up, that I might shew my power in thee, and that my name might be declared throughout all the earth."[184] This is a quotation from Exodus[185] as God addresses Pharaoh. Though God spoke it, it is recorded in Scripture by the apostle Paul in a unique fashion. Under the inspiration of the Holy Spirit, the apostle Paul equates God speaking with Scripture speaking.[186]

Jesus Himself clearly believed in the *verbal-plenary inspiration* of Scripture. The very words ("verbal") of Scripture (not just the general thoughts as many evangelicals teach) are fully ("plenary") inspired. Jesus said: "For verily I say unto you, Till heaven and earth pass, one jot or one tittle shall in no wise pass from the law, till all be fulfilled."[187] The "jot" and "tittle" refer to the smallest part of a letter—like the dot over an "i" and the cross beam of a "t." Regretfully, C. S. Lewis did not display this view of Scripture, or even anything remotely resembling it. His condescending view of Scripture is especially dangerous from someone so highly esteemed by men. The Lord Jesus Christ warned about those who were held in such high regard by men. "Woe unto you, when all men shall speak well of you! for so did their fathers to the false prophets."[188]

---

183 Ephesians 5:15.

184 Romans 9:17.

185 Exodus 9:16.

186 See also Galatians 3:8.

187 Matthew 5:18.

188 Luke 6:26.

Lewis and the Substitutionary Death of Christ

Christ's substitutionary death is one of the cardinal, foundational doctrines of the Christian faith. Without believing that Christ died in the place of unworthy sinners for the purpose of receiving the sinner's penalty, Christ's crucifixion simply becomes an unfathomable fact of history. The sacrifice of Christ was an event so basic that it was planned from eternity past, for Christ is described as "the Lamb that hath been slain from the foundation of the world."[189] Sin did not take God by surprise and neither was God's provision for sin a sudden improvisation.

Yet, C. S. Lewis was unbelievably confused on this point too. His writings reject the very heart of the gospel. In his famous *Mere Christianity,* Lewis claims that Christ came to teach, and then plunges on to indicate that even the apostles missed this "truth" and put too much emphasis on His death.

> **What did he [Jesus Christ] come to do? Well, to teach of course; but as soon as you look into the New Testament or any other Christian writing you will find they are constantly talking** about something different—**about His death** and His coming to life again. **It is obvious that Christians think the chief point of the story lies there.** They think the main thing He came to earth to do was to suffer and be killed.
>
> Now before I became a Christian I was under the impression that the first thing Christians had to believe was one particular theory as to what the point of this dying was. According to that theory God wanted to punish men for having deserted and joined the Great Rebel, but Christ volunteered to be punished instead, and so God let us off. Now I admit that **even this theory does not seem to me quite so immoral and so silly as it used to be**; but that is not the point I want to make. What I came to see later on was that **neither this theory nor any other is Christianity.** . . . Theories about Christ's death are not Christianity.[190]

---

189   Revelation 13:8

190   Lewis, *Mere Christianity*, p. 53–54.

Lewis' thoughts on the substitutionary death of Christ are simply heretical! According to his own words he disagrees with what the Bible teaches. Shockingly, Lewis questions the New Testament emphasis on the gospel—Christ's death, burial, and resurrection. Lewis, like many other religious academicians, misses the whole point for Christ's becoming a man. It was not first and foremost to teach—it was to take away the sin of the world. That involved His personal sacrifice and shed blood, not the manner in which He taught. Many passages prove this point; however, John's proclamation upon first seeing Christ is quite revealing. "The next day John seeth Jesus coming unto him, and saith, **Behold the Lamb of God, which taketh away the sin of the world.**"[191]

John the Baptist associates the sacrificial Lamb of God with His taking away the sin of the world. The apostle Paul continues this line of thought, indisputably revealing why Christ died. He died for the ungodly—He died for us!

> For when we were yet without strength, in due time **Christ died for the ungodly**. . . . But God commendeth his love toward us, in that, while we were yet sinners, **Christ died for us.** [192]

According to Lewis the biblical emphasis upon Christ's supernatural sacrifice should be redirected away from His death and focused upon His teachings. This helps explain the popularity of Lewis. The unregenerate man can handle the moral teachings of a religious figure, but he does not want to be faced with the absolute necessity of accepting Christ's singular substitutionary blood atonement. This is the dividing line between accepting Christ as Saviour or simply recognizing Him as a wonderful prophet or teacher.

Apart from the atoning death of Jesus Christ, and all of the various types of it found in the Old Testament, there could be no access to God by sinful man. About a hundred years ago, Dyson Hague, Canon of St. Paul's Cathedral, London, Ontario, who came from the same liturgical tradition as did Lewis, correctly wrote:

---

191 John 1:29.

192 Romans 5:8.

The Atonement [the death of Christ on the cross to bring about reconciliation] is Christianity in epitome. It is the heart of Christianity as a system; it is the distinguishing mark of the Christian religion. For Christianity is more than a revelation; it is more than an ethic. Christianity is uniquely a religion of redemption.[193]

Hague continues by showing how the atonement of Christ is tied in with the Old Testament sacrificial system, based on the shedding of the blood of the victim.

In one word: the whole system was designed to teach the holiness and righteousness of God, the sinfulness of men, and the guilt of sin; and **above all, to show that it was God's will that forgiveness should be secured,** not on account of any works of the sinner or anything that he could do, any act of repentance or exhibition of penitence, or performance of expiatory or restitutionary works, but **solely on account of the undeserved grace of God through the death of a victim guilty of no offence against the Divine law, whose shed blood represented the substitution of an innocent for a guilty life.**[194]

Christians are to be involved in reconciling the world unto God. The only way to do this is through the gospel. The apostle reveals that gospel in a nutshell, as follows: "Moreover, brethren, I declare unto you **the gospel . . . how that Christ died for our sins** according to the scriptures; And that he was **buried,** and that he **rose again** the third day according to the scriptures."[195]

No true Christian with any true spiritual sensibilities would ever dare to belittle the gospel. Christ came into the world "to save sinners." Our

---

193   Dyson Hague, "At-One-Ment by Propitiation," in *The Fundamentals: A Testimony to the Truth*, ed. by R. A. Torrey, A. C. Dixon, and others, Vol. III. (Grand Rapids: Baker Books, 1993), originally issued by the Bible Institute of Los Angeles in 1917), p. 78.

194   Ibid., p. 79.

195   1 Corinthians 15:1–4.

Lord did more than teach certain ethical principles; He taught about the purpose of His death. Jesus Christ was born to die: "This is a faithful saying, and worthy of all acceptation, that **Christ Jesus came into the world to save sinners; of whom I am chief.**"[196] Prior to Christ's birth, the angel announced the following:

> But while he thought on these things, behold, the angel of the Lord appeared unto him in a dream, saying, Joseph, thou son of David, fear not to take unto thee Mary thy wife: for that which is conceived in her is of the Holy Ghost. And she shall bring forth a son, and thou shalt call his name JESUS: **for he shall save his people from their sins.**[197]

No man can effectively communicate the gospel after having missed the whole point of the substitutionary death of Christ. If you are wrong on this, you are wrong on sin and on the very character of God. Yet, according to J. I. Packer, Lewis' command over the English language enabled him to be a powerful and effective communicator of the gospel.

> The combination within him of insight with vitality, wisdom with wit, and imaginative power with analytical precision made Lewis **a sparkling communicator of the everlasting gospel.** Matching Aslan in the Narnia stories with (of course!) the living Christ of the Bible and of Lewis' instructional books, and his presentation of Christ could hardly be more forthright. [198]

Lewis' command of the English language actually enabled him to speak out of both sides of his mouth. Each opposing group could find something within his writings that eloquently proved their respective positions. This is an amazing feat for this is said from groups that adamantly oppose each

---

196 1 Timothy 1:15.

197 Matthew 1:20–21.

198 J. I. Packer

other—even those on opposite sides of the truth of the gospel.

Packer could look at Aslan and believe that Lewis' works clearly communicate the gospel, yet a pagan could read the same materials and come away satisfied that Lewis was really one of them. Biblical Christianity and paganism are mutually exclusive—pagans are not Christians and Christians are not pagans. No true Christian living the life of Christ can both promulgate the gospel and at the same time affirm one's belief in pagan teachings.

Lewis and Evolution

It is evident from Lewis' writings that he simply did not believe the literal story of creation as revealed in the Word of God. Here's what he wrote in his book, *Reflections on the Psalms:*

> I have therefore no difficulty in accepting, say, the view of those scholars who tell us that the account of **Creation in *Genesis* is derived from earlier Semitic stories which were Pagan and mythical. . . . Stories do not reproduce their species like *mice. They are told by men.*** [199]

Lewis simply did not believe in the reliability and accuracy of the Genesis account of creation. He believed the account was man-made. Lewis' unscriptural views of the creation of man are profoundly corrupt and put him in the same camp with Charles Darwin. In the same book, Lewis wrote:

> For on any view man is in one sense clearly made "out of" something else. He is an animal; but an animal called to be, or raised to be, or (if you like) doomed to be, something more than an animal. **On the ordinary biological view (what difficulties I have about evolution are not religious) one of the primates is changed so that he becomes man; but he remains still a primate and an animal.** [200]

---

199   C. S. Lewis, *Reflections on the Psalms,* p. 110.

200   Ibid., 115.

Lewis' ideas are, indisputably, catching on with many churches. In an *Answers in Genesis* report dated February 6, 2006, we read that hundreds of congregations in the United States will be having a "Darwin praise service . . . celebrating. . . the 197th anniversary of the birth of Charles Darwin. It's called 'Evolution Sunday.'" How did all of this come about? The authors of the article, Ken Ham and Mark Looy, explain:

> Two years ago, Prof. Michael Zimmerman at the University of Wisconsin (its Oshkosh campus)—and also its dean of the College of Letters and Sciences—began what became known as "The Clergy Letter Project."
>
> Using the university's website, Zimmerman encouraged clergy across America to sign a letter that supports evolution and rejects the Genesis account of creation as literal history. . . .
>
> The next step for Zimmerman (again, using the university's website) was to solicit donations so that funds could be obtained to publicize this clergy letter and to gain exposure across the nation. He set up an arrangement with an organization called The Christian Alliance for Progress (CAP) to accept tax-deductible donations for his national project. . . . [201]

Christians clearly need to distance themselves from this kind of thinking, whether it comes from a university professor or someone of the stature of C. S. Lewis.

Evolution says that we evolved from something in the universe, yet the Bible attributes the creation to God Almighty. "And God said, Let us make man **in our image**. . . ."[202] The word "image" emphasizes the likeness and conformity between two separate beings—in this case, man and God. When something is made in the image of another, it can be likened to a die used in coin production. The picture in the die reappears, in some measure, on the coin. The image of God in man suggests three things:

---

201   www.answersingenesis.org/docs2006/0206evol_Sunday.asp?vPrint=1   (2/8/06).

202   Genesis 1:26.

1. Man's natural likeness with God (intellect, emotions, and a will). Man's capacity to worship and honor the Creator distinguishes him from the animals.
2. Man's moral likeness with God. Man is a moral being who can distinguish between right and wrong.
3. Man's positional likeness with God. Man was created to have "dominion" over the creation.[203]

This doctrine of special creation is one of the fundamental tenets of the Christian faith. Man neglects, or ignores, this foundational truth to his own peril. Public schools, universities, society in general, and many so-called Christian schools have all become evolutionary. So where does C. S. Lewis stand regarding special creation?

Lewis' views on evolution parallel some of his other aberrant views. One Christian author and teacher points out that although Lewis rejected naturalistic evolution, "he accepted theistic evolution and thought that the Old Testament contained mythical materials." Lewis "stressed the uniqueness of Christ, the historicity of the resurrection of Christ and the need for faith in order to be saved," but "he also believed in purgatory and in praying for the dead—claims that rankle many evangelicals who otherwise appreciate his work." [204]

No doubt, Lewis was weak on many cardinal issues of the Christian faith, but one author seeks to soften Lewis' views on special creation by observing: "Lewis produced most of his works before the birth of the modern creationist movement. For this reason (and because his background was in English Lit and not in science) he seems to be rather accommodating at times to the theory of evolution."[205] We wonder, however, if this really exonerates Lewis for his infidelity to Scripture. Here are some of his words on the subject.

---

203 Genesis 1:28.

204 *C. S. Lewis & Francis Schaeffer: Lessons for a New Century from the Most Influential Apologists of Our Time,* book review by Douglas Groothuis. pp. 2–3.
www.denverseminary.edu/dj/articles1999/0500/0501.php

205 www.ldolphin.org/cslevol.html (12/19/05), p. 1.

If by saying that man rose from brutality you mean simply that **man is physically descended from animals, I have no objection.** [206]

Lewis believed that the evolutionary process extolled today would be superseded by something else in the future.

> . . . I should expect the next stage in Evolution not to be a stage in Evolution at all: [I] should expect that Evolution itself as a method of producing change will be superseded. And finally, I should not be surprised if, when the thing happened, very few people noticed that it was happening. [207]

> For long centuries **God perfected the animal form which was to become the vehicle of humanity and the image of Himself.** He gave it hands whose thumb could applied to each of the fingers, and jaws and teeth. . . . The creature may have exited the ages in this state before it became man. . . .[208]

These are statements from Lewis' own pen, driven by the view that Lewis considered man simply the highest of the animals. In *Mere Christianity* he wrote: "When we come to **man, the highest of the animals. . . .**" [209] Some might object to calling Lewis a "theistic evolutionist." Was he?

Theistic evolution is the view that God simply superintended and guided the natural evolutionary processes. Lewis wrote:

> Century by century God has guided nature up to the point of producing creatures which can (if they will) be taken right out of nature, turned into "gods." . . . Until we follow Christ we are still parts of Nature, still in the womb of our great mother. Her pregnancy has been long and painful and anxious, but it has reached its climax.[210]

---

206 Lewis, *The Problem of Pain*, p. 67.

207 Lewis, *Mere Christianity,* p. 220.

208 Lewis, *The Problem of Pain*, p. 72.

209 Lewis, *Mere Christianity*, p. 158.

210 Ibid., p. 222.

This is theistic evolution.

Lewis and Heaven

Lewis' theistic evolution was certainly wrong, as were his views of Heaven itself. The fact that Lewis allegorized much of the biblical description of Heaven is frequently overlooked by his supporters. For example, he considered the crowns and streets of gold simply to be "scriptural imagery" to express the inexpressible.

> **All the scriptural imagery (harps, crowns, gold, etc.) is, of course, a merely symbolic attempt to express the inexpressible.** Musical instruments are mentioned because for many people (not all) music is the thing known in the present life which most strongly suggests ecstasy and infinity. **Crowns are mentioned to suggest** the fact that those who are united with God in eternity share His splendour and power and joy. **Gold is mentioned to suggest** the timelessness of heaven (gold does not rust) and the preciousness of it. [211]

Lewis' rejection of the biblical description of Heaven, along with his flimsy views of life's origin, is quite astounding when one considers that he rashly incorporated extrabiblical elements into his belief system. Lewis, for example, pictures animals in Heaven partaking the Christ-life flowing from their owners. This was consistent with his belief that animals could gain redemption through their masters. In *The Problem of Pain* Lewis wrote: "And in this way it seems to me possible that **certain animals may have an immortality, not in themselves, but in the immortality of their masters.**"[212]

What influenced Lewis' theological views of animals and his inclusion of them in his many works? As a child, Lewis entertained himself by writing and illustrating stories about animals.[213]

---

211   Ibid., p. 137.

212   C. S. Lewis, *The Problem of Pain* (New York, New York, HarperCollins, 1996) p. 144.

213   "Did You Know?" *Christianity Today* (7/1/85)

According to those who knew him, he was famous for his love of animals. His Oxford home, the Kilns, was overrun by cats and dogs. Sean Connolly, a priest studying Lewis for his doctoral thesis at the University of Oxford, referred to Lewis' views as "animal eschatology." He wrote that Lewis believed that "the beasts are to be understood only in their relation to man and through man . . . **the pets I had as a child—and indeed those I have now or may come to have later—may well be caught up in my experience of the heavenly realm when I died."**[214]

In *The Problem of Pain* we also read of his view that man had a redemptive function to perform concerning his pets. "If this hypothesis is worth considering, it is also worth considering whether **man**, at his first coming into the world, **had not already a redemptive function to perform. Man, even now, can do wonders to the animals. . . ."** [215]

In *The Great Divorce*, Lewis expressed his views concerning a woman's animals that followed her to Heaven.

> What are all these animals? A cat—two cats—dozen cats. And all these dogs . . . why, I can't count them. And the birds. And the horses . . . they are her beasts. "Did she keep a sort of zoo? I mean, this is a bit too much." **"Every beast and bird that came near her had its place in her love. In** her they became themselves. **And now the abundance of life she has in Christ from the Father flows over into them."**[216]

Sadly, Lewis did not take at face value the statements of the Bible concerning Heaven; however, he fearlessly and foolishly plunged ahead to design a "heaven" of his own making! Is this not a somber warning for those who take

www.ctlibrary.com/6276

214 Sean Connolly, "Animals and the Kingdom of Heaven," priest of the Diocese of East Anglia, doctoral work at the University of Oxford. www.all-creatures.org/ca/ark-194-animals.html
215 Lewis, *The Problem of Pain*, 140.
216 Lewis, *The Great Divorce*, pp. 119–120.

a similar kind of creative approach to their study of Scripture?

We find in all of this that Lewis had a fundamental disrespect for the Word of God. Lewis is so secular at times that he was uncomfortable with the Bible. In *The Silver Chair* Lewis describes Eustace's school, Experiment House, as a place where the Bible is discouraged. The bullies there are encouraged by the school authorities because their deeds are not seen as wrong, but as something that makes them "interesting psychological cases." Lewis speaks volumes in *The Silver Chair*: "The Head said they were interesting psychological cases and sent for them and talked to them for hours.... (When I was at school one would have said, 'I swear by the Bible.' **But Bibles were not encouraged at Experiment House**)...."[217]

Why would Lewis find it necessary to state that his fantasy school discourages the Bible? From the information already presented regarding Lewis' views on Scripture, this exclusion of the Bible seems to stem from the fact that he had very little respect for it. He had a low regard for what the Bible says about Heaven, and places the biblical revelation on par with the wisdom of the sages and pagan myths.

Lewis supporters have continually tried to minimize the significance of his statements on the Bible, but according to a study posted on the Christian Research Institute's website—certainly not a hard-nosed fundamentalist ministry—"**Lewis did not believe in an inerrant Bible,** though he did believe that Scripture was in some sense inspired. Some have tried to harmonize Lewis' words with biblical inerrancy and infallibility; unfortunately, this attempt is futile." [218]

Lewis and Hell

While Lewis spiritualized much of what the Bible says about Heaven, he flatly rejected what the Bible says about a literal Hell. In fact, he simply considered Hell to be a state of mind. His views are exhibited in *The Great*

---

217   C. S. Lewis, *The Silver Chair*, (New York, NY: Harper Collins, 1981), pp. 2, 6.

218   Steven P. Mueller, "Beyond Mere Christianity: An Assessment of C.S. Lewis." Christian Research Institute.
www.equip.org/free/JAL400.pdf

Divorce. "**Hell is a state of mind**—ye never said a truer word. And every state of mind, left to itself, every shutting up of the creature within the dungeon of its own mind—is, in the end, Hell."[219]

Lewis frequently wrote to, and confided in, a Catholic nun whom he referred to as "Sister Penelope." His biography identifies her as his friend of the Community of St. Mary the Virgin in Wantage.[220] In this next letter to her, he reveals to what extent he was willing to reject the plain teachings of Scripture in order to preserve his own heretical belief system. He wanted to find out how to "get over" (ignore) the plain teaching of Scripture.

> On October 24, 1940, Lewis wrote to Sister Penelope: "**About Hell; how do we get over Matthew 7:13, 14?** [Enter ye in at the strait gate: for wide is the gate, and broad is the way, that leadeth to destruction, and many there be which go in thereat: Because strait is the gate, and narrow is the way, which leadeth unto life, and few there be that find it.] **But I agree we *must* get over that one somehow or go mad. And leaving that one out, perhaps we can accept your argument that tho' hell exists, we are not absolutely forced to hold that anyone will reach it.**"[221]

From this letter and his quotation of Scripture within it, Lewis was obviously aware of the scriptural teachings concerning Hell; yet, he decided to pick and choose which passages of Scripture to accept or reject based on his own personal prejudices. He simply did not want to believe the Word of God. Being more interested in attempting to explain away the simple and direct truths of the Bible—especially ones that addressed issues he found hard to accept—he sidestepped upsetting verses like a pedestrian sidesteps bird droppings on a sidewalk.

May we suggest that Lewis did not simply have a problem with Hell.

219 C. S. Lewis, *The Great Divorce*, p. 70.

220 Roger Lancelyn Green, *C. S. Lewis: A Biography,*(Harvest Books Revised Edition, 1994), p. 198.

221 Roger Lancelyn Green, p. 221–222.

His real problem was with what Scripture teaches about God as Judge and dispenser of retribution upon those who reject His Son. What saith the Scripture?

> And the LORD God of their fathers sent to them by his messengers, rising up betimes, and sending; because he had compassion on his people, and on his dwelling place: **But they mocked the messengers of God, and despised his words, and misused his prophets, until the wrath of the LORD arose against his people, till there was no remedy.** Therefore he brought upon them the king of the Chaldees, who slew their young men with the sword in the house of their sanctuary, and had no compassion upon young man or maiden, old man, or him that stopped for age: he gave them all into his hand.[222]

> And these shall go away into everlasting punishment; but the righteous into life eternal.[223]

> And whosoever shall offend one of these little ones that believe in me, it is better for him that a millstone were hanged about his neck, and he were cast into the sea. And if thy hand offend thee, cut it off; it is better for thee to enter into life maimed, than having two hands to go into hell, into **the fire that never shall be quenched:** Where their worm dieth not, and the fire is not quenched.[224]

> Which is a manifest token of the righteous judgment of God, that ye may be counted worthy of the kingdom of God, for which ye also suffer. **Seeing it is a righteous thing with God to recompense tribulation to them that trouble you;** And to you who are troubled rest with us, when the Lord Jesus shall be revealed from heaven with his mighty angels, **In**

---

222 2 Chronicles 36:15–17.

223 Matthew 25:46.

224 Mark 9:42–44.

flaming fire taking vengeance on them that know not God, and that obey not the gospel of our Lord Jesus Christ: Who shall be **punished with everlasting destruction** from the presence of the Lord, and from the glory of his power. . . .[225]

Lewis and Universalism

In 1956, C. S. Lewis wrote *Till We Have Faces*. Even this late in his life—just a few years before his death, he strongly hints at Universalist teachings by claiming that we are all part of the *Whole*. **"We're all limbs and parts of one Whole. Hence, of each other, Men, and gods, flow in and out and mingle."**[226] It is this universal oneness evident in Lewis that makes him acceptable to the world at large that believes that any religion is acceptable so long as it accepts all others. Govindini Murty and Jason Apuzzo explain:

> "The Lion, the Witch and the Wardrobe" . . . is worthy of support from anyone, whether conservative or liberal, who believes in classic, **humanistic storytelling.** . . . Aslan, it has been debated, is intended by Narnia's author C. S. Lewis to be a symbol for Christ (the King of Kings) but of course the lion is also a royal and **divine symbol throughout world religion**; there are numerous lion-like divine figures in ancient Egyptian, Babylonian, Greek, Hindu and Buddhist religious symbolism. . . .
>
> The White Witch herself seems to be a throwback to various witches and goddesses of Celtic and Greek mythology. Her hair is dressed in the snake-like coils of Medusa. . . . It is perhaps that like a shamaness, the White Witch dons the lion's garb in order to assume his magical powers, or to signify some deeper connection with the figure of Aslan—**a connection that surmounts the duality of good and evil?** Why would the White Witch be garbed in leonine costume at the end, except perhaps as a sign that **she and Aslan are two halves of one whole,** and that they are playing out in ritual fashion an eternal cosmic struggle, where good and evil,

---

225 2 Thessalonians 1:5–9.

226 *Till We All Have Faces*, pp. 300–301.

light and dark, summer and winter alternate in ascendancy throughout the round of time?...

"Narnia" might have been written as a Christian allegory, but this is a movie that also draws on classical and world mythology, and can be enjoyed by people of all religious faiths.[227]

Lewis' concept of a universal oneness comes forth in the final book of the Narnia series, *The Last Battle*. In the following quotation, *Aslan* represents Christ and *Tash* represents Satan. Assuming that this correlation holds true, Lewis' premise would enforce the heresy of universalism by teaching that those who serve Satan all their lives have been unwittingly and ignorantly really serving God!

Then I fell at his feet and thought, Surely this is the hour of death, for the Lion (who is worthy of all honor) will know that **I have served Tash all my days** and not him. .... But the Glorious One bent down his golden head and touched my forehead with his tongue and said, Son, thou art welcome. But I said, Alas, Lord, I am no son of thine but **the servant of Tash.** He answered, **Child, all the service thou hast done to Tash, I account as service done to me.** Then by reason of my great desire for wisdom and understanding, I overcame my fear and questioned the Glorious One and said, Lord, is it then true, as the Ape said, that thou and Tash are one? The Lion growled so that the earth shook (but his wrath was not against me) and said, It is false. Not because he and I are one, but because we are opposites, **I take to me the services which thou hast done to him.** For I and he are of such different kinds that no service which is vile can be done to me, and none which is not vile can be done to him. **Therefore if any man swear by Tash and keep his oath for the oath's sake, it is by me that he has truly sworn, though he know it not, and it is I who reward him.** And if any man do a cruelty in my name, then, though he says the name Aslan, it is Tash whom he serves and by Tash his deed is accepted.

---

227   Newsmax (12/9/05), Murty and Apuzzo: "Narnia a Classic Tale of the Ages."

Dost thou understand, Child? I said, Lord thou knowest how much I understand. But I said also (for the truth constrained me), **Yet I have been seeking Tash all my days.** Beloved, said the Glorious One, unless thy desire had been for me thou wouldst not have sought so long and so truly. For all find what they truly seek.[228]

Lewis' message seems clear: those who do not know Jesus Christ are ultimately accepted by Him. In *Mere Christianity* Lewis defines his dangerous proposition even further.

> Here is another thing that used to puzzle me.... **Is it not frightfully unfair that this new life should be confined to people who have heard of Christ and been able to believe in Him?** But the truth is that God has not told us what His arrangements about the other people are. We do know that no man can be saved except thorough Christ; **we do not know that only those who know Him can be saved through Him.**[229]

But is the Bible really silent on this issue? Had Lewis not read of Cornelius, the sincere seeker in Acts 10?[230] Most Sunday school students know the inspired account. Cornelius and his whole family were devout. They gave generously to those in need and prayed to God. But that was not enough. Did his sincerity *in ignorance* mean that it was not necessary for him to hear the gospel and personally trust Christ? An angel came to Cornelius and revealed that his prayers had been heard. Yet, his works were not enough to save him.

> He saw in a vision evidently about the ninth hour of the day an angel of God coming in to him, and saying unto him, Cornelius. And when he looked on him, he was afraid, and said, What is it Lord? And he said unto him,

228 C. S. Lewis, *The Last Battle* (New York, NY: Harper Collins, 1984), pp. 204–206.

229 Lewis, *Mere Christianity*, p. 64.

230 See Acts 10:1–48.

> Thy prayers and thine alms are come up for a memorial before God. And now send men to Joppa, and call for one Simon, whose surname is Peter: He lodgeth with one Simon a tanner, whose house is by the sea side: he shall tell thee what thou oughtest to do.[231]

The biblical account reveals that Cornelius's sincerity was insufficient to save him. His sincerity did get a response from God. This indicates that God honors the requests of sincere seekers, but God's response was to send a preacher, Peter, who proclaimed Christ to Cornelius and his whole family.

This is not a hard or obscure doctrine.

> For God sent not his Son into the world to condemn the world; but that the world through him might be saved. He that **believeth on him is not condemned;** but he that believeth not is condemned already, because he hath not believed in the name of the only begotten Son of God.[232]

Willful unbelief or simple ignorance are both equally condemnatory.

Lewis mouths the fact that no man can be saved "except through Christ"; however, he openly denied that acceptance of Christ as Saviour was absolutely necessary for salvation. Lewis, and all who walk in his steps, have "two saviors": Jesus Christ, and "sincere ignorance." People may be saved by Jesus, in Lewis' thinking, but also by being sincerely ignorant. Yet the Bible plainly declares, "And this is life eternal, that they might know thee the only true God, and Jesus Christ, whom thou hast sent."[233]

The Christian faith, as revealed in the Scriptures, speaks of God's grace and love. In one sense God's love is unconditional. God accepts those who believe upon Him by faith unconditionally. He does not require that they first "clean up their lives" or "turn over a new leaf." He invites sinners to come as they are and He will make the heart change necessary for a renewed life.

---

231   Acts 10:3–6.

232   John 3:17–18.

233   John 17:3.

On the other hand, divine acceptance of the sinner is conditional: acceptance with God is for those who have put their faith in Jesus Christ and in Him alone: "He that believeth on the Son hath everlasting life: and he that believeth not the Son shall not see life; but the wrath of God abideth on him."[234] The Bible reveals two groups—believers and unbelievers; the forgiven and the condemned.

In our world of tolerance for everyone and everything, politically correct speech is elevated to the proverbial pedestal. The teaching of the Bible on this point seems terribly narrow and restrictive. Yet, there can be no mistaking Jesus on this. "Enter ye in at the strait gate: for wide is the gate, and broad is the way, that leadeth to destruction, and many there be which go in thereat: Because strait is the gate, and narrow is the way, which leadeth unto life, and few there be that find it."[235]

Contrary to popular belief, the way that leads to life is narrow and restrictive and very few find it. On the other hand, multitudes are going down the broad way—it's a superhighway with many lanes—to eternal destruction. It is the duty of every Christian to rescue as many people as possible from the road to destruction. Influential people who undermine the need for spreading the gospel should not be afforded access to others lest their influence convince others that evangelism is unnecessary.

One's faith must be focused on Jesus, who is the only Saviour. The Bible unequivocally says, "Neither is there salvation in any other: for there is none other name under heaven given among men, whereby we must be saved."[236] Yet in Lewis' modernistic theology sincerity is the deciding factor—the object of one's faith seems not to matter so long as the individual sincerely believes that he is right in whatever he believes.

Lewis further reveals what his unorthodox beliefs in chapter ten of *Mere Christianity*. He seeks to answer the question: "If Christianity is true why are

234   John 3:36.

235   Matthew 7:13–14.

236   Acts 4:12.

not all Christians obviously nicer than all non-Christians?"[237]

Part of the problem, observes Lewis, is that people

> may demand not merely that each man's life should improve if he becomes a Christian: they may also demand before they believe in Christianity that they should see the whole world neatly divided into two camps—Christian and non-Christian—and that all the people in the first camp at any given moment should be obviously nicer than all the people in the second.

Lewis, in his own revealing way, shows why this is unreasonable, but in doing so further reveals his spiritual infidelity and misunderstanding. Can a Christian slowly cease to be a Christian? Can a non-Christian, like a Buddhist, belong to Christ without knowing it by following those parts of his religion which are in agreement with Christianity?

> The world does not consist of 100 percent Christians and 100 percent non-Christians. There are people (a great many of them) **who are slowly ceasing to be Christians** but who still call themselves by that name: some of them are clergymen.
>
> **There are other people who are slowly becoming Christians though they do not yet call themselves so. There are people who do not accept the full Christian doctrine about Christ but who are so strongly attracted to Him that they are His in a much deeper sense than they themselves understand.** There are people in other religions who are being led by God's secret influence to concentrate on those parts of their religions which are in agreement with Christianity, **and who thus belong to Christ without knowing it.** For example, **a Buddhist of good will** may be led to concentrate more and more on the Buddhist teaching about mercy and to leave in the background (though he might still say he believed) the Buddhist teaching on certain other points. Many of the good Pagans long before Christ's birth may have been in this position. [238]

---

237 Lewis, *Mere Christianity*, p. 207.

238 Ibid., pp. 208–209.

Comments like this one—and there are many others—ought to make every doctrinally sound Christian unwilling to give a blanket endorsement of C. S. Lewis. Unfortunately, he would have made Larry King happy on "Larry King Live" when asked about the end of all non-Christians. Billy Graham, Joel Osteen, and Rick Warren, along with many other nationally-recognized Christian personalities, have consistently failed to give the right answer—God's answer—to Larry King when asked about the eternal consequences of those who fail to accept Christ.

So was C. S. Lewis really a universalist? Mueller, who seeks to give Lewis all the benefit of any doubt, writes concerning Lewis' desire for everyone to be accepted regardless of belief:

> Lewis was not a universalist; nevertheless, his description of salvation lacks biblical support. **Lewis said salvation is through Jesus Christ our Lord but also asserted that a person might belong to Christ without realizing it or explicitly knowing Him.** The only way to the Father is through the Son, but "we do not know that only those who know Him can be saved through Him." In other words, there can be **anonymous Christians**. It appears that here the medieval conception of the "righteous pagan" influenced Lewis. The passage from *Mere Christianity* describes such "good pagans" who *may* have belonged to Christ. Elsewhere Lewis suggested Akhenaten, Plato, and Virgil as examples of righteous pagans.[239]

Despite all of this incriminating evidence, major Christian leaders are holding Lewis up without reservation. In truth, however, C. S. Lewis should be regarded as one of the leading gurus for a watered-down, corrupted New Age Christianity that will save no one. His letters reveal much.

Lewis came to believe that virtuous heretics or pagans could be saved through Christ. "I think every prayer which is sincerely made even to a false god or to a very imperfectly conceived true God," he wrote to

---

239 Mueller, p. 5.

Mrs. Ashton on 8 November 1952, "is accepted by the true God and that Christ saves many who do not think they know Him."[240]

Lewis and Bible Prophecy

What did C.S. Lewis think of Bible prophecy? *Decision Magazine* (May 7, 1963) featured an interview with Sherwood Wirt, who asked Lewis: "What do you think is going to happen in the next few years of history, Mr. Lewis?" Lewis answered:

> I have no way of knowing. We have, of course, the assurance of the New Testament regarding events to come. **I find it difficult to keep from laughing when I find people worrying about future destruction of some kind or another.** Didn't they know they were going to die anyway? Apparently not. . . . The world might stop in ten minutes; meanwhile we are going to go on doing our duty. The great thing is to be found at one's post as a child of God, living each day as though it were our last but planning as though our world might last a hundred years.[241]

This is so typical of C. S. Lewis. Some of it is good: "We are to go on doing our duty," and we are "to be found at one's post as a child of God." And we certainly are not to be worrying about "future destruction." Yet there are other statements that reflect that he totally missed the mark. Lewis claims "I have no way of knowing" what will happen in the next few years. While we are not to date set or engage in "newspaper exegesis," we can know much about the direction of society, and gain a deeper understanding of current events, from Bible prophecy.

Lewis asked about those worrying about future destruction. "Didn't they know they were going to die anyway?" Yet, Scripture clearly says, "We shall not all sleep, but we shall all be changed. In a moment, in the twinkling of an

---

240 C. S. Lewis, *The Collected Letters of C.S. Lewis*, Vol. 2 (New York, NY: Harper Collins, 2004), p. 125.

241 William F. Jasper, "Discovering the World of Narnia," *The New American* (12/12/05), p. 24.

eye, at the last trump: for the trumpet shall sound, and the dead shall be raised incorruptible, and we shall be changed."[242] When Lewis asked "Didn't they know they were going to die anyway" he obviously was not aware of this most important New Testament passage. It teaches that there will be a "terminal generation" of Christians who will not die, but be translated. He failed to affirm the imminent return of Jesus Christ to catch away all believers.

Lewis and Suicide

Surely, some will instantly blurt out—Lewis did not believe in suicide. Let's hope not. However, an author can covertly reveal his true feelings regarding certain issues by portraying the chief protagonist in his novel as the purveyor of wisdom. In his book, *Till We All Have Faces*, the chief protagonist conveys his approval of suicide. "Have I not told you often that to **depart from life of a man's own will** when there is good reason is one of the things that are according to nature?"[243]

What could Lewis have meant by someone departing from life of his own free will? This little tidbit added to his other misstatements certainly paints an unfortunate, yet clear picture from a man that seemed gifted in saying what he meant to say.

---

242   1 Corinthians 15:51–52.

243   C. S. Lewis, *Till We All Have Faces: A Myth Retold* (Orlando, FL: Harcourt, Inc., 1984), p. 17.

Chapter 4

C. S. Lewis and the Ecumenical Movement

The Bible and Christian Unity

The Bible speaks about Christian unity, but it also speaks about contending for the faith. Before we look at the ecumenical views of C. S. Lewis, we need to examine one of the most misunderstood passages in all of Scripture, John 17. In this chapter Jesus prays to the Father: "That they may be one, even as we are one." There are several things that we must notice, however, lest we put words in the Lord's mouth and make Him say what He never intended to say.

For one thing, Jesus is praying for an organic unity of believers. He prays that the disciples may be one "even as we are one." The unity between the first and second Persons of the Godhead is the model. This is not an external, ecclesiastical unity where people get together in some kind of an ecumenical mix and forget their differences.

All too often we have heard sermons and messages that use this text to promote an ungodly unity of believers and unbelievers or apostates with other apostates. It is frightfully dangerous to liken the relationship of the Father and Son to this kind of an earthly, devilish unity that men are trying to produce!

Secondly, there is a distinctive unity of believers in verses 14–15. Jesus prays: "I have given them thy word; and the world hath hated them, because they are not of the world, even as I am not of the world." Jesus is not praying that they would mix with the world and become more like the world, but that they would continue to maintain their distinctives as His followers. In verses

16–17 He reinforces this and says: "They are not of the world, even as I am not of the world. Sanctify them through thy truth: thy word is truth."

We believe that this kind of unity is biblical and God-honoring. Ecumenists have no justification for claiming that Jesus' high priestly prayer supports their efforts at uniting all believers in some kind of an ecumenical hodge-podge. Clearly, that would be another example of a text without a context, making it a pretext.

This all means that judging and exercising discernment is not wrong. Jesus commanded, "Judge not according to appearance, but judge righteous judgment."[244] It is wrong to judge according to appearance, but Jesus makes it clear that there is such a thing as "righteous judgment." In fact, the apostle Paul taught: "He that is spiritual judgeth all things." [245]

The Bible gives several limitations and restrictions on judging, but these limitations and restrictions certainly do not condemn all judgment. It's important to remember that the abuse of a practice does not argue against the legitimate application of that practice. What are some of the limitations on judging?

For one thing, hypocritical judgment is wrong. "Judge not, that ye be not judged"[246] would seem to condemn all judgment, but the context reveals the meaning: "And why beholdest thou the mote that is in thy brother's eye, but considerest not the beam that is in thine own eye? Or how wilt thou say to thy brother, Let me pull out the mote out of thine eye; and, behold, a beam is in thine own eye?"[247]

Jesus was confronting the religionists of His day. He certainly was not addressing those who sincerely desire to expose error and to help others avoid error. In fact, what Jesus said a dozen verses later *requires* careful judgment: "Beware of false prophets, which come to you in sheep's clothing, but inwardly they are ravening wolves." What you see is NOT what you get. They

244 John 7:24.

245 1 Corinthians 2:15.

246 Matthew 7:1.

247 Matthew 7:2–3.

wear "sheep's clothing" but they are really "ravening wolves."[248]

The Bible also warns us against judging in matters of personal preference. Our personal tastes are not to be equated with God's will. While Christians may have certain personal opinions about a variety of matters, these opinions are not to be elevated to the position of divine law. It is imperative that we not judge people by human, non-moral standards, or by religious standards that are not binding on the conscience.

Paul makes this clear in Romans 14, where he deals with the issue of foods and days.

> Let not him that eateth despise him that eateth not: and let not him which eateth not judge him that eateth: for God hath received him. . . . One man esteemeth one day above another: another esteemeth every day alike. Let every man be fully persuaded in his own mind. He that regardeth the day, regardeth it unto the Lord; and he that regardeth not the day, to the Lord he doth not regard it. He that eateth, eateth to the Lord, for he giveth God thanks; and he that eateth not, to the Lord he eateth not, and giveth God thanks.[249]

C. S. Lewis and Christian Unity

Lewis seemed to advocate that anyone willing to be called a Christian is a Christian. If he felt that a particular doctrine conflicted with his hope of reunifying those who claim to be followers of Christ, the doctrine was dismissed as being unimportant. He also believed that Christians created their own "Sects and dividing Parties" within their own ranks when they got into matters beyond the scope of our proper concern. For Lewis, Christians must stick as closely as possible to "the belief that has been common to nearly all Christians at all times." [250]

---

248 Matthew 7:15.

249 Romans 14:3–6.

250 Alan Jacobs, *The Narnian: The Life And Imagination of C. S. Lewis* (New York: HarperSanFrancisco, 2005), p. 215.

This philosophy may seem logical on the surface; however, it is rooted in the assumption that the majority must be right, or at least that there is a higher likelihood of the majority being right versus those holding the minority viewpoint. Both Scripture and history, however, reveal that this is not necessarily so. Jesus said: "Enter ye in at the strait gate: for **wide is the gate, and broad is the way, that leadeth to destruction, and many there be which go in thereat:** because strait is the gate, and narrow is the way, which leadeth unto life, **and few there be that find it.**"[251]

Christian conformity, and exegesis by consensus is simply the wide path that leads to destruction. It is certainly unwise to join the majority when it is heading in the wrong direction. Therefore, Lewis' position of commonality among so-called Christians as the measuring rod for truth is simply unwise. There is only one way that leads to life eternal with no parallel path alongside that narrow way that leads unto life. The majority is often like the riotous crowd at Ephesus of which it was said, "and **the more part** knew not wherefore they were come together."[252]

The Philosophy of the Mega Church Movement

Lewis was a forerunner of the philosophy of the mega church phenomenon. Common today among the super church builders is the elimination of doctrine and an emphasis on the world's desperate need for a unified effort to fight the world's ills. This may sound commendable; however, it leads to damnable heresies and relegates the gospel to a lesser degree of importance, eventually dismissing the great commission altogether. The gospel must be given first place.

Symptomatic of this approach is the claim of mega church leaders, like Rick Warren, who is pushing a "global warming initiative":

Despite opposition from some of their colleagues, 86 evangelical Christian leaders have decided to back a major initiative to fight global warming,

---

251   Matthew 7:13–14.

252   Acts 19:32.

saying "millions of people could die in this century because of climate change, most of them our poorest global neighbors." Among signers of the statement, which will be released in Washington on Wednesday, are the presidents of 39 evangelical colleges, leaders of aid groups and churches, like the Salvation Army, and pastors of megachurches, including Rick Warren, author of the best seller "The Purpose Driven Life."[253]

Cal Thomas's comments on this, as found in *The Oklahoman* for Tuesday, February 14, 2006, expose the evils of this:

What is it with evangelical Christians that so many of them need a cause beyond the commission they've been given? Having witnessed the damage to the church's fundamental message of redemption from a too-close association with the "kingdom of this world"—first in the liberal National Council of Churches and World Council of Churches, and more recently with various conservative religious-political movements—some evangelicals have decided to give it another go. This time, the issue isn't abortion, gay rights or cleaning up offensive TV programs. They want to clean up the planet.

Various evangelical groups seem to be finding causes which drive them to join forces for global and humanitarian issues, but in the process they compromise their doctrinal stand. Groups with differing doctrinal beliefs can only join ranks if they compromise down to the lowest common denominator. This level of association based on compromise is unacceptable to any student of the Bible. One reviewer of Lewis' *Mere Christianity* on Amazon.com expressed his views when he wrote the following on April 16, 2002: "I like his 'lowest common denominator' approach to the fundamentals of Christian discipleship. . . ."[254]

---

253   Laurie Goodstein, "Evangelical Leaders Join Global Warming Initiative" (2/8/06) www.nytimes.com/2006/02/08/national/08warm.html?ex=1140066000&en=cf8adf44bb

254   [http://www.amazon.co.uk/exec/obidos/tg/stores/detail/-/books/0006280544/customer-reviews/203-0755764-5551136]

This lowest common denominator philosophy will one day allow a unified body to be controlled by someone perceived to be the great conciliator holding the key to solving all of man's ills and divisions. In order to facilitate this worldwide control, the groups with differences must surrender their conflicting standards or else be eliminated. This one-world political/religious organization prophesied for the end times will control through compromise until gaining complete control. At that time it will control the masses through fear and intimidation and offer no alternatives but total submission or death.

Lewis' writings are a common thread used to unite differing groups that might not normally find much common ground. Lisa Miller of *Newsweek* even connects Rick Warren of the *Purpose Driven Life* with Jim Wallis of *Sojourners,* stating: "Even Christians who might disagree about other things can agree on Lewis." Rick Warren, pastor of Saddleback Church praises *Mere Christianity* for its simplicity. "I don't mean it's shallow," Warren said. "The trick is to translate [the gospel] so a truck driver gets it."[255]

Jim Wallis, the left-leaning editor of *Sojourners,* loves Lewis because "he was not a narrow, legalistic Christian." "Wallis recounts how he recently took a C. S. Lewis tour of Oxford with his 80-year-old father. Their guide, a local cabby, knew Lewis when he was a boy and liked him—especially his love for beer."[256]

Who is Jim Wallis and what does his magazine stand for? Reading from the online Wikipedia encyclopedia:

Sojourners is a Christian magazine and a religious community based in Washington, D.C., though it has promoted itself with the slogan "Not from the Left, not from the Right, but from the Spirit," the magazine's content is generally left-leaning in political outlook, and is probably the most widely read publication among Christian progressives in the United States. Its founder and editor is Jim Wallis.

---

255   Lisa Miller

256   Ibid.

Rick Warren and Jim Wallis and their respective organizations are not the only ones coming together under the Lewis umbrella. Even evangelical Christians and Mormons are uniting under the banner of *The Lion*.

The local news station KSL5 TV in Salt Lake City, Utah, reported:

> Members of two faiths are using the premier of *The Lion, the Witch and the Wardrobe* as a way of continuing to "bridge the religious divide" in our state. The evangelical group, Standing Together Ministries, and the Latter-day Saints have shared the cost for the theatre. These two faiths disagree on many points in their beliefs, but about the works of C. S. Lewis, a man of faith, and this family-friendly film, they do agree.[257]

The same story, reported by hollywoodjesus.com, gives a similar perspective:

> At least in Salt Lake City, Narnia is a uniter, not a divider. An evangelical Christian group and a Mormon group are jointly offering free tickets to an opening night screening of the Narnia film, explicitly using the screening as an opportunity for bringing people of the two faiths together. This is not insignificant. Most Christians consider Mormons to be heretics, and the Mormons obviously consider themselves the True Church. And relations between the two groups in Salt Lake City often become quite heated.[258]

These outcomes should not be surprising when Hollywood is doing the pushing. When will Christians wake up? Should we expect any less from this cesspool of hypocrisy? Christians must soon remove their blindfolds in order to effectively gauge this second "tool for evangelism" coming out of Hollywood in as many years. Here is how the associate Episcopal priest at

---

257 Carole Mikita, "Faiths Come Together for Premier of 'Chronicles of Narnia'"
     www.ksl.com/?nid=148&sid=133602

258 Greg & Jenn Wright, "Christians and Mormons Together" (11/29/05)
     www.hollywoodjesus.com/comments/narnianews/2005/11/christians-and-mormons-together.
     html

the Church of the Transfiguration, the Rev. Dr. Clair McPherson, views it:

> Lewis "makes it very clear . . . that his purpose is not to be biased toward any denominational point of view or even any theological point of view within Christianity," says Reverend McPherson, who's been leading about 50 adults this fall in a four-week study of Lewis' "The Lion, the Witch and the Wardrobe." "I would never say to evangelicals, 'you can't have him.' I would say, **he belongs to all of us.**" [259]

Was all the ecumenism revolving around Lewis simply accidental, or was Lewis a bit weak on even some of the basic doctrines? Lewis claims, in *Mere Christianity*, that if you don't want to believe in the forgiveness of sins through Christ or the efficacy of Christ's shed blood, you should find some other formula that works for you. He goes on to point out that no matter what you decide, it is not worth quarreling over. Lewis believed in unity at all costs.

> What, then, is the difference which He has made to the whole human mass? It is just this; that the business of becoming a son of God, of being turned from a created thing into a begotten thing, of passing over from the temporary biological life into timeless "spiritual" life, has already been done for us. Humanity is already "saved" in principle. We individuals have to appropriate that salvation. But the really tough work—the bit we could not have done for ourselves—has been done for us. We have not got to try to climb up into spiritual life by our own efforts; it has already come down into the human race. If we will only lay ourselves open to the one Man in whom it was fully present, and who, in spite of being God, is also a real man, He will do it in us and for us. . . .
>
> Of course, you can express this in all sorts of different ways. You can say that Christ died for our sins. You may say that the Father has forgiven us because Christ has done for us what we ought to have done. You may

---

259   G. Jeffrey MacDonald, *The Christian Science Monitor*, "Christians battle over 'Narnia'" www.csmonitor.com/2005/1208/p14so3-lire.html

say that we are washed in the blood of the Lamb. You may say that Christ
has defeated death. They are all true. **If any of them do not appeal to you,
leave it alone and get on with the formula that does. And, whatever
you do, do not start quarreling with other people because they use a
different formula from yours.**[260]

Lewis' appeasement theology differs greatly from the apostle Paul's proclamation that he was ". . . set for the defence of the gospel."[261] Are the things
Lewis mentions—"Christ died for our sins," "the Father has forgiven us
because Christ has done for us what we ought to have done," "we are washed
in the blood of the Lamb," "Christ has defeated death"—just theories? Can
we accept some of these statements, but not others? Are not each of these
matters worth "quarreling" over or debating with those who would reject
such basic foundational truths?

The first thing that comes to mind when reading Lewis' words to avoid
quarreling at all costs is when Neville Chamberlain, the British prime minister, stepped from the plane in London. He waived the agreement signed
by Adolph Hitler, which Chamberlain said guaranteed "peace in our time."
Peace at no cost can be quite costly over time.

Most were relieved by Chamberlain's rosy report. No one likes conflict. Yet, conflict is a fact of life while living in a fallen world as we do. We
shouldn't seek it, but it will seek out every person that stands for the truth.
Conflict and opposition come with opportunity. Paul testified of many
adversaries. "For a great door and effectual is opened unto me, **and there
are many adversaries.**"[262]

It matters what one believes. Salvation and doctrinal truths about the
death, burial and resurrection of Christ are not mere formulas that can be
accepted or rejected with impunity. The shed blood of Christ is of paramount
importance, yet Lewis liked to write about "the theories" of Christ's death.

---

260   Lewis, *Mere Christianity*, pp. 181–182.

261   Philippians 1:17.

262   1 Corinthians 16:9.

The central Christian belief is that Christ's death has somehow put us right with God and given us a fresh start. **Theories** as to how it did this are another matter. . . . Any theories we build up as to how Christ's death did all of this are, in my view quite secondary.[263]

Lewis is right about theories; however, the truth as to why and how Christ died for sinners cannot be lumped together and rejected with manmade theories. One would think that the so-called fundamentalists would stand firm against C. S. Lewis and his unorthodox beliefs and writings. However, this is simply not the case as Pheobe Kate Foster points out:

His track record in wooing the target audience to religious orthodoxy was so impressive that even dyed-in-the-wool fundamentalists were willing to overlook the fact that **Lewis' denomination of choice, the Church of England, did not preach the necessity of a "born-again experience" for salvation or hold literalist biblical interpretation** as part of their creed.[264]

Our modern mind-set erroneously believes that love and discernment are opposites and that they cannot live under the same roof, so to speak. But Paul prayed for the Philippians "that your **love may abound yet more and more in knowledge and in all judgment; that ye may approve things that are excellent. . . ."**[265]

Lewis and Mormonism

Lewis' penchant for ecumenicalism is clearly revealed in how Mormons are so accepting of both him and his teachings. In a 1998 issue of *Christianity*

263 Lewis, *Mere Christianity*, pp. 54, 56.

264 Phoebe Kate Foster, "When We're Old Enough To Read Fairy Tales Again," Part 1 of 3 www.popmatters.com/books/features/051209-narnia-1.shtml

265 Philippians 1:9–10.

Today, Robert Millet, dean of Brigham Young University, is quoted as saying that C. S. Lewis "is so well received by Latter-day Saints [Mormons] because of his broad and inclusive vision of Christianity." [266]

Mark Tauber, the vice president and deputy publisher of HarperSanFrancisco, the division of Harper Collins that publishes Lewis' non-fiction books, agrees. He observes that Lewis "wouldn't be comfortable, really, being co-opted by any one group." He goes on to say that he is continually surprised by the broad appeal of Lewis' books. Tauber relates how he recently received a call from a Mormon leader who mentioned that Mormon religious school teachers were using *Mere Christianity* in the classroom. Tauber states: "We had no idea that the Mormons were into Lewis."[267]

Lewis' lowest-common-denominator-philosophy brings everyone together on a common level of agreement excluding none, except for those who refuse to compromise the truth. His form of compromise breeds concepts alien to a consistent biblicism. Statements in *The Voyage of the Dawn Trader* help us understand Mormon acceptance of Lewis. On the very first page Lewis writes that Eustace's parents "were very up-to-date and advanced people. They were vegetarians, non-smokers and **teetotalers and wore a special kind of underclothes**." He also wrote that their sons did not refer to them as "Father" and "Mother" but instead by their first names, "Harold and Alberta."[268] Could Lewis' mentioning of special underclothing be just coincidental?

It would be easy for Mormons to see a connection in Lewis' writings to their own peculiar beliefs concerning the importance of the Mormon's undergarments. A few years ago the *Washington Post* ran an article entitled "Unmentionable No Longer" which exposed the long held and secretive teaching of the Mormons.

266   John Kennedy, "Southern Baptists Take Up Mormon Challenge," *Christianity Today*, 6/15/98, p. 30.
      www.cometozarahermia.org/others/mormons_on_the_rise.html

267   Sarah Price Brown, "'Narnia' Fuels Public Fascination with Christian Author C.S. Lewis'" www.biblicalrecorder.org/content/news/2005/10_14_2005/ne141005narnia.shtml

268   C. S. Lewis, *Voyage of the Dawn Trader* (New York, NY: HarperCollins, 1980), p. 1.

The underwear is part of a covenant with God that Mormons consider private . . . the Mormon garment is an unseen reminder to "saints" (as LDS church members refer to themselves) of who they are. In young adulthood, when and if a Mormon man or woman goes through the "endowment" ceremony at the temple, they are given the garment and told to wear one every day thereafter. . . . When a garment is worn out, according to "Mormon America: The Power and the Promise" by Richard and Joan Ostling, the sacred symbols are snipped off and the rest can be discarded or used as rags.[269]

One of the authors (DS) is personally aware of a Mormon acquaintance who died and his non-Mormon wife related that those in the local Mormon organization came to the house and took her husband's underwear. We wonder whether Lewis' inclusion of the special undergarments in his book was intentional or purely for "artistic effect." Regardless, the writings of C. S. Lewis has a tremendous draw among this Christ-rejecting cult.

How popular is C. S. Lewis among Mormons? DesertBook.com is an official Mormon bookstore site. It carries many of Lewis' books and biographies. A search of the word "Narnia" on the website shows sixty-six entries of C. S. Lewis' materials, suggesting how well Lewis is received in Mormon circles.

In a revealing book review of *C. S. Lewis: The Man and His Message* posted on a website offering Mormon material we read: "Arguably one of the greatest defenders of the Christian faith, C. S. Lewis has gained widespread respect and popularity among members of The Church of Jesus Christ of Latter-day Saints. His writings, in fact, strike a chord of familiarity with Christians throughout the world."[270]

Lewis is often cited by Mormon authors who are seeking to minimize the

---

269   Hank Stuever, "Unmentionable No longer: What Do Mormons Wear? A Polite Smile, if Asked About 'the Garment,'" *Washington Post* (2/26/00) www.hankstuever.com/mormon.html

270   Book review of *C. S. Lewis: The Man and His Message* by Andrew C. Skinner and Rober L. Millet. deseretbook.com/store/product?product_id=100011496&sku=3826168(12/26/05), p. 1

differences between evangelicalism and Mormonism. One statement that is found in both *Mere Christianity* and also *Beyond Personality* strikes a familiar chord with Mormons who believe that man can become a god.

> **[God] said (in the Bible) that we are "gods" and He is going to make good his words.** If we let Him—for we can prevent Him, if we choose— **He will make the feeblest and filthiest of us into a god or goddess,** a dazzling, radiant, immortal creature, pulsating all through with such energy and joy and wisdom and love as we cannot now imagine.[271]

What is the over-all effect of the fact that both Mormons and evangelicals are praising Lewis' works? The effect, undoubtedly, is that Bible-believing Christians who make the claim that Mormonism is a cult are now being viewed with suspicion. Defending the faith can now be perceived as causing division among the "faithful" with Mormons now included in that group.

Significantly, evangelical author Gretchen Passantino points out that Mormons frequently use Lewis' writings to downplay the differences between Mormon teachings and evangelical beliefs.

> By these and other quotes from Lewis, a growing number of Mormons attempt to blur the distinction between historic, creedal, and biblical Christian doctrine and the teachings of the Church of Jesus Christ of Latter-day Saints (LDS). Since Lewis is one of evangelicalism's favorite authors (he was recently listed among the top ten Christians of the twentieth century in *Christian History* magazine), a posthumous endorsement of Mormon theology from his writings would go a long way toward allying Christian charges that Mormon theology is heretical.[272]

Passantino also reports that the Spring 2000 Brigham Young University's

---

271   Gretchen Passantino, "Are We Destined To Be Gods and Goddesses? Does C.S. Lewis Defend Mormonism's 'Progression to Godhood?'"
        cornerstonemag.com/pages/show_page.asp?423 (12/19/05), pp. 1-2.

272   Ibid., p. 2.

Women's Conference includes a seminar entitled "Letting God Have His Way: A Conversation about C. S. Lewis." The seminar is described in the following provocative way: "Join prominent LDS scholars as they explore Lewis' writings on the relationship of God to man, the necessity for free will, the nature of man, opportunities for joy, the lessons of pain, and the Godhood of Jesus Christ."[273]

Passantino reports that among Mormons, Lewis "is the most read religious author outside the Mormon faith." C. S. Lewis Internet sites are among the favored non-Mormon sites read by Mormons. Journalists Richard and Joan Ostling quip: "Yeah, yeah, so he wasn't technically LDS. But his personal theology continues to speak to LDS believers to such a degree that he certainly deserves the status of honorary member."[274]

In all fairness to Lewis and his supporters, we should point out that, according to Passantino, "each of the Lewis citations have been taken out of their contexts and twisted. In addition, frequently in his writings about humanity's eternal destiny he carefully clarifies the eternal and impassable gulf between the only Creator and His creatures, including humans."[275] Therefore, his writings may be misinterpreted by Mormons to support their heretical beliefs, but it does not seem that this was Lewis' intention.

Yet this does not exonerate Lewis, nor does it destroy our thesis about Lewis. Lewis' writings are often so vague and noncommittal on essential issues that he has given hope to cults and heretics that "he is one of us." Any competent author knows that he can write plainly enough so that everyone can easily figure out where he stands, or he can write in such a way so as to placate the majority.

Surely with the wonderful intellectual and literary skills that C. S. Lewis possessed, he could have, and should have, been more articulate in his statements if he really desired to express himself in defense of orthodoxy. It is entertaining to see how Lewis defenders on the evangelical side of the debate,

273 Ibid.
274 Ibid., p. 3.
275 Ibid.

and Mormons who claim that Lewis was favorable toward their side, both quote Lewis to support their particular perspective.

While Lewis supporters defend him against the charge of bad theology, Lewis' writings are, nonetheless, problematic for them. No doubt, he had a fertile and imaginative mind, but he was certainly not gifted in saying what he meant and in meaning what he said on biblical and theological issues. Or he intentionally wrote in such a manner to pull together competing groups under one spiritual umbrella—a dangerous form of ecumenicalism. One can carefully read a couple of paragraphs of *Mere Christianity* and come up wondering whose side he is on and which position he believed in.

Adding to the confusion is the fact that the contents of *Mere Christianity* were originally given as radio broadcasts on the air and then published in three separate installments as *Broadcast Talks* (1942), *Christian Behaviour* (1943), and *Beyond Personality* (1944).[276] If C. S. Lewis can be so theologically imprecise and confusing in his writings, what confusion he must have engendered in his radio broadcasts where the listeners did not have the opportunity to read and re-read what he has just said!

The Not-So-Surprising Universal Appeal of C. S. Lewis

The information covered thus far proves that C. S. Lewis has an amazing universal appeal to a broad spectrum of people. Many people have been changed through Lewis' writings. Former atheists, agnostics and skeptics have had their beliefs changed by reading Lewis. William F. Jasper, writing for *The New American*, shares his story.

> Like so many other young "intellectuals" throughout history—and especially among the generation that came of age in the 1960s—I had thrown off my childhood "shackles" of Christian superstitions and bourgeois values. I was now a liberated, sophisticated (or so I thought) agnostic, and for a time, even convinced myself to enlist under the banner of militant Marxist atheism.
>
> C. S. Lewis played a major role in removing the scales from my eyes

---

276   Lewis, *Mere Christianity*, Preface.

and leading me back from the edge of the abyss of unbelief. His Narnia stories led me to his other works, such as *Mere Christianity* and the *Abolition of Man*. As a convert to Christianity from atheism and socialism, he had wrestled with the questions, doubts, and arguments that I was facing. The answers he had come to, his clarity of thought, and his style of expressions were intriguing, satisfying, exhilarating.[277]

There are many others who would testify in similar fashion regarding the influence of C. S. Lewis on their lives. He was, and is considered, the "apostle to the skeptics," and confronted many of the issues that the intellectuals of today face. His answers pointed toward God, and the Christian revelation. He showed that one could profess faith in Christ without committing, as it were, intellectual suicide. But once again we have to ask, "Does this mean that we should give him our unequivocal endorsement? Should we, because of his fame and reputation, not be as the noble Bereans who regularly measured what they heard by the yardstick of the Scriptures?"[278]

Granted, Lewis wrestled with some of the important issues of life, such as whether or not God exists. Yet there are large numbers of people who believe that God exists and who also believe in morality and decency. They are the "nice" people of the world who are faithful to their wives. They might have a good work ethic, have received a good education, are raising their children to be hard-working and to even attend church on a regular basis. They contribute to various charitable causes ranging from helping disaster victims to supporting wildlife conservation. They are contributors to society and to the betterment of mankind. But is that the goal that God has set for us? Is morality and the belief in some sort of a Supreme Being what we should be aiming at and pointing others to? Is God looking for those who can argue the merits of a free-market economy against atheistic communism? Or is He looking for those that will receive and trust in His Son who died for them?

---

277 Jasper, p. 23.

278 See Acts 17:11.

Those Jewish ecclesiastical leaders of the first century were a pretty decent bunch of people. They professed faith in the God of Abraham, Isaac, and Jacob. They could quote from the prophets, yet the Lord Jesus Christ said more harsh things to them than He said to the harlots of His day.

In the book of Mark we read about Jesus being in a home. The crowds were thronging Him and some friends were carrying a man who was sick of the palsy.[279] When they saw they could not get to Jesus because of all the people, they went to the rooftop, made a hole in the roof and lowered their friend into the room. Verse 5 states: "When Jesus saw their faith, he said unto the sick of the palsy, Son, thy sins be forgiven thee."

The passage continues and reveals that the scribes were unhappy with Jesus' pronouncement. "Why doth this man thus speak blasphemies? Who can forgive sins but God only?"[280]

Please note, these religionists were theologically correct, as is Lewis in many cases. They knew that only God could forgive sins, but Jesus was not speaking "blasphemies" as they contended. He is the eternal Son of God! *They were right about God but wrong about Jesus—and their souls were in danger of damnation for this very error!*

Yes, Lewis has a universal appeal—from the hippies who have been helped in finding God to those of a markedly different persuasion. However, some of been irrevocably harmed by him too. In a Web article entitled "How Narnia Made Me a Witch," the writer states, "C. S. Lewis' books not only taught me important values, they helped bring me to the Goddess. For me, one of her names is Aslan." The author explains:

When I was eight years old, the librarian at my elementary school handed me "The Lion, the Witch, and the Wardrobe." The book took me into a magic world, where animals talked and nature was shimmering with enchantment. I devoured the book and avidly read the rest of the series, over and over again. Narnia was my comfort when I was sick and my escape

---

279 Mark 2:1–12.

280 Mark 2:7.

when life was boring and dreary.

The books made me aware that something was lacking in my daily routine of school and Hebrew school, of TV cartoons on Saturday mornings and games of handball in the apartment garage. **I longed to step into another world, one that would be wilder, more fluid, and more infused with wonder than the decidedly unmagical San Fernando Valley where I lived.** [281]

Obviously, Lewis' writing was sufficiently vague and fluid on certain points as to make him fit in "almost anywhere."

Unlike nearly all other influential thinkers and writers within Christian history, C. S. Lewis is not known for his reformation of or separation from the popular religious beliefs. Instead, he is known for defining, defending, and uniting the community of Christendom on what it "merely" (or in his own term "purely") is. This is evidenced by the overwhelming appeal and popularity he has to all sections and denominational backgrounds within Christendom. I am amazed the extreme positions within Christendom that claim Lewis as the champion and defender of their own denominational faith. **These extremes are seen on a continuum between liberals and the fundamentalists; the Roman Catholics and the evangelical Protestants. Even within Protestant Christianity there are extremes of the most conservative Baptists to the most charismatic Pentecostals claiming Lewis as one of their own.** For example, there are John Willis and Christopher Derrick, both Catholic priests, who claim that if Lewis had lived long enough to see Vatican II, his true colors of Catholicism would have come through. You have a similar claim being made in a Pentecostal magazine in an article by Kathryn Linskoog, who asserts that if Lewis had lived to see the formation and branching out of the Pentecostal movement, he would have jumped on board.[282]

---

281 "How Narnia Made Me a Witch."
www.beliefnet.com/story/179/story_17993_1.html (12/16/05), p. 1.

282 Sprague, pp. 1–2

Lewis' universal appeal transcends denominational boundaries. One researcher observes that while Lewis did not emphasize certain points of Christian doctrine, this was because he was more concerned about "core beliefs" than about what some may consider "peripheral issues." C. S. Lewis tried to deal with "the Common Hall" as he called it, the common beliefs that all Christians hold.

This means that "nonbelievers find that he presents the central beliefs of Christianity clearly," and most "Christians generally find significant agreement with his presentation." Yet, this same researcher admits, "it is clear . . . that not all Christians share Lewis' beliefs on certain points . . . the authority of Scripture, the existence of purgatory, and the inclusivity of salvation." [283]

Lewis and Evangelicalism
C. S. Lewis is held in high esteem by evangelical leaders all over the world. In the book *Narnia Beckons*, published by a leading evangelical publisher, we read in glowing terms about the animated version of the new Disney movie.

> Back in 1980, when I was president of the organization that produced *The Chronicles of Narnia: The Lion, the Witch and the Wardrobe* on CBS television, I received a letter from a middle-aged gentleman who said that his wife had been witnessing to him about Jesus and his atonement for years, but he just couldn't understand the concept until he saw the animated *The Lion, the Witch and the Wardrobe* on CBS television. He suddenly understood and accepted Jesus Christ as his Lord and Savior. This was one of the many letters about how the Emmy Award-winning television special impacted the thirty-seven million people who saw it. [284]

There have been many similar testimonies coming from other productions

---

283   Mueller, p. 2.

284   Baehr, p. 3.

revolving around Christian themes. Mel Gibson's *Passion* movie was supposed to produce a revival in America and elsewhere. In fact, Harvest House Publishers put out a book documenting the "miracles" that had been produced as a result of the movie. The book, entitled *Changed Lives: Miracles of the Passion* by Jody Eldred, featured a back cover that reported:

> Mel Gibson's film *The Passion of the Christ* and its powerful portrayal of Jesus' sacrifice are profoundly changing lives. This book captures some of the thousands of incredible stories recounted by the people who experienced them—in their own words.[285]

According to "media theologians" the Bible is no longer sufficient for a devolving society and world. We need movies, books, testimonies, and now fairy tales steeped in godless mythology and pagan superstition to make the message of the gospel "plain." Add to this a plethora of "helpful modern translations" and paraphrases of the Bible that are supposed to bring "the message of Christ to life." But is the church stronger? Are multiplied thousands coming to know Christ as Lord and Saviour? Is revival sweeping the land and society being changed for the better? The answer that we can give is an emphatic "NO!" Evangelical movie mania has not helped, is not helping, and certainly is not the answer!

Rick Warren, Saddleback pastor and author of the famed *Purpose Driven Life,* recently participated in the C. S. Lewis Institute conference in Oxford and Cambridge, England, in the summer of 2005. Warren addressed the topic: "The Good, the True, and the Beautiful—To What End?" The spiritual hodgepodge of other speakers at the conference included Chuck Colson of Prison Fellowship who was one of the signatories to *Evangelicals and Catholics Together,* mystic and contemplative writer Richard Foster, and Roman Catholic apologist and former Protestant Peter Kreeft.[286]

---

285 Jody Eldred, *Changed Lives: Miracles of the Passion* (Harvest House Publishers, 2004), back cover.

286 "Rick Warren Brings New Dimension to C. S. Lewis Summer Institute." http://biz.yahoo.com/pz/050624/80515.html (12/19/05), pp. 1–2.

It is quite clear that obedience to the divine mandate for biblical separation is imperative. One wonders the extent that Lewis' works are playing in the continuing unfolding of the new universal Christianity we see taking root and flourishing in our own day. *U.S. News & World Report* provides a typical, albeit erroneously off-target, characterization of C. S. Lewis:

> He became arguably the leading popular Christian apologist of the 20th century, a defender and explainer of the faith who was hailed by popes, Protestant evangelists, politicians, and other world leaders for his brilliant yet accessible campaign against the rising tide of unbelief in the modern world.[287]

The readers of *Christianity Today* who identify themselves as evangelicals rated Lewis "the most influential writer in their lives." However, the same article points out that "Lewis did no such thing."[288] This was meant to confirm that Lewis did not try to evangelize those with whom he came into contact. No wonder our world is so confused—the most influential writer for evangelicals does not believe in evangelizing the lost!

Although it is not our intent to question Lewis' salvation, many of his contemporaries did just that. Lewis' unorthodox beliefs led "… the late, great Martyn Lloyd-Jones, for whom evangelical orthodoxy was mandatory, to doubt whether Lewis was a Christian at all." [289]

How do a variety of people and writers feel about C. S. Lewis? Perhaps the best summary is from the C. S. Lewis Institute:

> After C. S. Lewis went public with his conversion and commitment to Jesus Christ, controversy hounded him until his death. Fashionable agnostics dubbed him "Heavy Lewis," liberal Christians reviled him for his lack of theological sophistication, and fundamentalists attacked his interpretation of scripture and his ecumenical charity towards most Christian traditions.

---

287 Tolson, p. 48.

288 J. I. Packer

289 Ibid.

But neither these issues nor a host of other contentions stirred up anything like the furor that surrounded his marriage to Helen Joy Davidman. In the minds of many of C. S. Lewis' friends it was bad enough that a bachelor nearly sixty years old married a woman of forty. But to make matters worse, she was an American divorcee who also happened to be Jewish and the mother of two boys.[290]

In Lewis' ecumenicalism and lack of doctrinal clarity, we find beliefs that will provide the seeds for the formation of the false church that will form subsequent to the Rapture of the saints. It will be a "super church" that will attract an untold number and will be characterized by an unholy animosity against the true faith "once delivered to the saints." Walvoord describes the situation that will follow the Rapture as follows.

> In the absence of the redeeming presence of any true believers, the Catholic, Protestant, and Orthodox churches will combine into a powerful religious and political institution. The super-church will be able to command the obedience and devotion of hundreds and millions throughout the world and will have power to put to death those who resist its demands for adherence. The new world church will be in alliance with the political powers of the Middle East. This combined effort will prepare the way for a new government with absolute power over the entire world. This unholy alliance is portrayed symbolically in Revelation 17, which describes a wicked harlot riding a scarlet-colored beast. For centuries expositors have recognized the harlot as a symbol of religion and the scarlet beast as representing the political power of the Mediterranean Confederacy in the end time. While their alliance will bring a temporary stability to the world, it will also create a blasphemous religious system which will lead the world to new depths of immorality and departure from true faith in God.[291]

---

290   Lyle W. Dorsett, *Helen Joy Davidman (Mrs. C. S. Lewis) 1915-1960: A Portrait.* www.cslewisinstitute.org (12/20/05), p. 1.

291   John F. Walvoord, *Armageddon: Oil and the Middle East Crisis* (Grand Rapids: Zondervan, 1974), pp. 108–109.

Chapter 5

C. S. Lewis and Roman Catholicism

Roman Catholic teaching and influence is slowly affecting evangelical churches. Many of the churches are accepting and adopting Roman Catholic doctrines that were formally abhorrent to such groups.

Marian Devotion

This is demonstrated in an emerging pro-Marian view in some Protestant groups. A recent article in *Time* reported:

> In many Protestant congregations, Mary is rarely in the spotlight except for Nativity pageants and sermons. But a growing number of scholars and preachers are examining Mary's other significant moments during the life of her son, including her presentation of Jesus at the temple after his birth and her role at the wedding at Cana, where she urges him to perform his first miracle, turning water into wine. . . . In a shift whose ideological breadth is unusual in the fragmented Protestant world, a long-standing wall around Mary appears to be eroding.[292]

Various reasons can be cited, all showing why this dangerous slip into Mariolatry needs to be avoided:

---

292   David Van Biema, "Hail Mary," *Time* (3/21/05), pp. 62, 64.

Today Catholics and Protestants feel freer to explore each other's beliefs and practices. Feminism has encouraged popular speculations on the lives of female biblical figures and the role of the divine feminine (think *The Red Tent* and *The Da Vinci Code*). . . . And the influx of millions of Hispanic immigrants from Catholic cultures into American Protestantism may eventually accelerate progress toward a pro-Marian tipping point. . . .[293]

Before we further delve into our concerns over this improper emphasis upon Mary, we should consider exactly what the Bible reveals about Mary's relationship to her Son.

We know that Mary understood (by communication from God Himself via angels,[294] prophetic utterances,[295] etc.) that the child in her womb was conceived by the Holy Spirit.[296] She knew His God-given names[297] with their meanings. She knew that her Son was the Son of God the Most High, heir to David's throne.[298] She knew that she was the mother of the Lord; that Jesus was the promised Christ, the fulfillment of the promise to Abraham.[299] She knew that her Son was a light to the gentiles,[300] a great joy to all people; she witnessed the gentile Magi worship her young Son with gifts and prostrations;[301] she knew that Jesus was appointed for the fall and rising of many in Israel,[302] a sign to be opposed, a revealer of hearts and that all this would

293   Ibid., p. 63.

294   Luke 1:26.

295   Matthew 1:2; Luke 1:42.

296   Luke 1:35.

297   Luke 1:31, 35; 2:21.

298   Luke 1:32.

299   Luke 1:55.

300   Luke 2:32.

301   Matthew 2:11.

302   Luke 2:34

pierce her own soul as a sword.[303] Mary probably knew Him better than anyone else. Unlike many other followers of Christ during His last days, she followed Him all the way to Golgotha.

Never did Mary withdraw her initial submission to God's will concerning her role in the Saviour's life and mission, though it most assuredly cost her enormous pain as His earthly mother. The Bible also reveals that Mary was rather contemplative about exactly who her Son was. In each of the following three cases Mary pondered or kept the sayings in her heart.

- The sayings of the shepherds in the manger made Mary very meditative. "And all they that heard it wondered at those things which were told them by the shepherds. But **Mary** kept all these things, and **pondered them in her heart.**"[304]
- Joseph and Mary were surprised at what was said about Jesus when they brought Him to the temple as a baby. "And **Joseph and his mother marvelled** at those things which were spoken of him."[305]
- Again, when Jesus was twelve they once again brought Him to the temple. Mary hid the things said about Him in her heart. "And he said unto them, How is it that ye sought me? wist ye not that I must be about my Father's business? And they understood not the saying which he spake unto them. And he went down with them, and came to Nazareth, and was **subject unto them**: but **his mother kept all these sayings in her heart.**"[306]

Notice that the Word of God is careful to point out that Jesus was subject unto Joseph and His mother. Had Jesus not subjected Himself unto both of them as His parents, He would have been a sinner. He never disobeyed them nor

---

303   Luke 2:35.

304   Luke 2:18–19.

305   Luke 2:33.

306   Luke 2:49–51.

even contemplated any type of defiance. Although His subjection was earthly, it did not and does not extend up into Heaven following His death.

Having now pointed out how well Mary knew her Son within certain limitations, we must still caution those that have tended to artificially elevate her. Is the "accelerating progress toward a pro-Marian tipping point" mentioned earlier a good thing? We can only answer this question intelligently if we understand what the Roman Catholic Church believes about Mary. The *Catechism of the Catholic Church* is quite clear regarding its position on Mary: "Taken up to heaven she did not lay aside this saving office but **by her manifold intercessions continues to bring us the gift of eternal salvation.** ... Therefore the Blessed Virgin is invoked in the Church under the titles of Advocate, Helper, Benefactress, and Mediatrix." [307] The *Catechism* continues deifying Mary by stating:

> The Church's devotion to the Blessed Virgin is intrinsic to Christian worship. The Church rightly honors the Blessed Virgin with special devotion. From the most ancient times the Blessed Virgin has been honored with the title of "Mother of God," to whose protection the faithful fly in all their dangers and needs. ... This very special devotion ... differs essentially from the adoration which is given to the incarnate Word and equally to the Father and the Holy Spirit, and greatly fosters this adoration. The liturgical feasts dedicated to the Mother of God and Marian prayer, such as the rosary, an epitome of the whole Gospel, express this devotion to the Virgin Mary.[308]

A Dangerously Low View Of Scripture

There are other troubling aspects of Roman Catholic thought as well. Ruth Gledhill, religion correspondent for *The Times* reports:

> The hierarchy of the Roman Catholic Church has published a teaching

---

307   *Catechism of the Catholic* (New York: Doubleday, 1995), Par. 969, pp. 274–275.

308   Ibid., Par. 971, p. 275.

document instructing the faithful that some parts of the Bible are not actually true. The Catholic bishops of England, Wales and Scotland are warning their five million worshippers, as well as any others drawn to the study of scripture, that they should not expect "total accuracy" from the Bible.[309]

Sadly, the Catholic Church has not only superseded scriptural authority with its traditions, but in a bold new step it has elevated science over the Bible:

The Vatican warned Catholics that if they do not listen to the contentions of modern science—regarding the origin of life and other issues—they risk falling prey to "fundamentalism." Cardinal Paul Poupard made the comments at a press conference pushing a Vatican project to try to create more mutual respect between science and religion. . . . "We know where scientific reason can end up by itself: the atomic bomb and the possibility of cloning human beings are fruit of a reason that wants to free itself from every ethical or religious link," Poupard told reporters. "But we also know the dangers of a religion that severs its links with reason and becomes prey to fundamentalism."[310]

Thanks to the Catholic Church, non-believers are encouraged in their battle against "intelligent design." The following quote demonstrates why no sincere Christian should ever hope that the Catholic Church will ever consistently side with the truth. MSNBC reports:

The Vatican newspaper has published an article saying "intelligent design" is not science and that teaching it alongside evolutionary theory in school classrooms only creates confusion. The article in Tuesday's edition of L'Osservatore Romano was the latest in a series of interventions by

---

309   Ruth Gledhill, "Catholic Church No Longer Swears by Truth of the Bible."
      www.timesonline.co.uk/printFriendly/0,,1-13090-1811332-13090,00.html (10/5/05).

310   "Vatican to Catholics: Listen to scientists"
      www.worldnetdaily.com/news/printer-friendly.asp?ARTICLE_ID=47205 (11/3/05).

Vatican officials—including the pope—on the issue that has dominated headlines in the United States. The author, Fiorenzo Facchini, a professor of evolutionary biology at the University of Bologna, laid out the scientific rationale for Charles Darwin's theory of evolution, saying that in the scientific world, biological evolution "represents the interpretative key of the history of life on earth." He lamented that certain American "creationists" had brought the debate back to the "dogmatic" 1800s, and said that their arguments weren't science but ideology.[311]

These ridiculous sentiments are not a slip of tongue, or pen, but are reflective of the Vatican's low view of the Bible and willingness to compromise on a central, cardinal truth of the Christian faith. In a Fox News report we read:

> The Vatican's chief astronomer said Friday that "intelligent design" isn't science and doesn't belong in science classrooms, becoming the latest high-ranking Roman Catholic official to enter the evolution debate in the United States. The Rev. George Coyne, the Jesuit director of the Vatican Observatory, said placing intelligent design theory alongside that of evolution in school programs was "wrong" and was akin to mixing apples with oranges.[312]

In view of all of these developments, and many others which space does not allow us to enumerate, the issue of C. S. Lewis and his beliefs regarding Roman Catholic teaching is an extremely important one. Did C. S. Lewis support the Bible and did he maintain the distinction between Romanism and biblical Christianity, or do his beliefs hasten a merging of the two?

C. S. Lewis and the Mass

The Roman Catholic doctrine of transubstantiation is not taught in the Bible. This is the view that the bread and wine become the actual body and blood of Jesus Christ. The *Catechism of the Roman Catholic Church* states:

---

311   www.msnbc.msn.com/id/10932031/from RSS/print/I/displaymode/1098/ (1/20/06).

312   www.foxnews.com/printer_friendly_story/0,3566,176050,00.html (11/18/05).

> The sacrifice of Christ and the sacrifice of the Eucharist are *one single sacrifice:* The victim is one and the same: the same now offers through the ministry of priests, who then offered himself on the cross; only the manner of offering is different. In this divine sacrifice which is celebrated in the Mass, the same Christ who offered himself once in a bloody manner on the altar of the cross is contained and is offered in an unbloody manner.[313]

In the first five centuries of church history, differing and often conflicting, views of the Lord's Supper began to emerge. Some of the early teachers continued to hold that the elements used in the Lord's Supper were purely symbolic (Origen, Basil, Augustine). However, others began to set forth the view that, in some way, the actual flesh and blood of Christ are combined with the elements (Cyril, Gregory of Nyssa, Chrysostom). During this period beliefs foreign to Scripture were creeping into the church. Regretfully, key Bible truths were being replaced by pagan superstition.

The preaching and teaching of the Bible was being devalued and mystical powers were attached to physical objects. The preacher became a "priest," someone who offers a sacrifice. This development was a logical outgrowth of the changing views of the Lord's Supper. If the body and blood of Christ were physically present at the Supper and, if as part of the worship of God, Christ was to be offered again and again, a priest was necessary to make the offering.

The doctrine of transubstantiation came about as an evolutionary development. Roman Catholic apologists will argue that while its genesis is found in the Bible, it took succeeding generations of church councils and dogmatic developments before it was fully taught. Transubstantiation was given full definition by Hildebert of Tours in 1134. In 1215 the doctrine was officially adopted by the Roman Catholic Church at the Fourth Lateran Council. As a response to the Protestant Reformation, the Catholic Counter-Reformation, gave defense and further articulation to the doctrine at the Council of Trent in the mid-1550s.

---

313   *Catechism,* Par. 1367, p. 381.

In the twentieth century the Second Vatican Council (1962–1965) defined the Eucharist in terms of fellowship with Christ and with all believers. It set forth the view that no truly Christian community can be established in the absence of the celebration of the Eucharist.[314]

Why do we give the historical development of a particular view of the Lord's Supper? Because the same ideas of incorporating pagan concepts that led to the development of transubstantiation are found in C. S. Lewis. To follow C. S. Lewis and to commit to his views is to affirm that fifteen centuries of doctrinal corruption were a good thing.

It must be remembered that Lewis' desire was to be "open" and to offend no one. He frequently refrained from taking any type of definitive stand for the truth. He wrote: "The very last thing I want to do is to unsettle in the mind of any Christian, whatever his denomination . . . to represent to himself what is happening when he receives the bread and the wine.[315]

Lewis was a conciliator who desired to satisfy everyone—even if it meant sacrificing the truth. As Lewis put it, "the very last thing" he wanted to do was to unsettle the mind of any "Christian" whatever he believes takes place when he partakes of the bread and wine. But expressing the truth can be at times rather unsettling. Jesus warned, "Woe unto you, when all men shall speak well of you! For so did their fathers to the false prophets."[316] The most popular preachers will be those who have learned how to speak without telling the truth. If a person knows the Bible, but refuses to warn others concerning the falsehood of other teachings, his compromise is abominable.

While Lewis did not want to clearly articulate his views in *Letters to Malcolm*, his views are quite clear in his famous *Mere Christianity*:

> It explains why **this new life is spread not only by purely mental acts like belief, but by** bodily acts like **baptism and Holy Communion.** It is not

---

314   See Robert A. Baker, *A Summary of Christian History* (Nashville: Broadman, 1959), pp. 70–81, 135–139, 254–256.

315   Lewis, *Letters to Malcolm: Chiefly on Prayer,* p. 101.

316   Luke 6:26.

merely the spreading of an idea; it is more like evolution—a biological or super-biological fact. . . . **He uses material things like bread and wine to put the new life into us.**[317]

The Center of the Controversy—

This is such an important issue that is evidently missed by many evangelicals, that we must develop the scriptural teaching on this point. It seems that all that Lewis refused to stand for—biblical authority, human depravity, the centrality of the blood of Christ, the word of God as the instrument of regeneration—is reflected in his view of the Supper.

When our Lord Jesus Christ instituted the Lord's Supper, He took the bread and said, "This is my body."[318] Did our Lord mean, "This is really my physical body, a mystical event that will continue down through the ages in the Mass"? or did He mean, "This *represents* my body"?

Those who maintain transubstantiation seek to support their position by appeal to these words of institution. They also appeal to the words of the apostle Paul: "Wherefore, whosoever shall eat this bread, and drink this cup of the Lord unworthily, shall be guilty of the body and blood of the Lord."[319] They point out that partaking in an unworthy manner constitutes a sin against "the body and blood of the Lord."

However, the scriptural view can be defended from the same verse by reading it just as literally: "Whosoever shall eat *this bread* and drink *this cup*. . . ." The elements have not changed—he still refers to the bread as bread. He also refers to the *cup*—literally that would mean that you would be sinning against the cup?

The problem with the teaching of transubstantiation goes much deeper. It denies the once-for-all sufficiency of the death of Christ two thousand years ago. Christ has to be re-offered over and over again. This, it is believed, takes place "at the sacrifice of the Mass." According to this view, one cannot

---

317   Lewis, *Mere Christianity,* p. 64.

318   Luke 22:19.

319   1 Corinthians 11:27.

say, "Christ *died* for me"[320] but rather "Christ *dies* for me."

Historically, Protestants and other non-Catholics have found this teaching to be dishonoring to the finished work of Christ. Evidently many have changed their minds or are simply willing to overlook this disparity. The Bible indicates that Christ's work is a finished work, completely efficacious and totally meritorious. Nothing needs to be repeated, or added: "By **one offering** he hath perfected **for ever** them that are sanctified."[321]

Just before our Lord died on the cross He said, "It is finished."[322] Unlike the priests of the Old Testament, Christ "needeth not daily, as those high priests, to offer up sacrifices."[323] Is this such an insignificant matter that those who hold to a different view are still somehow "within the pale of orthodoxy"?

An "Invisible Miracle"?

Roman Catholic dogma teaches that a miracle takes place at the Mass. The bread and the wine become the body and blood of the Lord. There is, however, no miracle of this type in the Bible. It is totally without biblical precedent. Transubstantiation produces an "invisible miracle" because, as Rome teaches, the bread and wine still look and taste like bread and wine but have, allegedly, become the body and blood of Christ, though you can't know it through the senses. But when Jesus healed, when He turned water into wine, when He stilled the storm, when He multiplied the loaves—these were all open, visible, and manifest miracles for all to see. The water looked like wine and tasted like wine.

Transubstantiation Not Supported By Scriptures Used To Support It

When Jesus said, "This is my body," did His disciples understand Him to

---

320   Romans 5:6, 8; 14:15; 1 Corinthians 8:11; 15:3.

321   Hebrews 10:14.

322   John 19:30.

323   Hebrews 7:27; see also Hebrews 9:24–28.

mean, "This is my literal body"? Remember, Christ made this statement while He was yet before them in the body of His flesh. Did the disciples understand Him to mean, "This is the body of my flesh being held by the hand of my flesh"?

Jesus was speaking in a way that was common to His teaching method. Note the following scriptures. Are they to be literally understood or is figurative language present here too?

> *I am* the light of the world: he that followeth me shall not walk in darkness. . .[324]

> *I am* the door: by me if any man enter in, he shall be saved.[325]

> *I am* the true vine, and my Father is the husbandman.[326]

If the Lord meant that the bread was literally His body, did He also actually mean that He was a literal light, a literal door, and a literal vine? Jesus was speaking figuratively in all four cases. He was saying, "I am like a light because I dispel darkness." "I am like a door because I am the entranceway to eternal life." "I am like a vine because I provide sustenance to the branches." Understanding these passages figuratively produces an interpretation that is much more consistent with the teaching of the Bible and certainly keeps one free from some type of esoteric teaching that God is in everything.

Crass literalism leads to absurdity. First Corinthians states: "After the same manner also he took the cup, when he had supped, saying, This cup *is* the new testament in my blood."[327] Did Jesus mean to say that the cup He was holding in His hand was actually the testament, or covenant, itself, or did He mean that the cup represents the covenant? Or in fact did He mean

---

324   John 8:12.

325   John 10:9.

326   John 15:1.

327   1 Corinthians 11:25.

that what was in the cup was representative of the new covenant?

"Cup" is a metonymy, a figure of speech in which one thing represents something else with which it is normally associated. In this case "cup" is used metonymously for its contents which represents the covenant sealed in our Lord's precious blood.

A common usage of metonymy is the phrase "the White House" used to refer to the president, or his staff, as in the statement, "The White House decided to release the speech earlier than anticipated." It was the president, or some high official, who made the decision, not the building commonly known as "the White House." Unfortunately, literal Roman Catholic exegesis would lead us to conclude that a building determines the scheduling of press releases!

Figurative substitutions of this sort are common to our writing and speaking, and appear in everyday communications as well as in the biblical writings. In the account of the rich man and Lazarus, Abraham expresses why it is unnecessary for a representative from the place of the departed going to the land of living to warn the rich man's brothers. "Abraham saith unto him, They have Moses and the prophets; let them hear them."[328]

"Moses and the prophets" is a metonymy for "the *writings* of Moses and the prophets"—the Word of God. To use the interpretive approach of the transubstantiationists would produce erroneous results. "They have Moses and the prophets" literally understood would mean, "they have Moses and the prophets speaking to them face-to-face on earth."

Others argue that John 6 clearly supports transubstantiation: "Then Jesus said unto them, Verily, verily, I say unto you, **Except ye eat the flesh of the Son of Man, and drink His blood**, ye have no life in you. Whoso eateth my flesh, and drinketh my blood, hath eternal life; and I will raise him up at the last day."[329]

Transubstantiationists believe that the Eucharist makes it possible for the faithful to comply with these words. Since we have to eat the flesh of Christ

328   Luke 16:29.

329   John 6:53–54.

and drink His blood, transubstantiation provides the process whereby that flesh and that blood become available. However, three observations need to be made.

1. If this passage teaches that we must eat the literal flesh of Christ and drink the literal blood of Christ, it teaches more than even Rome is willing to admit. Literally understood, it can be used to demonstrate that whoever partakes of "the sacrament of the Mass" automatically goes to Heaven. "Whoso eateth my flesh, and drinketh my blood **hath eternal life.**" All one has to do is to partake of the transubstantiated elements and one has eternal life.

2. Jesus was not here teaching about the Lord's Supper. In fact, the words spoken in John 6 were uttered by our Lord more than a year before the Supper was instituted. The chronology doesn't fit the Last Supper and related events. It would have been unreasonable for our Lord to expect His disciples to understand something that He had not yet revealed. Such would be like a math teacher explaining a higher level of math than the students were prepared to receive since the requisite steps to the solution of the more complex problem had not yet been presented.

3. A study of John 6 will show that the Lord was not teaching about the Lord's Supper, nor was He advocating cannibalism. Rather, He was speaking about faith. Our Lord had just fed the five thousand and the multitudes were seeking Him. They were laboring for the food that perishes. Our Lord perceived what was in their hearts and gave them instruction about faith.[330] He spoke about bread and His audience asked Him for this bread. Jesus responded: "I am the bread of life: he that **cometh** to me shall never hunger; and he that **believeth** on me shall never thirst."[331]

Jesus was speaking about "coming" and "believing." The person who comes

---

330   John 6:26–29.

331   John 6:35.

to Christ eats, for he shall *never hunger.* The person who believes, drinks and shall *never thirst.* In the context, coming to Christ is what it means to eat, and believing is what it means to drink. The context demonstrates that this is what our Lord means.

> But I said unto you, That ye also have seen me, and believe not. All that the Father giveth me shall come to me; and **him that cometh to me I will in no wise cast out.** . . . And this is the will of him that sent me, that every one which seeth the Son, **and believeth on him, may have everlasting life**; and I will raise him up at the last day.[332]

It is often alleged by Lewis supporters, and others who don't appreciate a critique of Lewis' theology, that "C. S. Lewis was no theologian." Indeed, he certainly wasn't a biblical theologian. This is all the more reason why he shouldn't be our model. Yet, such simple truths that we have set forth concerning the Lord's Supper and other crucial issues do not require a trained biblical theologian. These are matters that most Sunday school students could effectively debate from the Bible. Hiding behind the "Lewis-was-no-theologian" argument is to accept error simply because the individual spoke and wrote outside of his area of expertise.

C. S. Lewis and Prayers for the Dead

The theological underpinnings of Lewis' works are definitely influenced by his beliefs. Here is one comment which is quite revealing concerning his absolute unorthodoxy. His writings here reveal that Lewis did not believe in eternal security of the believer and the condemnation and hopelessness after death for the unbeliever.

> **Of course I pray for the dead.** The action is so spontaneous, so all but inevitable, that only the most compulsive theological case against it would deter me. And I hardly know how the rest of my prayers would survive if those for the dead were forbidden

---

332   John 6:36–37, 40.

> ... **On the traditional Protestant view, all the dead are damned or saved.** If they are damned, prayer for them is useless. If they are saved, it is equally useless.... To pray for them presupposes that progress and difficulty are still possible. In fact you are bringing in something like Purgatory.
>
> Well, I suppose I am.... **I believe in Purgatory** ... the very etymology of the word *purgatory* has dropped out of sight.... The right view [of purgatory] returns magnificently in Newman's *Dream*. There, if I remember rightly, the saved soul, at the very foot of the throne, begs to be taken away and cleansed. It cannot bear for a moment longer "With its darkness to affront that light." Religion has reclaimed Purgatory.
>
> **Our souls *demand* Purgatory,** don't they? Would it not break the heart if God said to us "It is true, my son, that your breath smells and your rags drip with mud and slime, but we are charitable here and no one will upbraid you with these things, nor draw away from you. Enter into the joy"? Should we not reply "With submission sir, and if there is no objection, **I'd rather be cleansed first.**" "It may hurt, you know"—"Even so, sir."
>
> I assume that the process of purification will normally involve suffering.... But I don't think suffering is the purpose of the purgation.[333]

Lewis' position flies directly in the face of the plain scriptural teachings as revealed in the Bible. Scripture says that Christ purged our sins and there is never even the slightest hint that we have anything to do with the purging of our sins here or in the hereafter. To claim that we must still be purged from sin after death would mean that Christ's death was not efficacious.

> Who being the brightness of his glory, and the express image of his person, and upholding all things by the word of his power, when he had **by himself purged our sins,** sat down on the right hand of the Majesty on high.[334]

Christ paid the penalty for our sins. There is nothing meritorious in human suffering. God is not propitiated (satisfied) by our sufferings, no matter

---

333 Lewis, *Letters to Malcolm*, pp. 107–109.

334 Hebrews 1:3.

how profound. In fact, it takes the shedding of blood to purge sins, not the suffering that Lewis alleges. "And almost all things are by the law **purged with blood;** and without shedding of blood there is no remission."[335] Christ (God manifest in the flesh) shed His precious blood for our sin! Even our willingness to shed our own sinful blood would be ineffective and deficient. Only Christ's sinless blood could satisfy the justice of God.

> Whom God hath set forth to be **a propitiation through faith in his blood,** to declare his righteousness for the remission of sins that are past, through the forbearance of God; To declare, I say, at this time his righteousness: that he might be just, and the justifier of him which believeth in Jesus. Where is boasting then? It is excluded. By what law? of works? Nay: but by the law of faith. Therefore we conclude that a man is justified by faith without the deeds of the law. [336]

All of the scriptural admonitions to sanctification, holiness and purity are for the living. "Having therefore these promises, dearly beloved, let us cleanse ourselves from all filthiness of the flesh and spirit, perfecting holiness in the fear of God."[337]

Lewis' belief in purgatorial cleansing is found in several of his writings. Very late in his life he wrote to his Catholic nun friend and stated, after almost dying the previous month: "When I die, and if 'prison visiting' is allowed, come down to look me up in Purgatory."[338]

C.S. Lewis and Auricular Confession

Lewis approved of confessing his sins to a priest. He provided his thoughts concerning his first confession and his desire to continue the practice thereafter. He wrote to Sister Penelope on October 24, 1940: "I am going to make

---

335 Hebrews 9:22.

336 Romans 3:25-28.

337 2 Corinthians 7:1.

338 *C. S. Lewis: A Biography,* p. 302.

my first confession next week. . . . " After his first confession, he reported back to her: ". . . The proper method of dealing with that is to continue the practice, as I intend to do."[339]

Beginning in the 1940s throughout the remainder of his life, Lewis' "spiritual director" was a Catholic priest named Walter Adams. He also chose him to be his "confessor" to whom he confessed his sins. [340]

Augustine, Aquinas, "Mere Christianity," And Ignatius Loyola

Several authors have likened C. S. Lewis to the "giants" of the Roman Catholic tradition. In an article commemorating the hundredth anniversary of Lewis' birth, J. I. Packer called Lewis "our patron saint." *Christianity Today* said Lewis "has come to be the Aquinas, the Augustine, and the Aesop of contemporary evangelicalism."[341] Even the title of Lewis' most famous work, *Mere Christianity*, seems to have a Jesuit connection. William Griffin writes:

> The words "Mere Christianity" weren't original to Lewis. In the seventeenth century Richard Baxter, an Anglican divine with Puritan predilections, used the words "Mere Christianity" in his book *The Saints' Everlasting Rest*. The work was something like the sixteenth-century Spaniard Ignatius Loyola's *Spiritual Exercises* in that it prepared the soul, through a series of measured steps, for its heavenly home. The first ten chapters described heaven, who'll be there and who won't, and why one must pursue Heaven strenuously while on earth. The last six chapters prescribed the Anglican method, with Puritan overlay, of pursuing the heavenly, and indeed heavily contemplative, life.[342]

Evangelicals of all stripes are indeed slipping into Catholicism, and it is coming through a mystical medieval contemplative Christianity. This statement is not intended to reflect any lack of love for the individual Catholic,

---

339   Ibid., p. 198.

340   *The Narnian*, p. 224.

341   "Still Surprised By Lewis," *Christianity Today* (9/7/98).

342   www.explorefaith.org/lewis/mere.html (1/18/06).

simply a disdain for teaching contrary to the Scripture—a teaching that condemns its followers to an eternity without Christ—something that we deem totally unacceptable. Our desire is use whatever means at our disposal to help Catholics discern the false teachings.

"He's One Of Us"

Lewis' unorthodox beliefs have caused many Catholics over the past century to claim him as one of their own. Andrew Greeley, a priest who writes for the *Chicago Sun-Times,* remarked that "C. S. Lewis was not a Christian in the sense of the word that 'evangelicals' insist upon. He was an Anglican who sometimes skirted, in his writings at any rate, dangerously close to the thin ice of Catholicism. Indeed, **many in my generation of Catholics simply assumed he was one of us.**"[343]

Lewis credits J.R.R. Tolkien, a staunch Roman Catholic, with having a decisive role in his "conversion" although Lewis was heavily influenced by the writings of G. K. Chesterton throughout his life. Lewis stated that "the contemporary book that influenced me the most is Chesterton's *The Everlasting Man.*" Sherwood Wirt, the individual interviewing Lewis, commented on Chesterton by stating, "I believe it was Chesterton who was asked why he became a member of the church, and he replied, 'to get rid of my sins.'"[344]

What did Chesterton really believe? Here is a quote from his book *The Everlasting Man*: "And this is the light; that the Catholic creed is catholic and nothing else. The philosophy of the Church is universal."[345]

Rome delights in sensible realities—icons, statues, bread and wine, candles, masses, novenas—and hence the Catholic appeal to allegories. This is the reason, we believe, Tolkien and Lewis' animalistic representations of Christianity are so appealing to Catholics.

---

343   Andrew Greeley, "Relax, It's Only a Fairy Tale, *Chicago Sun-Times* (12/9/05). www.suntimes.com/output/greeley/cst-edit-greel09.html

344   C. S. Lewis, *God in the Dock: Essays on Theology and Ethics,* edited by Walter Hooper, trustees of the Estate of C. S. Lewis: 1970, p. 260.

345   G.K. Chesterton, *The Everlasting Man* (San Francisco:Ignatius Press, 1993), p. 179.

In an article by Rob Moll entitled "C. S. Lewis, the Sneaky Pagan," Moll writes that "Lewis' conversion was very much shaped by the arguments of Tolkien that the gospel narratives fulfill the very best of human storytelling and myth." Speaking of Lewis' agenda, Moll writes: "I think he wanted to create a climate in the reader, an imaginative and intellectual climate that would make the reader more able to receive the gospel when they heard it."[346]

It appears to us that evangelicals slip dangerously close to Catholic idolatry when they embrace a vivid allegory as a summary of the biblical story. Jesus is not and never was a lion like Aslan in the film. In His character and essential nature He is "the lion of the tribe of Judah,"[347] but to make figurative language the basis for a real presentation as a sensible reality is to miss the point of the figure and violates the second commandment not to make any graven image "or any likeness of any thing that is in heaven above"[348]—something frequently done by Catholics. No wonder Tolkien and Lewis had no qualms about doing so!

The misplaced evangelical enthusiasm about the sufferings of Jesus in Mel Gibson's movie *The Passion of the Christ* puts them but a step away from importing crucifixes and Stations of the Cross into their churches. It appears that the evangelical enthusiasm for *The Passion* along with *The Lion, The Witch and the Wardrobe* shows just how seductively effective this temptation is. Fallen and sinful unregenerate individuals delight in pictures, sensible realities, and allegories, along with symbols and signs because such appeal to the fleshly side of man's nature. We are to walk by *faith* and not by *sight*[349]—a very hard thing to do for anyone that has never experienced the saving grace of Christ, let alone for those of us who have.

How do we see this in C. S. Lewis? Simply in the fact that from a Catholic perspective there is a connection between the alleged efficacy of baptism and

---

346 Rob Moll, "C.S. Lewis, the Sneaky Pagan" (6/28/04).
      www.christianitytoday.com/ct/2004/126/12.0.html.

347 Revelation 5:5.

348 Exodus 20:4.

349 2 Corinthians 5:7 (For we walk by faith, not by sight).

the imagined symbolism in *The Chronicles of Narnia*. In a Catholic publication we read: "In another volume, a boy turns himself into a dragon by dwelling on his resentments. When he then wishes to regain his friendship with the other children, Aslan leads him to a pool of water—baptism—where he painfully rips off his scales and frees the boy within."[350]

Another convincing quote is found in Lewis' *Voyage of the Dawn Trader*:

Well, he peeled the beastly stuff right off—just as I thought I'd done it myself the other three times, only they hadn't hurt—and there it was lying on the grass: only ever so much thicker, and darker.... Then he caught hold of me ... and threw me in the water.... I found that all the pain had gone from my arm.... After a bit the lion took me out and dressed me—[351]

Jesuit cardinal, Avery Dulles, a one-time Presbyterian who converted to Roman Catholicism, described Lewis as "probably the most successful Christian apologist of the twentieth century." This statement was an assessment made by a high-ranking Jesuit theologian who also wrote that Lewis "excelled as a spiritual writer."[352]

C. S. Lewis has a broad appeal. *Touchstone* magazine, published by the Fellowship of St. James, is a prime example of Lewis' appeal. Their Web page reads: "*Touchstone* is a Christian journal, conservative in doctrine and eclectic in content, with editors and readers from each of the three great divisions of Christendom—Protestant, Catholic, and Orthodox." Richard John Neuhaus gives his endorsement and writes: "Edited by a bevy of mainly younger Protestants, Orthodox, and Roman Catholics, *Touchstone* advances an ecumenism of orthodoxy defined by the Great Tradition."[353]

350 Joe Woodward, "De-Fanging C. S. Lewis: Will New Narnia Books Lose the Religion?" www.catholiceducation.org/articles/arts/a10103.html

351 C. S. Lewis, *Voyage of the Dawn Trader*, p. 116.

352 Cardinal Avery Dulles, "Mere Apologetics," *First Things 154* (June/July 2005), pp. 15–20 www.firstthings.com/ftissues/ft0506/articles/dulles.html

353 www.touchstonemag.com/(1/12/06).

This is highly revealing of where C. S. Lewis stood, and where his followers must inevitably end up. Does Christianity really need a further dumbing down of biblical distinctives by teachers and writers accepted by "all Christendom," or must we "earnestly contend for the faith which was once delivered unto the saints"?[354]

In failing to contend for the faith and in stoking the fires of ecumenism, Lewis is a turn off to true Bible-believing Christians. Yet, the depth of his appreciation is even wanting on the Catholic side. Jesuit theologian, Cardinal Avery Dulles, though writing of Lewis with great approval, closes his article by stating:

> As Lewis' greatest weakness, I would single out his lack of appreciation for the Church and the sacraments. . . . **Lewis seems content with this rather weak defense of the sacramental system. But in his later years he developed a deeper appreciation.** Speaking of Holy Communion in his posthumously published *Letters to Malcolm*, he writes: "Yet I find no difficulty in believing that the veil between the worlds, nowhere else (for me) so opaque to the intellect, is nowhere else so thin and permeable to divine operation. Here a hand from the hidden country touches not only my soul but my body. Here the prig, the don, the modern in me have no privilege over the savage or the child." . . .
>
> In joining the Church he made a genuine and honest profession of faith—but he did not experience it as entry into a true community of faith. He found it possible to write extensively about Christianity while saying almost nothing about the People of God, the structures of authority, and the sacraments. My own experience has been different. In becoming a Catholic, I felt from the beginning that I was joining the communion of the saints, the body to which Augustine and Aquinas, Bernard and Ignatius, belonged. . . . The sacramental system and the authority of pastors were (and are) for me among the most attractive features of Christianity. [355]

---

354 Jude 3.

355 Avery Cardinal Dulles, "Mere Apologetics.

These are not surprising comments from one in a position of authority within the Catholic church. Although Dulles articulated these negative thoughts, Lewis support among Catholics remains strong because of his sympathies for Rome. *Christian History and Biography* reports:

Many people who read Lewis' first book after his conversion, *The Pilgrim's Regress,* assumed he was a Catholic, and, in fact, the second edition was published by a Catholic publisher. Lewis marveled in 1940 that "the two people whose conversion had something to do with me became Papists!" (Dom Bede Griffiths and George Sayer). This popularity among and influence on Catholics continued throughout Lewis' life and to the present day. Pope John Paul II spoke of *The Four Loves* as one of his favorite books.[356]

Some people will claim that we are simply anti-Catholic for pointing out the teachings that align Lewis with Rome. This is simply not the case. The following article conveys our sentiments concerning why we feel compelled to speak up against false teachings and warn others of the inevitable outcome of their error.

Is This Hate?[357]

When a man bows before an idol of ivory, begging for salvation, and you tell him it cannot answer . . . **is this hate?**

When someone's little girl, barely sixteen, must tell her thoughts, her emotions and temptations to an unmarried priest in the confession box, and you tell her she need only confess to Jesus . . . **is this hate?**

When a poor, grieving widow pays from her meager substance for Masses for her dead husband, desperately hoping to end his pain in purgatory, and you tell her there is no purgatory . . . **is this hate?**

---

356 Robert Trexler and Jennifer Trafton, "Interesting and Unusual Facts about C. S. Lewis." www.christianitytoday.com/ch/2005/004/2.02.html (1/06/06), p. 3.

357 *Battle Cry,* May/June 1996. http://www.chick.com/bc/1996/hate.asp

When one billion souls, for whom Christ died, trust a well-fed pontiff dressed in gold and fine linen to give them the keys to heaven, and you tell them they need no one but Jesus . . . **is this hate?**

When Jesus, God's gift of love to all mankind, pointed his finger at the Pharisees and called them so many snakes . . . **was this hate?**

When the Apostle Paul stood on Mars Hill, and dared tell the philosophers of pagan mystery religion that they were too superstitious . . . **was this hate?**

NO!

To free a man from Satan's chains, you must first tell him he is a prisoner. Convince him that he is lost and without hope. And if pained and angered by the conviction of sin, he says your message is one of hatred, then know that his anguish is conviction of sin. Didn't you become upset when told you were a sinner? . . .

True hatred hides the gospel in beautiful words that upset no one, and therefore bring no conviction of sin.

True hatred stands in selfish silence as hell's population grows.

Our true heart's desire is to simply speak the truth in love.[358] When this means pointing out the false religious extra-biblical teachings, our craving for comfort and acceptance must never silence our desire to stand firm for the truth. Like the apostle Paul, we ask the same question: "Am I therefore become your enemy, because I tell you the truth?"[359]

---

358 Ephesians 4:15.

359 Galatians 4:16.

Chapter 6

C. S. Lewis: The "Sneaky" Pagan

Contrary to typical seminary teaching today, the truths of Scripture were *not* arrived at by consensus from learned sages who grappled with the issues that constitute the Word of God. Nor is Bible truth the product of philosophical speculation and investigation. Rather, that which is revealed in Scripture is revealed by God. Had God not provided us with this revelation of truth, man would be totally ignorant of Scripture, and much of the truth would be beyond human comprehension.

When the apostle Paul came to the pagan city of Corinth, he did not seek common ground with pagans so that they would be able to understand his message. Instead, he preached to them the gospel—Christ crucified. Paul knew that it was simply futile to attempt to use his persuasive powers in lieu of the power of God to convince the unbelievers.

> **For I determined not to know any thing among you, save Jesus Christ, and him crucified.** And I was with you in weakness, and in fear, and in much trembling. **And my speech and my preaching was not with enticing words of man's wisdom,** but in demonstration of the Spirit and of power: That your faith should not stand in the wisdom of man, but in the power of God.[360]

The apostle Paul's assessment of the wisdom of man and the power of God reveals how interaction with the non-believers took place during the formative years of the church.

---

360   1 Corinthians 2:2–5.

The great need today is for Christians to once again appreciate the divine uniqueness of God's words as revealed and preserved in the Bible. C. S. Lewis, however, did not seek to preserve the uniqueness of Scripture. Rather, he sought out what he believed was common ground in Scripture and paganism. In doing this he depreciated the uniqueness of God's Word, elevating paganism to a position that it does not rightly deserve.

Christianity Today[361] published an interview with Colin Duriez, a Lewis expert, and entitled the article "C. S. Lewis, The Sneaky Pagan." Duriez states, "Lewis wove pre-Christian ideas into a story for a post-Christian culture."

Actually there was nothing "sneaky" about Lewis' paganism. According to Josh Hurt, writing in another issue of *Christianity Today,* "not only was Lewis hesitant to call his books Christian allegory, but the stories borrow just as much from pagan mythology as they do the Bible."[362] Another writer states:

> Much of *The Lion, the Witch* . . . owes more to English folktales or Norse and classical myth than to the New Testament. The passage of the four Pevensie children through the magic closet into a world laboring under a spell of eternal winter is not Christian, nor are the cruel white witch, talking animals, centaurs and even a duo of Roman gods who inhabit it. True, the description of the redeeming figure of the lion Aslan as "the Son of the Great Emperor-Beyond-the-Sea" is a big hint. **But even Aslan's sacrifice on a huge stone table (not a cross; and performed with a stone knife, Aztec-style), and his subsequent miraculous recovery could have been borrowed from any number of world religions.**[363]

Upon viewing the film the astute viewer is left with the impression that the

---

361   *Christianity Today,* 6/28/04.

362   *Christianity Today,* 11/7/05.

363   David Van Biema, "How To tell If the Lion, the Witch and the Wardrobe Is a Christian Film," *Time* (10/3/05).
        www.time.com/time/arts/Printout/0,8816,1113226,00.html

sacrifice of Aslan is somehow related to Stonehenge, a mysterious circle of giant "prehistoric" stones in southern England. Researcher Berit Kjos comments:

> **The enticing pagan worlds nurtured by C. S. Lewis and his myth-making friends** were not inspired by God's Word or Spirit. Their stories **grew out of lifelong immersion in the beliefs, values, ritual, languages and lifestyles of former pagan cultures.** The white witch, Jadis—the self-professed Queen of Narnia—emerged from that pagan worldview, not from a biblical frame of reference. Her ritual sacrifice of Aslan has more in common with the ancient blood sacrifices to cultural gods (whether Hindu, Mayan, Incan, or Babylonian) than with the crucifixion of our Lord. **Small wonder the movie director chose a sacrificial setting for Aslan that looks strangely like the ancient ritual stones and pillars of Stonehenge, now a gathering place for the world's fast-growing networks of neopagans.** [364]

In her book *Journey Into Narnia*, Kathryn Lindskoog notes:

> The stone that is lowest in Stonehenge is called the stone of sacrifice because people suspect that humans were bound and stabbed there in evil ceremonies thousands of years ago. . . . It is quite possible that humans were once sacrificed there, and it is almost certain that Stonehenge gave Lewis the idea of the Stone Table. [365]

Is it any surprise that a pagan world is raving about C. S. Lewis and the new movie from Disney?

The following review by Govindini Murty and Jason Apuzzo reveals how totally acceptable the C. S. Lewis books and movies are to the world at large.

---

364 Berit Kjos, www.cuttingedge.org

365 Kathryn Lindskoog, *Journey into Narnia*, p. 104.

The Lion, the Witch and the Wardrobe ... is worthy of support from any-one, whether conservative or liberal, who believes in classic, **humanistic storytelling**.... Aslan, it has been debated, is intended by Narnia's author C. S. Lewis to be a symbol for Christ (the King of Kings) but of course the lion is also a royal and **divine symbol throughout world religion**; there are numerous lion-like divine figures in ancient Egyptian, Babylonian, Greek, Hindu and Buddhist religious symbolism....

The White Witch herself seems to be a throwback to various witches and goddesses of Celtic and Greek mythology. Her hair is dressed in the snake-like coils of a Medusa.... Is it perhaps that like a shamaness, the White Witch dons the lion's garb in order to assume his magical powers, or to signify some deeper connection with the figure of Aslan—**a connection that surmounts the duality of good and evil?** Why would the White Witch be garbed in leonine costume at the end, except perhaps as a sign that **she and Aslan are two halves of one whole**, and that they are playing out in ritual fashion an eternal cosmic struggle, where good and evil, light and dark, summer and winter alternate in ascendancy throughout the round of time? ...

Narnia might have been written as a Christian allegory, but this is a movie that also draws on classical and world mythology, and can be enjoyed by people of all religious faiths.[366]

While the Christian revelation is totally unique because of its divine source and therefore not to be confused with pagan myth, Lewis had some very different ideas on this important point—a point made even more important by the times in which we live and the trend toward syncretism.[367] Evidently, Lewis picked up these unfortunate ideas from J.R.R. Tolkien who had come, at one point, to perceive that Lewis was in the throes of a spiritual quest.

---

366   NewsMax (12/9/05), "Murty & Apuzzo: 'Narnia' a Classic Tale of the Ages"
       www.newsmax.com/archives/articles/2005/12/8/230129.shtml

367   Syncretism—the attempt to reconcile theology and mythology by asserting their unity.

Tolkien, seizing on this vulnerability, said that the obvious-seeming distinction that Lewis made between myth and fact—between intimations of timeless joy and belief in a historically based religion—was a false one. **Language, and the consciousness it reflected, was intrinsically magical. One had to become religious in order to save the magic, not to be saved from it.**[368]

Evidently, Tolkien's views on myth and magic colored Lewis' understanding of the Bible and its message, and made Lewis willing to accommodate other religions and religious points of view. "Where for millennia the cutting edge of faith had been the difference between pagan myth and Christian revelation, Lewis was drawn by the *likeness* of the Christian revelation to pagan myth."[369]

To say the least, Lewis' views on myth and magic are troubling. In his second epistle, the apostle Peter wrote:

> **For we have not followed cunningly devised fables**, when we made known unto you the power and coming of our Lord Jesus Christ, but were eyewitnesses of his majesty. For he received from God the Father honour and glory, when there came such a voice to him from the excellent glory, This is my beloved Son, in whom I am well pleased. And this voice which came from heaven we heard, when we were with him in the holy mount. [370]

The events of Scripture are not mythical, nor are they magical. Peter affirms that redemptive gospel events are historical and occurred on a time-space continuum. If we had been there with a camcorder, we could have gotten it all on film. As we continue to read of Lewis' views we have to ask a question:

---

368   Adam Gopnik, "Prisoner of Narnia."
      www.newyorker.com/critics/atlarge/articles/051121crat_atlarge (12/20/05), p. 7.

369   Ibid., p. 6.

370   2 Peter 1:16–18.

How could Lewis speak as he does of magic and myth and put them on a level with Bible facts?

On September 19, 1931, Lewis invited J.R.R. Tolkien and Hugo Dyson to dinner. Tolkien excused himself at three o'clock the next morning, but Lewis and Dyson continued talking for another hour or so. A month later Lewis wrote a letter to a friend to explain what he had learned that night about what he considered "the vexed problem of the Atonement":

> Now what Dyson and Tolkien showed me was this: that if I met the idea of sacrifice in a Pagan story I didn't mind it at all: and again, that if I met the idea of **a god sacrificing himself to himself** . . . I like it very much and was mysteriously moved by it: again, that the idea of the dying and reviving God (Balder, Adonis, Bacchus) similarly moved me provided I met it anywhere *except* in the Gospels. The reason was that in Pagan stories I was prepared to feel the myth as profound and suggestive of meaning beyond my grasp even tho' I could not say in cold prose "what it meant."
>
> **Now the story of Christ is simply a true myth:** a myth working on us in the same way as the others, but with tremendous difference that *it really happened:* and one must be content to accept it in the same way, remembering that it is God's myth where the others are men's myths: i.e., **Pagan stories are God expressing himself through the minds of poets**, using such images as He found there, while Christianity is God expressing himself through "real things."[371]

Several points should be noticed. For one thing, Lewis was moved by the pagan idea of "a god sacrificing himself to himself." Secondly, Lewis believed that the story of Christ is "a true myth," meaning that it really happened. Thirdly, "pagan stories are God expressing himself through the minds of poets." It is no wonder that Lewis could write, "And if, as I believe, Christ, in transcending and thus abrogating, also **fulfils, both Paganism and Judaism.** . . ."[372]

---

371 Alan Jacobs, pp. 148–149.

372 Lewis, *Reflections on the Psalms* (Harvest Books, 1964), p. 129.

Lewis is not an anomaly in the world of scholarship, for there are other scholars of ancient lore who find all sorts of parallels with Christianity in pagan lore. According to the online encyclopedia, Wikipedia.org: "It is possible that Dionysian mythology would later find its way into Christianity. There are many parallels between the legends of Dionysus and Jesus; both were said to have been born from a mortal woman but fathered by a god, to have returned from the dead, and to have transformed water into wine." This idea has been developed by those who connect Dionysus with the Lord's Supper. "The modern scholar Barry Powell also argues that Christian notions of eating and drinking 'the flesh' and 'blood' of Jesus were influenced by the cult of Dionysus. Certainly the Dionysus myth contains a great deal of cannibalism, in its links to Ino."[373]

Lewis scholar Alan Jacobs believes that this kind of thinking clearly shows Tolkien's influence. Through Tolkien, Lewis came to believe that "the 'doctrines' we get *out of* true myth are of course *less* true: they are translations into our *concepts* and *ideas* of that which God has already expressed in a language, more adequate, namely the actual incarnation, crucifixion, and resurrection." Jacobs asserts that this means that "the language of actual historical event, such as can be narrated in mythical form, is a *more* truthful language than the language of "concepts and ideas."[374]

After reading much of C. S. Lewis, and much about him by others, these insights help us to understand Lewis' view of God's message to man through the Bible. He saw myth as a more adequate way to express the mind of God than the propositional revelation of the Bible. It is this tendency in Lewis to see true myth as more effectively conveying truth that leads him, at least in some measure, to be on friendly terms with other religions and their religious forms of expression. One sympathetic Lewis supporter put it succinctly when he wrote: "Lewis does not confine his religious views to the Bible but recognizes God's revelation in literary masterpieces, in other religions, in ancient world myths, and through human reason and intuition. Christianity

373 http://en.wikipedia.org/wiki/Dionysus
374 Alan Jacobs, p. 149.

is true . . . not just because the Bible says so but because God chooses to reveal himself through many different ways, yet supremely through Christ."[375]

This is not surprising. Both Lewis and Tolkien saw pagan myth as being, in some sense, a revelation from God. This came about, perhaps, as a result of Lewis' confusion over how pagan writings were viewed by some of his teachers. Lewis wrote: "My [Christian] faith was first undermined by the attitude towards *Pagan* religion in the notes of modern editors of Latin & Greek poets at school. They always assumed that the ancient religion was pure error," meaning they assumed that the beliefs of the pagan cultures were superstitious nonsense. The effect this had on the young Lewis was to extend their critique to his religion—Christianity. "Hence," he wrote, "in my mind, the obvious question 'why shouldn't ours be equally false'?"[376] Lewis settled the matter in his mind by his approval of both. Rather than totally rejecting one (paganism) and accepting the other (Christianity), he accepted both.

Jacobs states that it was around the time of these struggles that Lewis came under the influence of a Miss Cowie, a kind of all-purpose nurse and dorm mother. She was "the sort of person who today would be called a proponent of New Age spirituality." Miss Cowie dabbled in theosophy, Rosicrucianism, and spiritualism, along with "the Anglo-American Occultist tradition." [377]

We should point out that this was occurring at a time in the history of the Western world when the Bible's credibility was under fierce attack by Darwinists and unbelieving scientists who wanted to destroy biblical authority by destroying the Bible. It was these attacks, and the allegedly insurmountable "problems" laid bare in the Bible, that fueled the desire for some kind of spirituality that was not dependent on belief in a literal, inerrant Bible. Alan Jacobs continues:

---

375   John W. Robbins, p. 3.

376   Alan Jacobs, p. 38.

377   Ibid.

Messages of spiritual oneness and the possibility of occult experience were especially appealing to people whose belief in orthodox Christianity had been shaken or destroyed, but the aggressive "scientific" agnosticism or atheism espoused by many followers of Darwin or by the philosophical atheism of (for example) many Marxists.[378]

Jacobs summarizes these spiritual influences on the young Lewis by observing:

So the first kind of experience that shaped the adolescent Jack [C. S.] Lewis was the Christian religion; the second was Miss Cowie's spiritualism, which replaced that religion when it had been undermined by classical scholarship. Yet more important than either of them, and somehow related to both, was his imaginative life—his instinctive aesthetic responses to art but also to the natural world.[379]

No doubt, Lewis was religious and he came to be a theist, i.e., he believed that God was supreme over His creation and not to be identified with it. Theism is far different from pantheism, which believes that God *is* His creation. Lewis came to be accepted by many not because he was a defender of Christian orthodoxy but because he was a supporter of theism against materialism, the view that there is no spiritual dimension of reality. Supporters of Lewis see the *Lion* movie as an effective way of showing people that there really is a Supreme Being out there. Chattaway observes:

Many Christians, including those who hope to use this film as an evangelistic tool, tend to excuse the pagan elements in Lewis' books as just so much window dressing; as far as they are concerned, all that stuff is the fairy-tale bait he had to set to lure unbelievers into his Christian world. But there is much more to Lewis' use of pagan myth than that. **In all of**

378   Alan Jacobs, p. 39.

379   Alan Jacobs, p. 40.

his writings, Lewis was confronting a modern, skeptical, materialistic view of the world that had no room for the supernatural. Lewis believed that paganism and Christianity had more in common with each other on this point than either had with the modern, secularized world. In the essay "Is Theism Important?" he wrote: "When grave persons express their fear that England is relapsing into Paganism, I am tempted to reply, 'Would that she were.' For I do not think it at all likely that we shall ever see Parliament opened by the slaughtering of a garlanded white bull in the housed of Lords or Cabinet Ministers leaving sandwiches in Hyde Park as an offering for the Dryads." [380]

Both Tolkien and Lewis had this desire in common, that is, to show that materialism is unsatisfactory as a world-and-life view. Joseph Pearce, Tolkien's biographer and author of a new book on Lewis, illustrates how myth helps the reader to discover "the unseen hand of providence": "... the power of Tolkien lies in the way that he succeeds, through myth, in making the *unseen hand of providence felt by the reader.* ... In his mystical creations, or sub-creations as he would call them, he shows how the *unseen hand of God is felt far more forcefully in myth* than it is ever felt in fiction."[381]

From Plato to Owen Barfield, Theosophy, and Beyond

As we have seen above Miss Cowie, an individual who had a marked influence on C. S. Lewis in his formative years, "dabbled in theosophy." On page 50 of the book *Narnia Beckons* authors Ted and James Baehr speak about the "stream of Neoplatonism" that runs through Narnia. It is at this point that we will develop the implications of this. Neoplatonism has some problematic associations. For example, Dale Nelson, in writing about Lewis' study group, "The Inklings," states: "Yeats and Steiner, Gurdjieff and Ouspensky, **Madame Blavatsky** and Annie Besant, the theosophists and anthroposophists and

---

380   Peter T. Chattaway, "Comment: The Paganism of Narnia."
      www.canadianchristianity.com/cgi.bin/na.cgi?nationalupdates/051124narnia (1/06/06), p. 1.

381   Humphrey Carter, ed. *The Letters of J.R.R. Tolkien* (Boston:Houghton Mifflin Company, 1981, p. 201.

seancers all practiced a Gnostic neo-Platonism which **sought to overcome the mortal limits of time-bound flesh by human imagination alone.**"[382] Plato, it seems, is at the root of Lewis' "sneaky paganism." In the last book of the Narnia series we read:

". . . This is Narnia."

"But how can it be?" said Peter. "For Aslan told us older ones that we should never return to Narnia, and here we are."

"Yes," said Eustace. "And we saw it all destroyed and the sun put out."

"And it's all so different," said Lucy.

"The Eagle is right," said the Lord Digory. "Listen, Peter. When Aslan said you could never go back to Narnia, he meant the Narnia you were thinking of. But that was not the real Narnia. That had a beginning and an end. It was only a shadow or a copy of the real Narnia . . . all of the dear creatures, have been drawn into the real Narnia through the Door. And of course it is different; as different as a real thing is from a shadow or as walking life is from a dream."

His voice stirred everyone like a trumpet as he spoke these words: but when he added under his breath, **"It's all in Plato, all in Plato:** bless me, what do they teach them at these schools!" The older ones laughed.[383]

Of paramount importance is Lewis' world and life view. As we have seen even Lewis supporters argue that Neoplatonism is characteristic of Lewis. Tolson comments:

Add to this his [Lewis'] attraction to the Platonic idea that all true knowledge is remembering and that **the object of this remembering is the realm of the ideal forms behind the world of appearances.** Even after

382   Dale Nelson, "The Inklings: Lewis, Tolkien, Williams and Barfield explore Theosophy and Reincarnation."
www.crossorad.to/Quotes/spirituality/tolkien-Lewis.htm , p. 3.

383   C. S. Lewis, *The Last Battle* (NY: HarperCollins, 1984), pp. 211–212.

he became a Christian, Lewis would insist that all religions share with Platonism an appreciation of higher, absolute truth—the Tao, he called it, using the Chinese word for the "way"—and that all equally reject the relativism embedded in so much modern ethical thought.[384]

Others concur, including evangelicals who endorse Lewis' work. For example in a book published by a leading Christian publishing house, the authors write:

In fact, a stream of Neoplatonism runs through the Narnia Chronicles as the Great River runs through Narnia itself—like the Great River, created by Aslan on the very first day of Narnia's existence. Platonism is so basic to the landscape of the Chronicles that the books would not be the same without it.[385]

The authors explain:

Lewis redirects at least two ideas from Plato into the Christian stream of thought: first, the theory of forms, with its emphasis on the doctrine that there are two worlds, the real (ideal) world and the apparent world, and secondly, the necessity of moral formation and insight as preparation for death.[386]

This doctrine of "two worlds" is contained in Lewis' use of the term "Shadowlands":

Shadlowlands is a term Aslan used in *The Last Battle* as a metaphor for the earthly realm, indicative of the limited, unenlightened view of reality that its transitory inhabitants possess. Plato's cave dwellers in his story from

---

384   Jay Tolson, pp. 49–50.

385   Ted and James Baehr, p. 50.

386   Ibid.

Book VII of *The Republic* represent a similar situation as they only have a partial and shadowy view of existence. [387]

According to his supporters, Lewis had a Greek frame of reference. It was a world-and-life view that was rooted in Plato. Yet, the wisdom of the ancient Greeks was something that Paul repeatedly argued against. "Beware," wrote the apostle Paul, "lest any man spoil you through philosophy and vain deceit, after the tradition of men, after the rudiments of the world, and not after Christ." [388] It is this worldly wisdom—and in Paul's day he particularly meant the wisdom of the ancient Greeks—that is totally vain and empty:

> For the preaching of the cross is to them that perish foolishness; but unto us which are saved it is the power of God. For it is written, **I will destroy the wisdom of the wise, and will bring to nothing the understanding of the prudent.** Where is the wise? where is the scribe? where is the disputer of this world? **hath not God made foolish the wisdom of this world?** For after that in the wisdom of God **the world by wisdom knew not God**, it pleased God by the foolishness of preaching to save them that believe. For the Jews require a sign, and the Greeks seek after wisdom: **But we preach Christ crucified**, unto the Jews a stumblingblock, and **unto the Greeks foolishness;** But unto them which are called, both Jews and Greeks, Christ the power of God, and the wisdom of God. Because the foolishness of God is wiser than men; and the weakness of God is stronger than men.[389]

While leading evangelicals are condemning secular humanism they are at the same time embracing a Christian philosopher whose Platonism is at the very root of the world view they are condemning. Do we really want to give a blanket endorsement to a writer who espouses a world view that is repeatedly spoken against in the Word of God?

---

387   David Graham, "Shadowlands." In *We Remember C. S. Lewis: Essays and Memoirs,* David Graham, ed. (Nashville: Broadman and Holman, 2001), p. 78.

388   Colossians 2:8.

389   1 Corinthians 1:18–25.

Well if you have trouble answering that, here's another potentially perplexing question: What about Lewis' endorsement of "the Tao"? This is a view that is at odds with the clear teachings of Scripture too. The Bible says of Christ, "And he is before all things, and by him all things consist."[390]

In his famous 1947 book *The Abolition of Man*, Lewis expresses his view of the Tao:

> The Chinese also speak of a great thing (the great thing) called the *Tao*. It is the reality beyond all predicates, **the abyss that was before the Creator Himself.** It is Nature, **it is the Way,** the Road. It is the Way in which the universe goes on, the Way in which things everlastingly emerge, stilly and tranquilly, into space and time. It is also the Way in which every man should tread in imitation of the cosmic and supercosmic progression, conforming all the activities to that great exemplar.[391]

Eric Sheske, writing on a Catholic website, connects C. S. Lewis' belief in "the Tao" with his beer drinking. Sheshke writes that since the publication of *The Abolition of Man* "Lewis' name has been associated with the Tao because of his love and respect for the natural law it embodies. I, however, associate Lewis with the Tao for a different reason: his beer drinking."[392] Lewis evidently made a metaphysical distinction between enjoying something and being aware of enjoying it. Lewis wrote: "Enjoyment and the contemplation of our inner activities are incompatible. You cannot hope and also think about hoping at the same moment." This distinction can be traced to the Roman Catholic mystic Thomas Merton and his understanding of the Tao.

Into this philosophical and religious mix having an influence on Lewis we must add Owen Barfield who, according to Alan Jacobs, "would become one of the most important people in Jack's life. He was certainly the

---

390   Colossians 1:17.

391   Lewis, *The Abolition of Man*, (NY: HarperCollins, 1947), p. 18.

392   Eric Sheske, "C. S. Lewis and the Tao."
      www.catholicexchange.com/vm/index.asp?vm_id=1&art_id=27704, pp. 1-2

most intellectually gifted of Jack's friends."[393] Who has ever heard of Owen Barfield—hardly a household name—and why would anyone want to study his writings?

> Many people who look into the writings of Owen Barfield . . . are C. S. Lewis admirers who are curious about this man who was Lewis' close friend throughout his adult life, from 1919 till Lewis' death in 1963. Barfield was Lewis' legal and financial advisor, and became an executor of his estate. Lewis dedicated his first scholarly book, *The Allegory of Love* (1936) to this "wisest and best of my unofficial teachers," **stating in its preface that he had asked no more than to disseminate Barfield's literary theory and practice**, and dedicated the first Narnian chronicle to his friend's adopted daughter Lucy. [394]

The influences upon Lewis' life are quite obvious. Miss Cowie and Owen Barfield provided Lewis with an occult exposure to both theosophy, and its relative anthroposophy. According to its adherents, one of the goals of theosophy is to promote paganism through various means, such as literature. *Webster's Third New International Dictionary* defines theosophy in the following way:

> 1) a body of doctrine relating to deity, cosmos, and self and held to rest on direct intuitions of supersensible reality by preternaturally perceptive individuals and to give a **wisdom superior to that of historical religion** of empirical philosophy of science . . . a system of often occult and esoteric thought presented as a means of individual salvation and sometimes associated with **mysticism**, pantheism, or magic. 2) a syncretistic system of theosophy following chiefly Hindu philosophies and associated with a movement originating in the US in 1875, aiming to serve through its societies as the nucleus of a universal brotherhood of man and to guide

393   *The Narnian,* p. 90.

394   Dale Nelson, p. 1.

the individual toward perfect wisdom through **the study of world litera-ture** on the laws of the universe and through the development under the esoteric teachings of mahatmas of his latent inner senses responsive to the invisible cosmos, and **teaching physical and spiritual evolution** (as of the soul through reincarnations)....

While Lewis never publicly declared to be a theosophist (as far as we know), there is so much here that sounds just like Lewis—the mysticism and magic, "the study of world literature," and the "teaching [of] physical and spiritual evolution." Since salvation is "sometimes associated with mysticism, panthe-ism, or magic" and since theosophy purportedly gives "a wisdom superior to that of historical religion," the theosophist can bypass Scripture, as Lewis often does.

Barfield, who was so influential of Lewis, departed from the teachings of theosophy and was caught up in anthroposophy which, according to Rudolf Steiner (1861–1925), the founder of anthroposophy, is "a path of knowledge to guide the spiritual in the human being to the spiritual in the universe."[395]

Not Only Not Christian But Anti-Christian

The first of the C. S. Lewis movies released in December 2005 is simply the tip of the iceberg. In March 2001, when HarperCollins announced its exclusive rights to publish Lewis' works in English, it also revealed plans to "repackage Lewis' theological works, and to commission new Narnia picture books for preschoolers."[396]

According to the above-cited article HarperCollins was terribly con-cerned about the "Christian" aspects of a Narnia documentary and other related merchandise. Steve Hanselman, senior vice president of Harper-SanFrancisco wrote concerning the script of a proposed documentary by Carol Hatcher:

395   www.steinerbooks.org/aboutrudolf.html

396   "Mere Marketing," CT.

The pages of the script suggest that Narnia will be treated from the vantage of **children in need of hopeful fantasy,** with the inspiration coming from memories and pictures in his head. **If Stephen King and J. K. Rowling are the commentators on Narnia, as the script suggests, Simon [Adley] should be quite pleased.** "We'll need to be able to give emphatic assurances that no attempt will be made to correlate the stories to Christian imagery/ theology." Hanselman went on to write that the script does not characterize what "'true Christianity' is, and said it should stay that way."[397]

The general desire to eliminate any perceived Christian imagery goes hand-in-hand with a desire to avoid the pre-millennial doctrines found in Scripture. Writing for *The Christian Science Monitor,* Jeffrey MacDonald reports:

Adherents to "a sectarian style in **confrontational evangelical circles** could learn a lot from Lewis," says Stephen G. Post, a bioethicist at Case Western Reserve University in Cleveland.... Post contends, for instance, that Lewis' determination always to "embrace rather than alienate the other" in such books as "The Abolition of Man" means **he wouldn't have given the time of day"** to such contemporary hot sellers as the **'Left Behind' series, where fictional accounts imagine nonbelievers suffering on earth during the biblically forecast rapture.**[398]

Lewis' Influence on Others
Regretfully, many are increasingly classifying magic into distinct categories, as if some is good and other kinds are bad. It is unwise to classify magic into the "black magic" of *Dungeons and Dragons* and the "white magic" of C. S. Lewis' stories. Magic is magic and both are working together to indoctrinate everyone into the visually realistic and aesthetically satisfying world of the occult. Yet, this erroneous distinction persists. Ted Baehr's comments are characteristic.

---

397 Ibid.

398 G. Jeffrey MacDonald, *The Christian Science Monitor,* 'Christians battle over 'Narnia'" www.csmonitor.com/2005/1208/p14s03-lire.html

... the Harry Potter franchise promotes a decidedly pagan worldview that could lead impressionable young minds, particularly those who have never been given a moral compass, in the direction of the occult. **C. S. Lewis' *Narnia* series, on the other hand, presents a clearly biblical, Christian worldview.** Yet both *Narnia* and *Harry Potter* deal with magic. What's the difference? Some Christians are disturbed by C. S. Lewis' use of the word "magic" in *The Chronicles of Narnia*. **Magic is forbidden in the Bible.**[399]

Commendably, Baehr points out that the Bible forbids magic, but his distinction between good and bad magic is totally confusing. The magic in C. S. Lewis' materials will further indoctrinate millions of unsuspecting children in pagan beliefs and practices while parents stand in awe of their children's desire to read. The same excuse is used in defense of the *Harry Potter* books. The Bible condemns those who call evil good and would apply to those that use their persuasive powers to convince others of the acceptability of "wholesome" magic. **"Woe unto them that call evil good, and good evil; that put darkness for light, and light for darkness; that put bitter for sweet, and sweet for bitter!"**[400]

From the innocent looking "Pokémon" card games, the unsuspecting target graduates to "Magic the Gathering" and other role-playing games, ranging from "Dungeons and Dragons" to "Vampires." Just as marijuana is a "gateway drug" to a life lived in a drug-induced stupor, so C. S. Lewis opens individuals to the dangerous world of the occult. Television exposes young people to varying degrees of magic as they watch "Xena Warrior Princess," "Buffy the Vampire Slayer," "Sabrina the Teenage Witch," and "Angel." Daytime TV shows portray people like James Van Praagh and John Edwards "communicating" with the dead. All of this popular nonsense further misleads an already misled world into an overflowing cesspool of anti-Christian thought.

---

399   Ted Baehr, "Redemptive Rendition of Narnia," (12/26/05)
      www.thenewamerican.com/artman/publish/article_2818.shtml

400   Isaiah 5:20.

The *Harry Potter* books and movies and those of C. S. Lewis are simply another deceptive tool. They are all working together to further blur the already distorted lines between good and evil. In a confused generation, this is serious. This blurred reality is eerily similar to Hollywood's portrayal of the "good" vampires of "Angel" and the "good" witches of "Charmed" and "Buffy the Vampire Slayer."

All of this is interrelated in Satan's grand design for the destruction of mankind. Our youth are being indoctrinated into the world of witches and wizardry while parents remain oblivious to the real danger. One of the greatest occult influences on this generation is J. K. Rowling who has publicly admitted that she was greatly influenced by the writings of C. S. Lewis.

> **J. K. Rowling has said that Lewis had a huge influence on her,** yet many people have problems with Harry Potter. I've heard many writers say they've been influenced by Lewis and they try to copy him. It is often too similar; all these books are pale imitations.[401]

C. S. Lewis influenced J. K. Rowling who is one of the leading spiritual influences of our day. Does this suggest something about the influence of C. S. Lewis?

The Bible clearly warns us about our associations and what our response to such negative influences should be: "And have no fellowship with **the unfruitful works of darkness,** but rather reprove them. For it is a shame even to speak of those things which are done of them in secret."[402]

Charles Colson credits C. S. Lewis' *Mere Christianity* with playing a decisive role in his conversion to Christ:

> In 1973, in the midst of the Watergate crisis, I visited the home of a friend who read to me from *Mere Christianity*. **In that book, I encountered**

---

401 Michael Coren, "The Subtle Magic of C. S. Lewis' Narnia."
www.catholic.org/featured/headline.php?ID=2827

402 Ephesians 5:11–12.

a formidable intellect and a logical argument that I found utterly persuasive. That night in the driveway of my friend's home I called out to God in a flood of tears and surrendered my life to Christ. . . . Today because of Lewis, there are millions of readers like me who can attest that they too have found God.[403]

Colson "encountered a formidable intellect and a logical argument" that he found to be "utterly persuasive." Yet, the first three chapters of First Corinthians reveal God's thoughts concerning human wisdom's capacity to convince the unbeliever. Salvation comes through faith in the Christ of Scripture, not through rational argumentation. Those who have confidence in rational argumentation conclude that God's will regarding salvation is foolish. So says the Scripture:

For the preaching of the cross is to them that perish foolishness; but unto us which are saved it is the power of God. For it is written, I will destroy the wisdom of the wise, and will bring to nothing the understanding of the prudent. Where is the wise? Where is the scribe? Where is the disputer of this world? hath not God made foolish the wisdom of this world? For after that in the wisdom of God **the world by wisdom knew not God,** it pleased God by the foolishness of preaching to save them that believe.[404]

The world simply cannot come to understand God through wisdom, whether realized through reading a book written by a great intellect, like that of C. S. Lewis, or self-generated. The apostle Paul testified that he refrained from using enticing words since the individual's faith would lack a solid foundation that comes only from a truly biblical perspective.

If your faith rests in a logical argument, someone who has a better argu-

---

403   Charles Colson, "Three Died That Day" (11/21/03)
        www.townhall.com/opinion/columns/chuckcolson/2003/11/21/170460.html

404   1 Corinthians 1:18–21.

ment could eventually persuade you in another direction. This is especially true concerning spiritual matters. Today, increasing numbers of people are being "convinced" to get saved rather than "convicted" of their lost condition and the necessity of a personal decision for Christ. When the pressures of life mount, their turning over of this "new leaf" is short lived, resulting in their turning away from that which they simply perceived as truth at the time.

It is the power of God and the demonstration of the Spirit that will bring true faith to the individual—not one's ability to entice or manipulate the individual into "believing"—whether the manipulator be a "high powered evangelist," a moving orator, or a gifted philosopher. Although Lewis lacked a secure doctrinal foundation, he skillfully maneuvered many through the intricacies of the English language to convince them of the veracity of his arguments. The apostle Paul goes on to explain the utter foolishness of this approach:

> Let no man deceive himself, If any man among you seemeth to be wise in this world, let him become a fool, that he may be wise. **For the wisdom of the world is foolishness with God.** For it is written, he taketh the wise in their own craftiness.[405]

Colson is the prime mover behind publishing the symposium *Evangelicals and Catholics Together: Working Towards a Common Mission.* In his part of the symposium, Colson credited C. S. Lewis' writings as a major influence leading him to form this ecumenical outreach.[406] Colson writes: "Lewis' eloquent arguments in *Mere Christianity* on why Christians must stand together to defend the faith have motivated my work to bring evangelicals and Catholics together."[407] Colson argues that C. S. Lewis "was not

405 1 Corinthians 3:18–19.

406 See Chuck Colson, *Evangelicals and Catholics Together: Working Towards a Common Mission,* (Nelson Reference, 1995), p. 36.

407 Charles Colson, "C. S. Lewis and God's Surprises." *We Remember C. S. Lewis: Essays and Memoirs,* David Graham, ed. (Nashville: Broadman & Holman, 2001), p. 28.

only a keen apologist but also a true prophet of our postmodern age." His literary and philosophical insights, according to Colson, made him a keen discerner of the times and an observer of modern culture. Colson also wrote concerning C. S. Lewis:

> Why was Lewis so uncannily prophetic? At first glance he seems an unlikely candidate. He was not a theologian; he was an English professor. What was it that made him such a keen observer of cultural and intellectual trends?
>
> The answer may be somewhat discomfiting to modern evangelicals: **One reason is precisely that Lewis was not an evangelical.** He was a professor in the academy, with a specialty in medieval literature, which gave him a mental framework shaped by the whole scope of intellectual history and Christian thought. As a result, he was liberated from the narrow confines of the religious views of his day—which meant he was able to analyze and critique them.
>
> . . . You and I need to follow Lewis' lead. We must liberate ourselves from the prison of our own narrow perspective and immerse ourselves in Christian ideas "down the ages." Only then can we critique our culture and trace the trends.[408]

It *is* reasonable to liberate oneself from ineffective and unscriptural methodology. However, Lewis "liberated himself" through the use of paganism and myth. This is not liberation, but further condemnation because it stands in direct contrast to the truth.

Colson is by no means alone in his glowing endorsement of Lewis. Bob Fryling, the executive director of InterVaristy Press, was quoted as saying, "Outside of the Scriptures themselves, Lewis is probably the greatest authority and example of a thoughtful Christian faith." [409]

We seriously question such comments based on the existing facts.

---

408   Chuck [Charles] Colson, "Discerning the Trends: The Prophecy of C. S. Lewis," "BreakPoint" broadcast for November 29, 2004, pp. 1-2.

409   "C. S. Lewis Superstar"

Chapter 7

Distortions of the Lion Movie

Which Lion?

The Chronicles of Narnia is a seven-set series. In this series, the creation of Narnia and the other worlds is told by Lewis in a book whose storyline precedes *The Lion, the Witch and the Wardrobe*. In the first of the series, *The Magicians's Nephew*, the creator, Aslan the lion, is presented to the reader.

Because Aslan is the creator, he is an allegorical representation of the Lord Jesus Christ. That means that Christ is now associated with being the creator of the river god, fauns, satyrs, and dwarfs. *The Magician's Nephew* gives a true sense of the creation similarities, as in the creation of light.

> One moment there had been nothing but darkness; next moment **a thousand, thousand points of light** leaped out—single stars, constellations and planets, brighter and bigger than any in our world. . . .[410]

Lewis patterned chapter nine, entitled "The Founding of Narnia," after the creation of the world found in the Word of God. No one honestly analyzing Lewis' works could deny the obvious creation allegory. Light shows up on the first day of the Narnian creation much like it showed up on the very first day of the biblical creation. "And God said, Let there be light: and there was light."[411] The similarities are impossible to miss. The similarities are what make Lewis' deviations troublesome.

---

410   C. S. Lewis, *The Magician's Nephew*, (HarperCollins, 1983), p. 117.

411   Genesis 1:3.

> And now for the first time, **the Lion** was quite silent. He was **going to and fro** among the animals. And every now and then he would go up to two of them (always two of them) and touch their noses with his. . . . But the pairs which he had touched instantly left their own kinds and followed him. At last he stood still and all the creatures whom he had touched came and stood in a wide circle around him.[412]

Aslan the lion, the creator, is said to be "going to and fro." Repeatedly, the Bible mentions this phrase in relation to Satan's activities, not those of the Lord's. "And the LORD said unto Satan, Whence camest thou? Then Satan answered the LORD, and said, **From going to and fro in the earth**, and from walking up and down in it."[413]

As Lewis' creation narrative continues, he mentions *the roaring of the lion.* It too is eerily similar to the biblical account of Satan.

> The Lion, whose eyes never blinked, stared at the animals as hard as if he was going to burn them up with his mere stare. **The Lion opened his mouth . . . the deepest, wildest voice** they had ever heard was saying: "Narnia, Narnia, Narnia awake. Love. Think. Speak. Be walking trees. Be talking beasts. Be divine waters."[414]

Interestingly, the only biblical images of a roaring lion are negative and associated with the devil and not the Lord. For instance, the Bible states: "Be sober, be vigilant; because **your adversary the devil, as a roaring lion,** walketh about, seeking whom he may devour."[415]

We find it troublesome that the figure that purportedly represents Jesus Christ in Lewis' Narnia series has some definite associations with Satan in the Bible. No doubt, this could be simply coincidence, but it could be much

---

412 Lewis, *Magician's,* p. 136.

413 Job 1:7.

414 Lewis, *Magician's,* pp. 137–138.

415 1 Peter 5:8.

more. This is why we say it is "troublesome." We want to give Lewis the benefit of the doubt, but knowing how many strange views Lewis held, it is certainly not unreasonable to be troubled by it all.

Moreover, C. S. Lewis' claim to fame revolved around his ability to use occult fantasy to supposedly deliver "the gospel" in the form of magic, sorcery, and heathen mythology. This is troublesome for those of us who feel that spiritual truths should be regarded with the highest of standards and purest of associations. Does the following sound like it is parallel to the Bible's description of creation, or are there some elements that are totally foreign to the biblical presentation?

> Out of the trees wild people stepped forth, **gods and goddesses** of the wood; with them came **Fauns and Satyrs and Dwarfs. Out of the river rose the river god with his Naiad daughters.** And all these and all the beasts and birds in their different voices, low or high or thick or clear, replied: "**Hail, Aslan. We hear and obey.** We are awake. We love. We think. We speak. We know."[416]

Shockingly, Lewis makes Aslan (Christ) the creator of the very things which the Bible condemns. The first of the Ten Commandments—the moral law of God—states that man is to have no other gods apart from the one and only God. "Thou shalt have no other gods before me."[417] Man creates gods and goddesses out of his own desire to worship something tangible in direct violation of God's Word. Should we encourage our children to read books which allegorically attribute these unwholesome creations to God? Is this not conveying an unfortunate message that chimes in with the message of the world?

> "And now," said Aslan, "Narnia is established. We must next take thought for keeping it safe. I will call some of you to my council. Come hither to

---

416 Lewis, *Magician's*, p. 139.

417 Exodus 20:3.

> me, you **the chief Dwarf, and you the River-god**... For though **the world is not five hours old and evil has already entered it.**" [418]

The entering of sin and evil into the world is another of Lewis' parallels to the book of Genesis. He states that Adam's race did the harm and brought evil into Narnia.

> "... a force of evil has already entered it; waked and brought hither by this Son of Adam." The Beasts, even Strawberry, all turned their eyes on Digory.... **"And as Adam's race has done the harm, Adam's race shall help to heal it."** [419]

The Narnian influence is inestimable. This generation has already seen the Bible completely replaced in the public schools by books like the *Harry Potter* series. It would seem that once a half dozen of these movies is completed, Disney will have completely replaced the biblical account with the Narnian account of creation in the minds of millions of impressionable minds. The visual images of creation, redemption, and every other important biblical truth will have been supplanted by Disney's visual stimuli. Will these visual stimuli mean nothing to those who read of them and view them on the screen? As Berit Kjos observes:

> Carried on the emotional impact of dramatic movies, the images we see will lodge in our minds and memories long afterwards. Many of those suggestive scenes will never be erased, no matter how hard we try. Sometimes they give rise to cravings or obsessions that drive the victim toward more and stronger emotional stimuli. [420]

The sinful desires of man are insatiable. His *intense longings* for stronger emotional stimuli simply become the infrastructure for new and greater

---

418   Lewis, *Magician's*, pp. 142.

419   Ibid., p. 161.

420   Berit Kjos, part 2, p. 3.

obsessions. Once his initial cravings are fulfilled they simply become the catalyst for needing ever increasing stimuli. In the end, the individual's insatiable appetite and lust drives him even further away from God.

How we picture reality has an impact on our devotion to God, His ways, and His Word. The sin of fallen humanity is that they professed "themselves to be wise" and "they became fools, and changed the glory of the uncorruptible God into an image made like to corruptible man, and to birds, and fourfooted beasts, and creeping things."[421] The issue is whether the universe is as God says, or is it made up of mythological, co-mingled creatures foreign to Scripture?

Berit Kjos asks, and answers, the most pertinent question of all:

> Can those who are captivated by myth and magic also love God with *all their heart*, mind, strength and soul? No! For when their hearts are divided between God's good and the world's counterfeits, they become blind both to the wonders of God and to the darkness of sin.[422]

The Distortions of a "Lion Savior"

The futility of pagan myth to accurately convey Bible truth, and the facility with which such myth conveys *un*truth, should be obvious to those who understand how completely incompatible these two are. Presenting *truth* all dressed up in myth, steeped in pagan lore, is at best confusing and self-defeating. Yet the movie's promoters have effectively duped churches and other organizations into accepting another of Hollywood's money-making gimmicks.

One report indicates that elementary school children and teenagers in Bible study groups booked whole theaters to see the first Narnia movie.[423]

The advertising experts have effectively done their job and the Christian community has again fallen prey to the Hollywood movie moguls. Should

---

421   Romans 1:22–23.

422   Berit Kjos, part 2, p. 4.

423   Jim Meyers, "Disney's 'Narnia': Christ Need Not Apply"

we feel good about the fact that the headlines reveal that Bible study groups are booking theaters anxiously awaiting the next Hollywood blockbuster?

The Lion movie has several distortions and departures from biblical truth. For example, *The Lion, the Witch and the Wardrobe* distorts biblical teaching about Adam and Eve by inferring that Adam had a wife prior to Eve. Speaking of the "White Witch," Mr. Beaver says that

> ... she's no daughter of Eve. She comes of **your father Adam's ... first wife,** her they call Lilith. And she was one of the Jinn. That's what she comes from on one side. And **on the other side she comes from the giants.** No, no, there isn't a drop of real human blood in the Witch.[424]

This movie subtly contradicts the story of creation by inferring that Adam and Eve were not the first man and woman created. Does this matter to the general public? Some will claim that it is all just make-believe, so what's the big deal? Well, if it is just all make-believe, then don't advertise it as a Christian allegory which implies a connection with reality and a conveyance of truth.

As sad as it is to see a Hollywood blockbuster blatantly contradicting basic biblical truths while being touted as a Christian film, its treatment of the Lord Jesus Christ is of greatest concern. Christ did not use magic to save man from his sin.

The movie and book describes Aslan's magic (remember, Aslan represents Christ) as more powerful than the magic of the witch—a magic that brings him back to life and destroys the witch's power.

Magical powers are increasingly coveted by more people every year as information on how to dabble in magic is more readily accessible through the Internet and the public school systems. In fact, public schools have become a breeding ground for witchcraft by increasingly exposing students to various aspects of witchcraft. Should Christians really be contributing to this rising interest and lust for magical powers by endorsing an allegedly Christian movie that has magic as its primary focus?

---

424   *The Lion,* p. 81.

We know there are those who will argue that we are making a mountain out of a molehill. But consider the words of a careful researcher who presents a critical vantage point.

> Many of the characters in this set of books are **gods and demons** from **pagan mythology!** Aslan is the god-like lion who very obviously depicts Christ in the stories; and yet in heathen mythology **this lion represents the sun!** In *The Lion, the Witch and the Wardrobe* Aslan is said to be "coming and going"; to have "golden" eyes, face and fur; to have "warm breath"; to scatter golden beams of light; to be big and bright; etc. And according to the *Dictionary of Mythology, Folklore and Symbols,* by Gertrude Jobes, the sun is seen as a *lion, golden* in colour; with its breath symbolizing the sun's rays; etc. In addition, the ancient sun-worshippers believed that the sun died as it reached its southernmost point, bringing winter. It was "reborn," or resurrected, when it returned northward, bringing spring. In the *Narnia* series, when Aslan returned to Narnia, it became *spring*; and after dying at night, he was resurrected in the early morning![425]

We know that many of our readers are not steeped in witchcraft; however, some of the readers of Narnia are. Suppose as a result of this that that person comes to believe that there is no difference between Christianity and witchcraft. If he or she gets influenced by the witchcraft and eventually rejects Christianity, will this person's blood be on your hands for failing to warn him or her? The apostle Paul said that the only way to be pure from the blood of all men was to declare all the counsel of God. "Wherefore I take you to record this day, that **I am pure from the blood of all men.** For I have not shunned to declare unto you **all the counsel of God.**"[426]

Should the "champions of the faith" shy away from being critical of Lewis because he was so widely popular? Some of his supporters may believe that

425 Peter T. Chattaway, "Comment: The Paganism of *Narnia*." www.canadianchristianity.com/cgi-bin/na.cgi?nationalupdates/051124narnia

426 Acts 20:26–27.

we are reading into Lewis' writings what is not there and that the associations we find are purely coincidental and unintended. Well, we do *not* believe that they are purely coincidental or unintended in most cases.

C. S. Lewis reveled in mythology and understood the mythological terminology, clearly recognizable to those steeped in paganism. Christians who wish to believe that Lewis used allegorical terms and figures to represent the truth of the gospel must understand that occultists make the same claim and find Lewis sympathetic to their point of view. Regretfully, the symbolism of Lewis more closely resembles occultic figures than Christian ones.

But for argument's sake let's assume that this allegory represents Christianity. That would make Aslan the incarnate Christ and the White Witch would be Satan. Here are five obvious allegorical similarities to prove our premise:

- ✦ The arrival of Aslan signals the arrival of Christmas. Christmas is celebrated by many as Jesus' birthday, i.e., His arrival in the world.
- ✦ Aslan frees all of Narnia from the wicked ways of the evil witch who represents Satan.
- ✦ The breaking of the stone table upon the death of Aslan could be likened to the veil in the temple being torn in two when Christ died.
- ✦ Aslan dies for a sinner, taking away his sins through the shedding of his own blood much like Christ paid for the sins of all mankind.
- ✦ Aslan is resurrected and recreates a new world.

These parallels to the biblical account do exist. They are real and evident; yet that does not give the overall story or theme of the books or movies a positive evangelical representation of the gospel.

Along with these very real compatibility issues there are several allegorical distortions evident in the books and movies that further confuse youthful as well as adult readers and viewers.

Love and Adored vs. Despised and Rejected

Aslan is a powerful lion, adored by all of his subjects and filled with all temporal power. A true Christian allegory would necessitate Aslan being an animal that was despised and rejected, not one that is the noble and mighty king of the beasts, with all worldly power and prowess.

This is an important matter because failure to be biblically accurate here not only perverts prophecy, but it also distorts historical reality. Unlike Aslan, Christ was despised, rejected, and certainly *not* revered for His physical strength or prowess. **"He is despised and rejected of men**; a man of sorrows, and acquainted with grief: and we hid as it were our faces from him; **he was despised, and we esteemed him not."**[427]

It is obvious from Scripture that Christ was far from being adored and admired. Contrary to the alluring and angelic paintings of "Jesus," one of the central points of the gospel is that people would not find a magnetic beauty that would make Him desirous. The desire for Him or rejection of Him would be based on who He was. "For he shall grow up before him as a tender plant, and as a root out of a dry ground: **he hath no form nor comeliness;** and when we shall see him, **there is no beauty that we should desire him."**[428]

God intended the gospel to draw men to Himself—not to His perceived beauty while clothing Himself in human form. Jesus Christ was God manifest in the flesh, but His humble birth was to be representative of a life of humility, and a death in shame. His earthly presence did not reveal that He was truly King of Kings and Lord of Lords, otherwise it would have appealed to man in a fleshly way. Though this is a serious distortion from the movie, there are others too.

Fulfillment of Prophecy

Christ did not die in our place in order to appease Satan. He died in our place to satisfy the righteous demands of His own holy and righteous law.

---

427   Isaiah 53:3.

428   Isaiah 53:2.

We don't have a sentimental pardon; we have an honorable pardon by Christ Himself on our behalf.

> Whom God hath set forth to be a propitiation through faith in his blood, to declare his righteousness for the remission of sins that are past, through the forbearance of God; **To declare, I say, at this time his righteousness: that he might be just, and the justifier of him which believeth in Jesus.**[429]

In the movie scene prior to Aslan's sacrifice for the young boy, the White Witch claims his soul by saying, "Because he has sinned, he is mine." Aslan replies on Edmond's behalf, "But I can give myself in his place." The witch agrees to this and kills Aslan in Edmond's place. Aslan is then resurrected from the dead.

Because of the faint and often ambiguous similarities to Christ's substitutionary sacrifice, many people claim that Aslan accurately depicts the Lord's payment on the cross of Calvary. A more in depth analysis completely dispels this erroneous conclusion. The Lord did *not* sacrifice His life for us after negotiating with Satan concerning His payment for sin. Christ's sacrifice was a fulfillment of prophecy promised before the world began, for Scripture states: "In hope of eternal life, which God, that cannot lie, **promised before the world began.**"[430]

Christ Laid Down His Life

The Lord Jesus Christ's sacrifice for sin was not only prophesied and foretold before the world began, but Satan was the instrument used by God, and not the other way around. Unlike the workings of Aslan and the White Witch, the Bible says no one took Christ's life from Him. He laid it down and He had the power to take it again.

> Therefore doth my Father love me, because **I lay down my life,** that I might take it again. **No man taketh it from me, but I lay it down of myself.** I

---

429   Romans 3:25–26.

430   Titus 1:2.

have power to lay it down, and I have power to take it again. This commandment have I received of my Father.[431]

And **Jesus** cried with a loud voice, and **gave up the ghost.**[432]

Thinketh thou that I cannot now pray to my Father, and **he shall presently give me more than twelve legions of angels?**[433]

The fact that Christ could have chosen not to go to the cross for us is powerfully portrayed in the song written in tribute to Jesus' statement in the Garden as the soldiers come to take Him away. The song entitled, "Ten Thousand Angels"[434] says "He could have called ten thousand angels." The second stanza reads:

He could have called ten thousand angels
To destroy the world and set him free.
He could have called ten thousand angels,
But He died alone, for you and me.

The White Witch may have taken Aslan's life when she stabbed him with the dagger, but it should be obvious that no mere creature had the power to take the life of the Son of God. Christ gave His life for us. Aslan died to satisfy the "Deep Power" and the White Witch rather than shedding his blood to satisfy the righteous demands of God's law. One must not underestimate this crucial distinction because Satan has only the power relegated to him by Almighty God.

Unlike Aslan when stabbed on the stone altar, Jesus could have come off the cross at any time He chose to do so. The power of life and death was

431 John 10:17–18.

432 Mark 15:37.

433 Matthew 26:53.

434 "Ten Thousand Angels"—words and music by Ray Overholt.

never in the hands of those who put Him on the cross. However, the power of life and death was in the hands of the witch, who immediately took Aslan's life from him when she plunged the knife into him. This crucial distortion of truth is indicative of changing the truth of God into a lie. [435]

The Distortion of Child Empowerment

Dr. Ted Baehr, founder and publisher of MOVIEGUIDE* gives the following synopsis. Note the shift in focus from the Christological figure (Aslan) to humanity providing its own redemption.

> A prophecy says that **four sons and daughters of Adam and Eve** will come to Narnia and **help Aslan . . . free Narnia from the White Witch.** To thwart the prophecy, the White Witch has told everyone that, if they see a son or daughter of Adam and Eve, they should kidnap and bring them to her. . . .
>
> . . . The resurrection romp with Aslan, Lucy and Susan has also been eliminated, and the movie focuses more **on the children being the solution to the evil** in Narnia when, in fact, the victory is Aslan's. . . . [The children] are heirs to the victory that **Aslan wins on the stone table,** and Jesus Christ won on the cross. . . .
>
> In fact, the movie is a very clear Christological allusion, or imagining, of the story of Jesus Christ. The minor changes do not take away from the meaning in the book. . . .
>
> Andrew Adamson . . . understands the element of sacrifice and redemption, but his concern was for the **empowering of the children** . . . his love for the original source ultimately keeps the movie on target. [436]

This story, according to almost everyone except the author of the book and the movie's director and producer, is supposed to represent an allegorical

435   See Romans 1:25.

436   "Absolutely Thrilling! Disney's Chronicles of Narnia."
      www.assistnews.net/Stories/s0511091.htm

account of Christ's sacrifice. How can so many people unintentionally depict the greatest spiritual truths known to man? It cannot be done! Since many people believe that the movie and books are accurate biblical allegories, the changes to the biblical account take away from the most important book—the Bible.

Narnia's prophecy does not coincide with the Old Testament prophetic utterances of a Saviour. In stark contrast to the biblical prophesies, the movie's prophecy promises that *four humans* will come and save the land. What a sham to call this deceptive story a picture of truth and even a remote allegory of Christ's redemption of mankind! Rather than exclusively exalting the Christ figure, it exalts man and his nonexistent redemptive qualities. Error prevails when truth and error are mixed. Contrast the movie director's rather candid comments to NewsMax.com to his interview meant for a Christian audience above. ". . . The film's director, Andrew Adamson, also has **pooh-poohed the idea that the allegory reveals Christ's resurrection,** saying that concept is a common theme."[437]

The film's director admits that he did not intend for the movie to convey Christ's resurrection. He simply stated that the sacrifice of oneself is a common theme amongst many religions.

Should parents allow the images from this movie to cleave to their children's mind when the pagan settings are so intentional? Who decides what message the film really conveys? Can the movie portray Christ's resurrection contrary to the intentions of everyone involved with the movie? In order to ward off any suggestion that Adamson's comments were merely a slip of the tongue, here are his thoughts from another interview.

"When director Andrew Adamson was asked recently how he dealt with **the books' religious content** in making *The Chroniocles of Narnia: The Lion, the Witch and the Wardrobe,* he chuckled and said: **"I ignored it."**[438]

437   Meyers, Jim, "Disney's 'Narnia': Christ Need Not Apply."
      www.newsmax.com/archives/articles/2005/12/8/204407.shtml

438   Simon Houpt, "God's Blockbuster"
      www.theglobeandmail.com/servlet/ArticleNews/TPStory/LAC/20051203/WALDEN03/
      TPEntertainment/Film

In addition to the outright denial by the film's director of any Christological tone in the movie, we see that children become their own redeemers in the movie, as mentioned earlier. This deceptive tool used by Satan confuses and confounds the world. The Bible tells children the real way to please the Lord on this earth. "Children, obey your parents in all things: for this is well pleasing unto the Lord."[439]

Submission is the key to happiness (and long life). According to the Bible, the children's welfare revolves around their personal relationship with their parents. Contrary to the prevalent social welfare mentality, it is certainly not their self-coronation on the throne of their own hearts. Yes, we are a world gone crazy with *personal rights.*

For instance, pro-abortionists coined the phrase "a woman's right to choose" to imply the right of a woman to terminate the life of her pre-born child. This madness extends to children, too.

Parental responsibility should preempt this so-called child empowerment. This philosophy has been taken to alarming extremes. For instance, the same child needing a signed parental permission slip to go on a school field trip has the "right" to thwart her parents' wishes and have a life-changing medical procedure to abort a baby. This is simply inconceivable.

Shamefully, the courts and our legislative bodies are no better than Hollywood as they squander the opportunities to positively reinforce basic family cohesion and authority. Yet, these basic biblical principals are the very things that made this country strong for so many years. The Word of God promises long life to children who live obediently under their parent's authority. "Children, obey your parents in the Lord: for this is right. Honour thy father and mother; (which is the first commandment with promise;) **That it may be well with thee, and thou mayest live long on the earth.**"[440]

The promise of a long life as a result of obedience to one's parents makes even more sense today with the ever increasing teen suicide rates. However, the chaotic state of our public school system reflects the disintegration of

---

439 Colossians 3:20.

440 Ephesians 6:1–3.

parental respect and authority. Some good old-fashioned discipline in lieu of child empowerment would work wonders on our crumbling society. Should we trust Hollywood or the tried and true biblical principles that have sustained so many families for so long?

The Distortion of a Powerless Christ Figure

According to C. S. Lewis, he never intended for his fantasies to represent any greater Christian spiritual truth. He was simply fascinated by mythology and fantasy. Yet, most people seem to want to apply deeper spiritual truths from this movie as though some greater spiritual truths were to be purposefully conveyed by the author. With this in mind, we must realize that no truly reverential movie that includes a character mimicking the Lord Jesus Christ would ever tone down His omnipotent nature and authority.

Some movie reviewers familiar with the books were disappointed because the movie producers increased the power of the witch while diminishing Aslan's power and authority. Should this surprise us? Jeffrey Overstreet in *Christianity Today* rightfully complains about this very thing.

> While other characters' roles have been expanded, the lion's appearances are painfully brief. He doesn't have the time onscreen to earn our affection and awe the way we might have hoped. And scene by scene, the writers consistently **skirt the issue of Aslan's authority**, eliminating most references to his history, power, and influence. **Aslan's father, the Emperor-beyond-the-sea, is never mentioned.** Instead, the lion waxes philosophical like Obi-Wan Kenobi, mentioning the Deep Magic that "governs" his "destiny." Huh?
>
> Just as **Aslan's majesty has been diminished, the strength of the witch has been upgraded.** She bears little resemblance to the sorceress who made Mr. Beaver declare, "If she can stand on her two feet and look [Aslan] in the face it'll be the most she can do and more than I expect." In the novel, Jadis went into terrified hysterics at the mere mention of Aslan's name—here she barely flinches. When they face off, she's fearless. Did Adamson make the White Witch a more threatening villain to increase

suspense? That's a practical idea. But Lewis would have objected. This Aslan is essentially muzzled and bound long before the Stone Table scene.[441]

Here are four clear examples where *The Lion, the Witch and the Wardrobe* movie and book erodes Aslan's authority and thereby communicates a dethroned Christ figure:

+ The responsibility for redemption is placed on human children and not upon Aslan. Father Christmas declares, "Aslan is on the move." As a result of the children showing up, he says that "the witch's magic is weakening."
+ It is the children's arrival in Narnia that prompted Aslan into action as reflected in Mr. Beaver's statement. He says that Aslan's arrival in Narnia is one of several things that have happened "because of you," i.e., because of the children's presence in Narnia.
+ The children are told, "The hope brought by Your Majesties is starting to weaken the witch's power."
+ The book makes a distinction between the power of Aslan and that of his father. Aslan's power is referred to as "Deep Magic" and his father's is referred to as "Emperor's Magic." Aslan seemed to figure out the "Deeper Magic" in a way that the witch did not, rather than being equal with his father. In reality, Jesus Christ did not simply outmaneuver Satan during the temptation—He is Almighty God manifest in the flesh.

Reviews of *The Lion* movie are correct when they liken the death and resurrection scenes, power to heal, *et. al,* as being depicted in many other popular movies without any hint that they are "Christian allegory." This would include *E.T.: The Extraterrestrial, Star Wars,* and *The Matrix.* Simply because a movie depicts a struggle between good and evil does not make

---

441   Review by Jeffrey Overstreet, "The Chronicles of Narnia: The Lion, The Witch and the Wardrobe," *Christianity Today* (12/08/05).
www.christianitytoday.com/movies/reviews/lionwitchwardrobe.html

the movie "Christian." Mark Johnson, the **producer** of the Lewis movie, likens the sacrifice in his movie with the same type of sacrifice in *Star Wars* and *The Matrix*. His questioner states, "Unmistakably C. S. was a Christian allegorist." To which, Johnson replies:

> Although he claims that *The Chronicles of Narnia* are not Christian allegories. We know he was a Christian and a Christian writer, so it's not as though it doesn't have sort of his beliefs and traits, whatever.... There are Christians and non-Christian (readers). And if you say, **"Well, there's a character who sacrifices his life and then is reborn," you can find that character in *Star Wars* and *Matrix* or whatever else,** so we did not set out to be true to anything other than the novel.[442]

The producer's words here are revealing. The fact that he finds parallels in *The Lion* movie to the sacrifice and rebirth sequences in *Star Wars* and *The Matrix* shows that *The Lion* movie intentionally conveys no more Christian truth than a host of other popular movies. In fact, it is actually harmful because of these sacrilegious associations. Another author's comments further prove this point.

> ... Many fans of the Narnia books who've put up with or ignored the novels' Christian subtext (or overtones, depending on how you look at it) may be fearful that "Narnia," which has been heavily marketed by Christian groups, is really a religious movie in disguise. **But I am not sure the Jesus imagery in "Narnia" is any more overt than what you get in "E.T." (he does, after all, have the power to heal and to rise from the dead).** ... This is a movie that achieves a level of craziness that feels more operatic than it does outright Christian.[443]

---

442 "Is the Film 'The Lion, the Witch and the Wardrobe' Faithful to C. S. Lewis' Book?" http://preview.gospelcom.net/interviews/narnia.html

443 Stephanie Zacharek, "The Chronicles of Narnia: The Lion, the Witch, and the Wardrobe" http://dir.salon.com/story/ent/movies/review/2005/12/09/narnia/index_np.html

All of these reviewers and commentators are correct. Just because the movie has a "die-for-others" plot interwoven into the production does not make it a Christian allegory.

Only God can deliver us from the erroneous notion that any self-sacrificing individual is a Christ figure if enough basic similarities exist. Historically there have been many cults and even Hitlerian regimes with crackpots who gave their all for "the Cause." Their self-sacrifice does not make them Christian.

Disney Sanitized

According to a recent report in *World* magazine,

> The marketing of this film will be the most comprehensive program for faith and family groups that Disney has ever undertaken.... As with *The Passion,* that will entail meetings with church and education leaders, public events at churches and schools, advance screenings, corollary educational materials, outreach to youth groups and colleges, and a strong emphasis on internet resources.[444]

Andrew Greeley of the *Chicago Sun-Times* reports:

> According to an unnamed Disney executive in a recent issue of the *New York Times,* Narnia will provide the company with a "Christian niche," among the lucrative fantasy "franchises" such as "Harry Potter and "The Lord of the Rings."[445]

Pastor Rick Olsen of Costa Mesa, California, looks at the movie production from another angle. His views and actions represent the typical Narnia/Hollywood movie sermonette preacher of the twenty-first century. Elaine Dutka,

---

444   Andrew Coffin, "Winter Wardrobe," *World Magazine.*
       www.worldmag.com/displayarticle.cfm?id=10307

445   Andrew Greeley, "Relax, It's Only a Fairy Tale," *Chicago Sun-Times* (12/9/05).
       www.suntimes.com/output/greeley/cst-edt-greel09.html

writing for the *Los Angeles Times,* articulates her perspective.

> When it comes to connecting with young people, some clergy believe,
> storytelling is far more effective than an academic approach. While "The
> Passion" was "powerful and specific," "Narnia" provides some "very real
> answers to problems in the universe," said Rick Olsen, senior associate
> pastor at Harbor Trinity Church in Costa Mesa.
>
> Olsen was contacted by Outreach to record a segment for Disney's
> promotional DVD on "Narnia," one of his favorite pieces of literature.
> He's also conducting a series of pre-sermon talks about the movie and
> trying to rent the Irvine Spectrum for a night, just as he did with "The
> Passion." . . .[446]

Elaine Dutka also wrote that Outreach, Inc., one of Motive's partners and
a *Passion* veteran, is producing resource materials such as a DVD aimed at
ministers. Disney is reaching out to 40,000 youth ministers across America
and has marshaled the support of leading clergymen such as Robert Schul-
ler of Crystal Cathedral in Garden Grove, California, and Rick Warren of
Saddleback Church in Lake Forest. The movie's producers hope that Christians will "buy into" the movie and support it, yet they want to downplay
any type of perceived Christian connection.

Evidently, many Christians are in the dark about the animosity between
Disney and Christian groups like the Southern Baptist Convention. The
1997 Southern Baptist Convention resolution identifying Disney as the
target of an economic boycott has been lifted as a result of Disney's removal
of Michael Eisner as the chairman, and Disney's partnering with Walden
Media in financing *The Lion* movie. According to Richard Land, president
of the SBC's Ethics and Religious Liberty Commission:

> Hollywood is slowly discovering that America is a very religious country.

---

446 Elaine Dutka, "'The Lion, the Witch,' the Faithful," *Los Angeles Times* (10/5/05).
     www.calendarlive.com/printedition/calendar/cl-et-lion5oct05,0,4692411.story?coll=cl-cal-
     endar

> Many in Tinsel Town were shocked at the box office success of Mel Gibson's movie *The Passion of the Christ*. Southern Baptists and others of faith saw Disney's decision to partner with Walden Media in financing and distributing *The Lion, the Witch and the Wardrobe*, part of C. S. Lewis' Chronicles of Narnia series, as a gesture for reconciliation. [447]

Americans are not the only ones being drawn in by this Hollywood type hypocrisy. It seems that the theater-style seating in the movie house has replaced sermons heard from the church pulpit in Europe, too. Twenty years ago, ministers preached against going to the movies; now it seems they are going to the movies for their preaching material. Here is the scoop from the European version of *Christianity Today*, entitled *Christianity Magazine*:

> A new film adaptation of C. S. Lewis' classic children's story, "The Lion, The Witch and the Wardrobe" (LWW), will be screened in your local cinema from early December—**providing local churches with a fantastic evangelistic opportunity.** In the wake of various initiatives to use "The Passion of the Christ"—Mel Gibson's gory re-telling of the death of Christ last year, churches in the US and the UK **are exploring creative ways to link into what is widely predicted to be the must-see blockbuster movie this Christmas.** [448]

Instead of distributing Bibles, tracts, or other sound evangelistic literature, British churches are now supporting Hollywood and giving out free tickets to the movie. St. Luke's Anglican Church gained much media coverage when it distributed free tickets to *The Passion of the Christ* and it is doing the same thing for the Narnia extravaganza.

The Methodist organization, Methodist Children, put together a special Narnia service. Manchester Cathedral staged a Narnia day. St. Luke's An-

---

447   Richard Land, "Looking Back on the Disney Boycott," *Faith & Family Values* (July-August 2005), p. 5.

448   John Buckeridge, "The Narnia Opportunity," November 5 issue, *Christianity Magazine* www.christianitymagazine.co.uk/engine.cfm?I=92&id=421&arch=1

glican Church in Maidstone gave out free tickets to single parents, as it had done with *The Passion* movie. According to a spokesman for the church: "We are giving away £10 000 pounds worth of tickets to single-parent families in and around the area."[449] At the current exchange rate of 1.7:1 that equals $17,188 US dollars.

Movie ticket distribution is just another one of the many new trends helping these churches make themselves appear "relevant" and "progressive." Their interpretation of visiting the fatherless and widows seems to be to provide free movie tickets. The Bible, however, defines pure religion in another way: "Pure religion and undefiled before God and the Father is this, **To visit the fatherless and widows in their affliction**, and to keep himself unspotted from the world."[450]

Separated Christians or Gullible Christians?

Hollywood's constant abuse of Christian beliefs and standards has worn down and worn out Christians. They hungrily wait for entertainment that would positively reflect Christian beliefs. When the product comes along deceptively-packaged by professionals adept in the art of manipulation, almost anything remotely similar to the truth becomes acceptable. That is why the Narnia advertising campaign is being orchestrated by the same group that implemented the very successful *Passion* advertising extravaganza.

> "Many people put churchgoers and Hollywood on the opposite sides of the equation," said Paul Lauer, whose Motive Entertainment orchestrated the "Passion" campaign and has been working on doing the same for "Narnia" since early this year. **"But churchgoers are hungry for movies reflecting strong values** —like 'Narnia.' . . ."
>
> . . . Outreach, Inc., one of Motive's partners and a "Passion" veteran, is producing resource materials such as a DVD aimed at ministers. . . .

---

449   Shaun Willcock, "The Chronicles of Narnia": Occult Fantasy of a Closet Roman Catholic." www.biblebasedministries.co.uk/indexRomeUpdate.htm

450   James 1:27.

> Disney is also reaching out to **40,000 youth ministers** nationwide and has marshaled the support of leading clergymen such as **Robert Schuller of Crystal Cathedral** in Garden Grove and **Rick Warren** of Saddleback Church in Lake Forest. Group sales—many organized by churches—are in the works. . . .[451]

Many people have come to believe that if a nationally-recognized popular personality supports a movie production, it must be acceptable. Nothing can be further from the truth. Historically, the higher up one sits in the world's estimation, the more susceptible he or she becomes to the pressure of political correctness. The Billy Graham ministry is another of the nationally-recognized groups supporting the film.

Lon Allison, director of Illinois' Billy Graham Center said: **"We believe that God will speak the gospel of Jesus Christ through this film."** [452]

The Narnia movie has no more chance of speaking the gospel to viewers than *The Matrix* movie. This fraudulent and dishonest advertising has carried over into other movies that have no distinctive "Christian" element to them. Elaine Dutka comments:

> . . . A movie doesn't have to be overtly religious, though, to connect with the church-based audience. The promotional campaigns for New Line's "Secondhand Lions," Universal's "Cinderella Man" and Screen Gems' "The Exorcism of Emily Rose"—just for starters—**were directed at a grass-roots evangelical component."**[453]

"It's All About Money, Stupid!"

If Hollywood continues to produce and market so-called Christian themed movies or simply movies with good moral messages, we may need to create

---

451 Elaine Dutka.

452 Jim Meyers, "Disney's 'Narnia': Christ Need Not Apply." www.newsmax.com/archives/articles/2005/12/8/204407.shtml

453 Elaine Dutka.

a **Gullibility Index Meter (GIM).** This GIM would track and record how deceptively effective each subsequent film dupes the church-going public. Elaine Dutka points out that Walt Disney Studios, while denying any Christian connections, used the same kind of church-based campaign as the *Passion* promoters.

> Walt Disney Studios is hoping that the same kind of church-based campaign that helped turn "The Passion of the Christ" into a blockbuster will convert C. S. Lewis' children's classic "The Chronicles of Narnia: The Lion, The Witch and the Wardrobe" into a **big-screen franchise....**[454]

Jim Meyers of NewsMax.com wrote an excellent article entitled "Disney's Narnia: Christ Need Not Apply." He wrote that Disney hoped to tap the same audience that Mel Gibson drew to the theaters while at the same time downplaying its "supposed links to Christianity."

> While Disney clearly hopes to **tap** into the same audience that made Mel Gibson's "The Passion of the Christ" a huge box office hit, **the same people behind the film version of "Narnia" are vocal in downplaying its supposed links to Christianity....** A Hollywood insider who has dealt with Disney's marketing executives told NewsMax that the media giant has had great apprehension promoting the film to Christian groups and has done so only in a low-key manner. "Disney is loathing the idea that the likes of Rush Limbaugh, Sean Hannity or a preacher like Jerry Falwell will actively promote the film. **They want the Christian community's money, but not their viewpoint,"** the source said. [455]

What is the underlying motive for this movie and the others that will inevitably follow? Obviously, it does not seem to be a desire for Christian conversions, nor a sincere love for the truth. If people are converted through

---

454   Ibid.

455   Jim Meyers, "Disney's 'Narnia': Christ Need Not Apply"

it Disney will regard that as "collateral damage." As has been shown, the comments by the movie's *director* reveal that he did not direct the movie to reflect Christian truth. The movie's *producer* voices the same sentiments. Mark Johnson said that he never thought of the lion as a Christ-figure when he read the book.

> "Narnia's" producer, Mark Johnson said: "When I read the book as a child, I accepted it as a pure adventure story. It never occurred to me Aslan was anything more than a great lion rather than a Christ figure." Said producer Johnson: "We're not selling the movie to any particular group. With a movie this size, we're trying to sell it to everybody." Put another way, **Disney would like to sell "Narnia" minus Christ—but still have Christians pay the bill."** [456]

The motive, according to those in the know, is "profit margin." The Walt Disney Company hopes that the Narnia movie will help recoup some of its recent losses. Corporations generally exist to bolster the bottom line. A fat bottom line avoids a disappointing showing in the stock exchanges and keeps shareholders happy. Walt Disney Co. is no different from any other corporation out to make a buck.

> For Walt Disney Co. the film based on **the C. S. Lewis classic offers a chance to recover at the box office after its latest quarterly losses.** . . . Christians are now recognized by Hollywood as a valuable niche market after Mel Gibson's "The Passion of the Christ" was a surprise $600 million worldwide hit. . . .[457]

Disney worships mammon—the god of money. Take note of the love-hate antithesis in Matthew, where Jesus says: "No man can serve two masters: for either he will hate the one, and love the other. **Ye cannot serve God and**

---

456   Ibid.

457   Phoebe Kate Foster, "When We're Old Enough To Read Fairy Tales Again," Part 3 of 3
      http://popmatters.com/books/features/051209-narnia-3.shtml

mammon."[458]

Since Disney is serving mammon, the Bible says it is impossible for that organization to be serving God. Should Christians be supporting such an organization, and bringing its product into their churches, hearts, and minds? Or should Christians just close their eyes to the sheer hypocrisy of the whole matter and appreciate the mere morsel of red pottage from the movie makers? [459]

---

458 Matthew 6:24.

459 See the story of Esau selling his birthright to Jacob for a bowl of red pottage because he was faint (Genesis 25:29–34).

Chapter 8

C. S. Lewis and "Esoteric Christianity"

In the Garden of Eden, Satan promised Eve that if she ate of the forbidden fruit she would receive a marvelous impartation of knowledge. "And the serpent said unto the woman, Ye shall not surely die: For God doth know that in the day ye eat thereof, then your eyes shall be opened, and **ye shall be as gods, knowing good and evil.**"[460]

The philosophy of esotericism has been making the same satanic appeal since being influenced in the Garden. According to Lutzer and DeVries:

> This philosophy, known as esotericism, lies at the heart of the New Age Movement. We are told that there is a "transformation of consciousness" that initiates us into true spirituality. Historically, the esoterics believed they were privy to special knowledge that was hidden from the masses. We must leave religion behind and venture into a new dimension of knowledge and enlightenment. The eventual goal is spiritual conversion.[461]

Sadly, this same philosophy has made its way into evangelical churches. "Esoteric Christianity" is a term applied to this New Age/Gnostic "Christianity" which the apostolic church rejected. The churches today need to be equally skeptical of such a teaching and philosophy. However, it has been gaining popularity in modern times through the efforts of influential evangelical leaders who are appealing to the mass of malcontents.

---

460   Genesis 3:4–5.

461   Erwin W. Lutzer and John F. DeVries, *Satan's Evangelistic Strategy for the New Age* (Wheaton, IL: SP Publications, 1989), p. 20.

Many people, unhappy with what they consider a dogmatic Christianity promoting an angry deity, are diluting the message of the Bible with a mystical, contemplative Christianity that is less offensive to stargazers, chanters and cultic vegetarians. In a chapter entitled "The Yoga of the West" author Ray Yungen explains the subtle advance of this phenomenon.

> One day, I wandered into a secular bookstore to investigate their religion section. The section was divided into two equal parts. The one on the left had the heading *Spirituality: The New Age*. It accordingly contained titles reflecting that viewpoint. On the right was *Spirituality: Judeo-Christian*. In this section, one would expect to find titles in line with traditional concepts of Judeo-Christian orthodoxy. Not so! The basic principles of the New Age movement were represented, with only a few exceptions, in both parts. How is this possible?[462]

Although repeatedly warned not to intermingle or be overly influenced by the world,[463] the church is becoming increasingly like the world. Roman Catholic writer William Johnston answered how this is possible when he penned the following observation:

> Something very powerful is emerging. . . . We are witnessing a spiritual revolution of great magnitude in the whole world. . . . The rise of a new school of mysticism within Christianity. . . . It is growing year by year.
>
> For the most part, the evangelical church has very little awareness of this rapidly growing spiritual revolution. Most evangelicals seem unaware there has even been a paradigm shift in spirituality. . . .[464]

---

462 Ray Yungen, *A Time of Departing: How A Universal Spirituality Changing the Face of Christianity* (Silverton, OR: Lighthouse Trails Publishing, 2002), p. 33.

463 For example: 1 John 2:15–16, "Love not the world, neither the things that are in the world. If any man love the world, the love of the Father is not in him. For all that is in the world, the lust of the flesh, and the lust of the eyes, and the pride of life, is not of the Father, but is of the world."

464 Ibid.

We believe that this "paradigm shift in spirituality" explains the widespread, careless acceptance of J.R.R. Tolkien and C. S. Lewis by large numbers of evangelicals. In addition to the acceptance of Tolkien and Lewis, *Harry Potter* has its advocates within the evangelical churches too. The dangers of *Harry Potter* have been clearly delineated in various works, including *Harry Potter: Innocent Entertainment? or Darkness Disguised?*[465]

When trying to discuss Lewis' deficiencies with his supporters, the effect of this spiritual paradigm shift rears its ugly head most vehemently. The reason for this is quite simple. Millions of professing Christians have been programmed to automatically reject anything that doesn't fit into this new way of thinking. Much like virus scan software, the paradigm shift has produced a "spirituality" that weeds *out* truth—indeed, a powerful reminder of the gravity of the scriptural exhortation to "gird up the loins of your minds."[466]

Fantasy and the "New" Spirituality

In order to understand the fantasy movies of J.R.R. Tolkien and C. S. Lewis, it is necessary that we delve into any possible connections with hermetic thought, often referred to as hermeticism.

Hermeticism comes from the name Hermes, the Greek-Egyptian god who is considered to be the founder of the occultic arts—astrology, alchemy (magic), and the revealer of occult messages from spirit entities. Hermeticism has a long and varied history in Satan's attempts to change, modify, and alter the word of God. B. F. Westcott, associate and co-worker of Fenton John Anthony Hort, notoriously associated with the Westcott-Hort text of most modern translations, was an original member of the Philological Society, later known as "Hermes."[467]

---

465   DVD or VHS available from www.McCowenMills.com, P.O. Box 1611, Millbrook, AL 36054, (866)344-1611 (toll free).

466   1 Peter 1:13.

467   Kerby F. Fannin, *While Men Slept: A Biblical and Historical Account of the New Universal Christianity* (Addison, MI: Life's Resources, Inc., 2002), pp. 162–163.

While we often equate fantasy with harmless, religiously-neutral children's stories, the evidence suggests that there is much more than meets the eye. A. E. Waite, Catholic mystic writer who formed an allegedly Christian-oriented group associated with Golden-Dawn hermeticism in 1903, wrote *The Book of Ceremonial Magic*. This following brief synopsis, although rather esoteric, will help the reader to understand hermetic teaching.

Beyond these fields and this borderland there lies the legendary wonder-world of theurgy, so called, **of Magic and Sorcery,** a world of fascination or terror, as the mind which regards it is tempered, but in any case the antithesis of admitted possibility. There all paradoxes seem to obtain actually, contradictions coexist logically, the effect is greater than the cause and the shadow more than the substance. Therein the visible melts into the unseen, the invisible is manifested openly, motion from place to place is accomplished without traversing the intervening distance, matter passes through matter. There two straight lines may enclose a space; **space has a fourth dimension**, and untrodden fields beyond it; without metaphor and without evasion, the circle is mathematically squared. **There life is prolonged, youth renewed, physical immortality secured.** There earth becomes gold, and gold earth. There words and wises possess creative power, thoughts are things, desire realizes its object. There also, the dead live and the hierarchies of extra-mundane intelligence are within easy communication, and become ministers or tormentors, guides or destroyers of man. There the Law of Continuity is suspended by the interference of **the higher Law of Fantasia.** [468]

Fantasy is far from simply make-believe, but make-believe that presents another world and life view. In the above quotation "the hermetic or magical world view" is presented—a view quite different from the world view found in Scripture and predominant in societies that have been founded on a Judeo-Christian belief system.

---

468   Charles A. Coulombe, "hermetic Imagination: The Effect of the Golden Dawn on Fantasy Literature.
http://www.cheetah.net/~ccoulomb/hermeticimagination.html, pp.1-2.

Charles A. Coulombe claims:

> While the Magical world-view may not be popular among us today, it is an integral part of practically all pre-industrial societies. In Europe, the country folk from time immemorial to this century (and in some out-of-the-way places even yet) saw this everyday life of ours as interpenetrated with beings and actions from other worlds co-existent with this one.[469]

We have, in another section, made note of Lewis' Neoplatonism, and how this was noted in his writings even by Lewis' supporters. This is significant because Lewis' Neoplatonism helps us to understand his use of fantasy. Significantly, there were many in the annals of Christian history who held to Neoplatonism, at least until the Reformation broke its sway—for a time. Coulumbe notes that the educated folk shared the concept of the magical world when hermeticism and Neoplatonism met up with a form of Christianity. Columbe continues:

> In the philosophical world, **the meeting of hermeticism** (the belief that the visible world is an analogy of the invisible, summed up in the phrase "as above, so below") **and Neoplatonism** (with its insistence that the Platonic Archetypes were the realities, of which earthly expressions were mere shadows) **with Christianity produced several waves of educated folk who shared this magical concept of the world.** First came such Neoplatonic Church Fathers as St. Dionysius the Areopagite, St. Clement of Alexandria, Origien, and St. Augustine. Then came the Ultra-Realist scholastics such as John Scotus Eriugena, Pope Sylvester II, Williamn of Auvergne, Roger Bacon... **many of whom looked to Alchemy, Astrology, and the Qabalah as a means of interpreting the revelation implicit in creation**—a revelation supplementary, but inferior to, Holy Writ. Lastly, the Classical Humanists such as Reuchlin, Pico della Mirandola, Cardinal Bessarion and Aeneas Piccolomini, were similarly inclined. The Reformation put an end to such developments....[470]

---

469   Ibid., p. 2.

470   Ibid., p. 4.

As incredible as these associations are with the teachings, some readers might find it incredible that hermeticism is also associated with the modern versions on the market today. The words "as above, so below," which, according to the preceding quote, are a summary of hermeticism, are also found in Eugene Peterson's *The Message: The Bible in Contemporary Message:*

> Our Father in heaven,
> Reveal who you are.
> Set the world right;
> Do what's best—
> **As above, so below.**
> Keep us alive with three square meals.
> Keep us forgiven with you and forgiving others.
> Keep us safe from ourselves and the Devil.
> You're in charge!
> You can do anything you want![471]

The symbolism and meaning of "as above, so below," was well known in times past, and even reflected in the architecture of European cathedrals. Picknett and Prince write that "all the lofty symbolism that can be found in the cathedrals was understood by the initiates at the time to reflect the age-old hermetic adage: *As above, so below.*" They explain that the phrase can be traced to the *Emerald Tablet* of Hermes Trismegistus.

These words mean that everything on earth has a counterpart in Heaven, and vice versa, something that Plato made popular with his notion of the *Ideal.* **They believed that everything that exists was merely a shadow of its ideal.** Pickett and Prince point out that "the magicians—or magi—went further, believing that every thought or act was mirrored on another plane, and that both dimensions somehow effected each other irresistibly. There

---

471   *The Message: The Bible In Contemporary Language* (NavPress: Colorado Springs, 2002), p. 1754.

are resonances of this concept in **the modern scientific idea of parallel universes.**"[472]

It is hard to believe that Peterson was not aware of the meaning, background and significance of the words "as above, so below" in his "paraphrase"—or, more accurately, "his theological rewriting of the Bible." *The Message* has many other New Age-type phrases and references. *The Message*, for example, changes the word "Lord," when used in reference to Jesus Christ, to "Master," a common New Age designation for transcendence. Here are three examples comparing the King James Bible to *The Message*:

◆ **KJV**—Go home to thy friends, and tell them how great things **the Lord** hath done for thee....[473]

◆ *The Message*—Go home to your own people. Tell them your story— what the **Master** did, how he had mercy on you.[474]

◆ **KJV**—The Lord said to my **Lord**, Sit thou on my right hand till I make thine enemies thy footstool. David therefore himself calleth him **Lord**; and whence is he then his son?[475]

◆ *The Message*—God said to My **Master**, "Sit here at my right hand until I put your enemies under your feet..." David here designates the Messiah "**My Master**"—so how can the Messiah also be his son?[476]

◆ **KJV**—... Even so, come, **Lord** Jesus. The grace of our **Lord** Jesus Christ be with you all, Amen.[477]

---

472   Lynn Pickett and Clive Prince, *The Templar Revelation: Secret Guardians of the True Identity of Christ* (New York: Simon & Schuster, 1998), p. 112.

473   Mark 5:19—King James Bible.

474   Mark 5:19—The Message.

475   Mark 12:36–37—King James Bible.

476   Mark 12:36–37—The Message.

477   Revelation 22:20–21—King James Bible.

- *The Message*—. . . Yes! Come, **Master** Jesus! The grace of the **Master** Jesus be with all of you. Oh, yes![478]

Supporters of *The Message,* as well as Church Growth devotees, argue against this by claiming that the King James Bible also uses the word "Master" in reference to Jesus. For example, Richard Abanes, in his *Rick Warren and the Purpose That Drives Him* writes: "But Such scrutiny can also be turned against the classic King James Version of the Bible (KJV), which also translates the Greek word *kurios* (normally rendered *Lord*) as *Master* in reference to Jesus (see Ephesians 6:9 and Colossians 4:1). Is the KJV now New Age?"[479]

This argument, on the surface, may appear to have some merit. However, it is hard to see how the criticism leveled against *The Message,* namely that it communicates New Age teachings, can also be applied to the King James Bible. For one thing, when the King James translators used "Master" in reference to Christ, the word "Master" did not, in the seventeenth century, have the New Age meanings and connotations that it has today.

Moreover, the King James Bible has none of the other New Age phraseologies and implications inherent in *The Message.* It certainly does not use the phrase "as above, so below," nor does it endorse, or even suggest, pantheism, as in Ephesians 4:6 where the newer translations state that God is "**in** everything," as compared to the KJV which states: "One God and Father of us all, who is above all, and through all, and **in you all.**" Christ is in Christians[480] but He does not indwell matter.

Interestingly, even Eugene Peterson has some reservations about his work, *The Message.* In an October 2002 *Christianity Today* interview Eugene Peterson was asked: "Do you think *The Message* will be well suited for reading in worship?" Peterson answered:

When I'm in a congregation where somebody uses it in the Scripture read-

---

478 Revelation 22:20–21—The Message.

479 Richard Abanes, *Rick Warren and the Purpose that Drives Him: An Insider Looks at the Phenomenal Bestseller* (Eugene: Harvest House, 2005), p. 141, note 39.

480 See Colossians 1:27.

ing, it makes me a little uneasy. I would never recommend it to be used as saying, "Hear the Word of God from the Message." But it surprises me how many do. You can't tell people they can't do it. But I guess I'm a traditionalist, and I like to hear these more formal languages in the pulpit. [481]

Magic That Unifies

Recent current events indicate that Europe is coming together and being unified in a way that has never taken place in the past. The description of the European Union's flag calls for a blue background representing the sky over the Western world. Upon this "sky" is a circle of twelve golden stars representing the solidarity and harmony between the peoples of Europe. Moreover, a new "global Mary," not entirely Roman Catholic but somewhat so, is being promoted to strengthen this solidarity and harmony.[482]

In this context, hermeticism, magic, fantasy, and myth take on new significance. The European Union (EU) frequently uses the image of the mythical goddess Europa as their unifying figure. In Greek mythology Zeus took the form of a white bull and met Europa, the daughter of Agenor, at the seashore. Appearing kind, he coaxed Europa to climb onto his back and then swam off with her across the sea to Crete where Europa had three sons by Zeus.[483]

The EU has chosen as its anthem "Ode To Joy," the prelude to Beethoven's Ninth Symphony. Though the EU has kept only the music and not the text, the text clearly speaks of the unifying effect of magic spells.

Joy, Oh! Divine scintillation
Sparkling from Elysium,
With a cheerful animation
Goddess, to thy shrine we come

481 www.christianityhtoday.com/ct/2002/011/33.107.html (1/25/06), p. 3.

482 See a fascinating discussion of this and many other related issues in Robert R. Congdon, "The European Union and the Supra-Religion," a paper delivered at the Fourteenth Annual Pre-Trib Study Group, December 5–7, 2005.

483 "Europa," *Encyclopedia Mythica*. http://www.pantheon.org/articles/e/europa.html

These our nations once divided
Now your magic spells unite
Where your wind does beat around them
Brotherhood and love delight.

With a kiss bestowed on millions
Embraced in fraternity,
Let us build a world of union
And peace for all humanity.[484]

Theosophy . . . and Beyond

In discerning the place of magic, hermeticism and some of the influences on Lewis and company, we must look at theosophy and its developments. Charles Coulombe writes:

> In 1875 Helena Blavatsky founded the Theosophical Society in New York, which soon spread through the English speaking world. Originally, very Western in emphasis, studying such topics as alchemy and the writings of Paraclesus, the Society took on a strongly Oriental tone after Mme. Blavatsky took a voyage to India, and claimed to have made contact with various Tibetan "Ascended Masters." A number of members took issue with this (among whom was **Rudolf Steiner,** who eventually founded his own Anthroposophical Society in Germany).
>
> A further objection to the course of the T.S. [Theosophical Society] was that its membership were encouraged only to study occult doctrine, not to practice it—that is, not to practice Magic. But an organization formed in 1888 soon attracted many Theosophists who wished either a more Western teaching or Magical practice, or both: **The Hermetic Order of the Golden Dawn.** [485]

It was in this same time period that "there came both the literature of the

---

484   See Robert R. Congdon, "The European Union and the Supra-Religion."

485   Cuolombe, "hermetic Imagination," pp. 6–7.

fantastic and the new phenomenon of spiritualism." The French term *occultisme* is thought to have been first used by Eliphas Livi (1810–1875). "Like the fantastic and the quasi religion of spiritualism, nineteenth century occultism showed a marked interest in supernatural phenomena, that is to say, in the diverse modes of passage from one world to another."[486] Some of those originally associated with the Theosophical Society re-worked this occultism into a pseudo-Christian context.

> From the very beginning, its membership [The Golden Dawn] fell roughly into two categories: those who were of a Western Theosophical bent (many of whom, as just noted, had left the T.S. for that particular reason), **and those of a more explicitly Christian orientation.** This uneasy mix would erupt later into open conflict; but at the very beginning both camps were united in declaring that **"to establish closer and more personal relations with the Lord Jesus, the Master of Masters, is and ever must be the ultimate object of all the teachings of our order."** Unexceptional as this goal was, the Order's means of reaching it were quite unusual. The G.D. [Golden Dawn] aspired to be not merely a complete academy of occult knowledge (as indeed the T.S. had claimed to be) **but also a forum for Mystico-Magical practise—which Magic was seen as being like that of Eliphas Levi. In the words of Stephan Hoeller, Magic in this sense is "an umbrella term for the growth or expansion of consciousness by way of symbolic modalities.**[487]

C. S. Lewis came into the sphere of hermetic thought through, among others, William Butler Yeats. Alan Jacobs writes: "Another characteristic figure, one (as we shall see) closer to Lewis, was the poet William Butler Yeats." Jacobs traces hermetic thought and the Hermetic Order of the Golden Dawn:

> As early as 1887, when he was just twenty-two, Yeats was initiated into a society called the hermetic Students—"hermetic" referring to an ancient

---

486   Ibid., p. 5.

487   Ibid., p. 7.

legendary magician, Hermes Trismegistus, and more generally to secret spiritual knowledge. Later he would be admitted into the Order of the Golden Dawn, an organization that also attracted **Aleister Crowley, a black magician and Satanist who liked to refer to himself as "The Beast of the Apocalypse."** Yeats was no Satanist, but the "new religion" he made developed into something that, at precisely the time when Jack [C. S.] Lewis was falling under the sway of Miss Cowie, he was happy to call simply "Magic"—"what I must call the evocation of spirits, though I do not know what they are." [488]

Other individuals can be cited as being in close connection with Lewis and with hermetic beliefs. Charles Williams, one of the other poets and writers influencing Lewis "stands out among the three because of both his overtly theological oeuvre, and because of his close (connection) with C. S. Lewis and J.R.R. Tolkien. He joined the Golden Dawn in 1917. . . . There can be no doubt that Williams' novels owed their themes to areas studied by the Golden Dawn." One of Williams' works "pulsates with the hermetic dictum 'as above, so below.'"[489] Lewis' Catholicism fits in with Williams' sacramental view of reality.

In Williams we see a proposal strikingly like Waite's in "Ceremonial Union," and reminiscent of Yeats' observations regarding "victims." This is deeply esoteric matter here. Yet it is also profoundly Christian, being a restatement of the idea of the "Mystical Body of Christ," exemplified by St. Paul: "We being many are one bread, one body; for we all partake of the one bread" (I Cor., x, 17). **Here we see at once the identification of the Church with her founder, with the Sacraments, particularly the Eucharist, binding all together.** In time, Williams felt the need to give some kind of structure to like-minded friends. He founded in 1939 a

488   Alan Jacobs, *The Narnian: The Life and Imagination of C. S. Lewis* (New York: HarperSanFrancisco, 2005, p. 39.

489   "hermetic Imagination," pp. 20–21.

loosely organized "Order of the Companions of the Co-inherence." To its membership were given seven guidelines. **One of these advocated the study "of the Co-inherence of the Holy and Blessed Trinity, of the Two Natures in the Single Person, of the Mother and Son, of the communicated Eucharist, and of the whole Catholic Church."** . . . Another set down **the Order's four feasts: the Annunciation, Trinity Sunday, the Transfiguration, and All Souls.** All of this is extremely reminiscent of Waite's version of the Golden Dawn. It is interesting to note that the Golden Dawn observed five feasts; these were the four solstices and equinoxes, and their high festival, the feast of Corpus Christi.[490]

The Hermetic Order of the Golden Dawn, and its ancient associations with hermeticism, is also significant because of the developing trend, popularly expressed in Dan Brown's *The Da Vinci Code*,[491] to develop the theme of "sacred sexuality." According to Picknett and Prince, "The power of female sexuality also lies at the heart of movements such as Rosicrucianism, hermeticism and even certain forms of Freemasonry."[492]

Many modern women have been caught up in the goddess movement. Claiming that the canonic Scriptures are male dominated, they claim that the Gnostic gospels give due honor and respect to women. The ancient, but heretical, *Gospel of Thomas*, has become their *Magna Carta*. Yet no one should be fooled about where it puts women. Without doubt, the concluding saying of the *Gospel of Thomas* hardly sounds a feminist note:

> Simon Peter said to them, "Let Mary leave us, for women are not worthy of life." Jesus said, **"I myself shall lead her in order to make her male,** so that she too may become a living spirit resembling you males. **For every woman who will make herself male will enter the kingdom of heaven."**[493]

---

490 Ibid., pp. 24–25.

491 See *The DaVinci Code* exposé available from www.McCowenMills.com, P.O. Box 1611, Millbrook, AL 36054, (334)285-6650.

492 Lynn Picknett and Clive Prince, *The Templar Revelation,* , plate facing p. 161.

493 James M. Robinson, ed., *The Nag Hammadi Library* (San Francisco: Harper and Row, 1988), p. 138.

In hermeticism, the cult of the goddess is developed to a high degree of sophistication. The goddess is the ideal woman with mystical powers, powers that sacramentalize eroticism. According to Dan Brown, Constantine squashed the early church's matriarchalism in favor of a "patriarchal Christianity by demonizing the sacred feminine." Is it purely coincidental that in his *Perelandra*—Lewis' science-fiction novel—that he describes Eve as a goddess and that she is the sum of truth and beauty and beyond the description of logical categories? We will let the reader decide, but here is the passage from *Perelandra*:

> There was no category in the terrestrial mind which would fit her. Opposites met in her and were fused in a fashion for which we have no images. One way of putting it would be to say that neither our sacred nor our profane art could make her portrait. Beautiful, naked, shameless, young—**she was obviously a goddess:** but then the face, the face so calm that it escaped insipidity by the very concentration of its mildness, the face that was like the sudden coldness and stillness of a church when we enter it from a hot street—**that made her a Madonna.** The alert, inner silence which looked out from those eyes overawed him; yet at any moment she might laugh like a child, or run like Artemis or dance like a Maenad.[494]

Perelandra (1943) is Lewis' second installment of his science fiction novels, the first being *Out of the Silent Planet* (1938). ReligionFacts.com explains the plot of *Perelandra*.

> After an awe-inspiring journey through space, Ransom finds himself in a warm sea surrounded by lush, green islands. He meets the Green Lady, who is the Eve figure of Venus. . . . After a long journey back to the surface, Ransom emerges into a paradise and witnesses a solemn ceremony granting Tor and Tinidril (the Green Lady) suzerainty of the planet. It is revealed

---

494   C. S. Lewis, *Perelandra* (New York: Macmillan, 1944), p. 64.

that Malacandra and Pearland (Mars and Venus) **are pure masculinity and pure femininity. . . .**[495]

Even a cursory study in early church history concerning the attacks on Christian doctrine and infiltration of dangerous teachings reveals that although the early church suffered great persecution, the majority enjoyed a high degree of purity until the emperor Constantine issued the Edict of Milan in January 313. The emperor allowed a situation to develop that resembles modern America: all people, including Christians, were free to observe the religion of their choice. In this new atmosphere of "religious liberty" and freedom of conscience, apostasy, false teachings, and cultic leaders proliferated. Mal Couch gives several examples:

+ Ebionites were humanizing disciples who brought many back under the law of Moses. They rejected what Paul taught, viewed Christ as a mere man, and used only Matthew in a mutilated form.
+ The Gnostic-like cult of Cerinthus who made a distinction between the early Jesus and the heavenly Christ. His views spread throughout Asia Minor.
+ The pseudo-Clementine homilies proclaimed that God dwelt on high in bodily form, and his spiritual image could be seen in humans here below. **The writings also speak of a feminine side to God.**[496]

Is there any warning here for Christians today? Are not the many parallels with today's religious scene a wake-up call for those who know history? Unfortunately, most people are ignorant of history and thus condemned to repeat it.

---

495 http://www.religionfacts.com/christianity/people/lewis.htm

496 Mal Couch, "Spiritual Apostasy and Doctrinal Confusion," in *Issues 2000: Evangelical Faith & Cultural Trends in the New Millennium,* Mal Couch, General Editor (Grand Rapids: Kregel, 1999), p. 131.

Sanitizing That Which Is Foul

We realize that C. S. Lewis is held in very high esteem by many evangelicals, something that is evidenced by the positive press the Narnia series is receiving. No doubt, we must be cautious in finding trends in Lewis that are not there. But others may be guilty of sanitizing that which is foul because they have gradually been desensitized and have become accustomed to the encroaching evil. In a chapter entitled "Capturing the American Mind" Erwin Lutzer and John F. DeVries tell the following story. It is indicative of how people are conned.

> A con artist in Chicago had a successful scheme that worked like this: he would contact a prospective client, assuring the man that a few hundred dollars invested in a specified business venture would double in a matter of months.
>
> The client was leery, but the sales pitch was so impressive that he decided to try it. A few hundred dollars was not much to lose.
>
> A few months later, the con man made good his promise; he returned to bring the man double his money. His extravagant claims appeared to be true.
>
> A month later the con man returned to his client with a similar promise. This time the investment was a few thousand dollars. Once again the investor returned an impressive dividend.
>
> So it went. Each time the client developed more confidence in his broker; each time the amount of money increased.
>
> Finally the happy client was willing to give his friend $50,000 with the promise of still higher profits.
>
> With that the broker disappeared.[497]

Satan too knows that a small risk brings him great dividends in confused souls. The Bible has many references to apostasy, both as a present reality, as well as a future prophecy. The apostles wrote against apostates and false teachers

---

497   Lutzer and DeVries, pp. 27–28.

bringing confusion and disharmony to the first century churches, as well as describing apostasy in the last days. Apostasy is both a present reality as well as something that will be manifest in the future. Charles Ryrie writes:

> Beyond any questions, apostasy is both present and future in the church. It was present when Paul wrote to Timothy, and Paul looked forward to a future great apostasy distinctive enough to be of the present-future antichrist. There were antichrists present in the church in John's day, and still he looked forward to the coming great Antichrist (1 John 2:18). Apostasy is something that plagues the church in every generation, though at the end of the church age the great apostasy will come on the scene before the Day of the Lord.[498]

There are many indications that apostasy is a present reality in the church, but there are also indications that we are quickly approaching the time when the end-time apostasy will be a full-blown reality.

The Bible tells us of the danger of worldliness, and tells us not to love the world:

> Love not the world, neither the things that are in the world. If any man love the world, the love of the Father is not in him. For all that is in the world, the lust of the flesh, and the lust of the eyes, and the pride of life, is not of the Father, but is of the world. And the world passeth away, and the lust thereof: but he that doeth the will of God abideth for ever.[499]

While people dress and act in a worldly manner, worldliness is more than simply the way people dress and act: **it is an attitude**.

People who think in a worldly manner are worldly. However, those who value the things that are important to people whose belief system is rooted in the world, rather than in God's truth as revealed in Scripture, are truly

---

498 Charles C. Ryrie, *Dispensationalism*, expanded ed. (Chicago: Moody, 1995), p. 140.

499 1 John 2:15–17.

worldly too. The evangelical church has departed from its biblical moorings and has become truly worldly. It has no problem in accepting paganism and Romanism into its life and worship.

The contemporary seeker-sensitive services, with their emphasis on feeling at home and casual dress, is but symptomatic of a new way of thinking. As Thomas Ice explains,

> Worldliness . . . is an organized system of ideas, concepts, attitudes, and methods that Satan uses to compete with God's view of life and how people should live on planet earth. Satan is the controller of this system of thinking. Whenever we think like the world, we are thinking just like Satan wants us to think.[500]

In his book *Who Are You To Judge? Learning to Distinguish Between Truths, Half-Truths and Lies*, Erwin W. Lutzer sounds a solemn warning about worldliness in today's churches.

> The church is to be in the world as a ship is in the ocean; but when the ocean seeps into the ship, the ship is in trouble. I fear that the evangelical ship is taking on water. The world is seeping into the church so rapidly that we might well wonder how long the vessel can stay afloat. The church, which is called to influence the world, finds herself influenced *by* the world.
>
> If we as Christ's representatives can scarcely stay afloat, how can we expect to rescue a society that is sinking around us? We have bought into the world's values; into its entertainment, its morals, its attitudes. We have also bought into its tolerance. . . .[501]

Standing Strong

It is important that we remember that there are only two systems of values,

500 Thomas Ice, "Growing Mysticism," in *Issues 2000: Evangelical Faith & Cultural Trends in the New Millennium,* Mal Couch, General Editor (Grand Rapids: Kregel, 1999), p. 54.

501 Erwin W. Lutzer, *Who Are You To Judge? Learning to Distinguish Between Truths, Half-Truths and Lies* (Chicago: Moody Press, 2002, p. 13.

ideas, and concepts. One system is that of God; the other is that of Satan. Worldliness reveals that we are under the wrong master. Those who are godly can only be so when Christ is Lord of their lives and His will and ways prevail in their lives. How can we be sure that we are not worldly and how do we guard against allowing Satan to control and direct our lives through worldliness?

First: reject the notion that little things are of little or no consequence. Both God and Satan gain great victories by using little things in our lives. Every journey begins with a few steps. The Great Commission was given to only a few poor individuals with no access to great fortunes. David fell into sin and brought grief to himself and his household after one look. Destructive forest fires frequently begin with one small spark . . . We could continue *ad infinitum*, but the point is clear. Beware when you begin to think that viewing such a movie, or reading such a book is just a small thing. It could be the spark that leads you or those you love down a dangerous path of no return.

Second: be serious about the things of God. Modern society is terribly superficial. People seem unaware of the consequences of their actions and reactions. It is as if we have a "cartoon view" of life. In cartoons no one really gets hurt. The rabbit falls off a mountain, is driven over by a huge truck and is flattened like a pancake, but suddenly the hapless rabbit pops out to his old original shape, none-the-worse for the experience.

But life is not like that. People do get hurt. Lives are ruined. Satan does influence our values—and his influence leads toward death. Jesus described him and said, "He was a murderer from the beginning, and abode not in the truth, because there is no truth in him."[502]

We have spoken in different churches, and at conferences, and have both been active in Christian work for decades. If there is one thing that characterizes all too many Christians today it is that they increasingly trivialize sin and evil. We are exposed to so much of it on television and elsewhere that we have become de-sensitized to its true nature.

Third: remember that it will be easy to be worldly, and to fall under

---

502   John 8:44.

the sway and influence of Satan. Human nature is weak and frail; even the best of Christians need to be on the alert. Paul wrote, "Let him that thinketh he standeth take heed lest he fall."[503]

We all have to make an effort to live a life that is honoring to Christ. Why? Because in order to do that we have to "swim against the current." Swimming with the current is easy and because it is easy, it is appealing. Similar in fashion to water naturally flowing down hill, people naturally follow the trends of the world. And never before have those trends been so attractive, powerful, and widespread. Never before have they been quite as deceptive.

Unfortunately, the church has not been doing its job to insulate Christians from the world's influences. Christians are becoming increasingly exposed to worldliness within the church. For example,

+ "Worship leaders" sounding eerily similar to cheerleaders have replaced godly pastors who used to preach the Word of God.
+ "Friendship evangelism" promoting personal relationships has replaced any type of confrontational soul winning.
+ Missions that once emphasized God's glory and redeeming power now focuses on meeting human social needs of underprivileged people groups.
+ Pastoral leadership is now rejected by those who want professionally trained individuals with management and psychology skills.

Should we be surprised that churches and ministries are now considered a very lucrative market by the entertainment industry? The entertainment industry has not changed; Christians have! Christians have moved ever closer to the world's standards.

Fourth: Satan never tells the whole truth. Satan is alive and active on planet earth, and he is having a field day in churches. He never tells the

---

503   1 Corinthians 10:12.

truth, but simply mixes truthful tidbits with lies in order to mask the lies. On the Mount of Temptation, Satan quoted Scripture to Jesus.[504] It would seem obvious that Satan would have used his most effective weapon against the Son of God. He simply twisted Scripture attempting to deceive Christ.

Satan also uses the same deceptive tools to effectively beguile man. He even transforms himself into something that he is not. The Bible says, "For Satan himself is transformed into an angel of light."[505] As an angel of light he presents just enough truth to ensnare the unwary soul and appear God sent.

When you add human carnality and love of fleshly indulgence to the fact that we are living in the last days, Satan has quite a foothold. Isn't it wise to stay alert? Shouldn't our first line of defense be to: "Prove all things; hold fast that which is good"?[506]

Fifth: An inability to see evil in something may be a result of the fact that worldliness is already dominating one's thinking. Once again, remember that worldliness is not simply certain acts, or ways of dressing, but that it goes back to one's value system. What we think and our values are inextricably woven together. If our thinking is wrong, our values will also be wrong.

In the book of Revelation we read: "Fear none of those things which thou shalt suffer: behold the devil shall cast some of you into prison, that ye may be tried; and ye shall have tribulation ten days; **be thou faithful unto death**, and I will give thee a crown of life."[507] Being "faithful" means to be fully convinced, that is, fully convinced that God will take care of the Christian even in the midst of the greatest of trials.

The things we purposefully allow to come into our lives should promote our faithfulness—promoting conviction in us about God and His Word. It is inconceivable for Christians to now be convinced that viewing occultic movies and reading Middle English fairy tales with the casting of spells and

---

504 Matthew 4:3–11.

505 2 Corinthians 11:14.

506 1 Thessalonians 5:21.

507 Revelation 2:10.

performing of magic is really helping one to be *faithful*.

Sixth: we don't have to perceive something to be evil for it really to be so. Wild mushrooms can be both delicious and deadly. If an individual, in all sincerity picks, cooks, and eats mushrooms that he really believes are harmless, does his ignorance cancel the effects of the poison should he make the wrong choice?

Lutzer observes that many people think that "if an occult object, game, or story is accepted as fantasy, then it is not to be feared. As long as one does not believe in the power of an Ouija board, then it is not dangerous. As long as one reads horoscopes for fun, there is nothing wrong with the practice."[508] This is simply not the case. Many times these "innocent" things are simply springboards into more advanced errors of deception.

Seventh: we win in this battle by submitting ourselves to God. The book of James says: "Submit yourselves therefore to God. Resist the devil, and he will flee from you." [509]

Due to the influence of many popular televangelist healers, many people now incorrectly believe that Satan is resisted by saying a few words, waving an object, or by using some other equally sensational gimmick. But according to Scripture the way to resist the devil is to submit oneself to God. Without this submission one has no power to resist him.

Missing Christ

A Christ-centered focus remains the key to a fruitful ministry and life and the only means of truly pleasing God. Yet most people completely miss the mark in this area allowing too many things to distract them from the object of their love and devotion. Churches and individual Christians desperately need to submit to God by completely submitting to His Son.

Yet, the increasing interest in talking about "God" and "religion" today seems to be making Christians much more evangelistically complacent. All of this talk turns out to be no more than an extremely effective satanic

---

508   E. W. Lutzer, *Who Are You To Judge?* p.175.

509   James 4:7.

smokescreen because when people are wrong about Jesus all of the talk about "God" and religion is futile.

Mark 2 reveals the story of Jesus in Capernaum. He was in the home in which He stayed, as Capernaum was His headquarters during the great Galilean ministry. A large crowd gathered, and the people kept assembling. Finally, there was no way for anyone else to enter the home. Four men brought a man "sick of the palsy"[510] meaning that the man was a paralytic. Unable to reach Jesus through conventional means, they made a hole in the roof and let the man down into the room where Jesus was teaching.

It must have been a quite a sight. In those days Middle Eastern rooftops were covered with mud, palm leaves, and straw. You can imagine the noise as Jesus was speaking to the others in the room. As the men were breaking through the roof, bits of straw, dirt, and dust were surely falling upon those in the room and filling the air. This was Jesus' response to their actions: "When Jesus saw their faith, he said unto the sick of the palsy, Son, thy sins be forgiven thee."[511]

Jesus' proclamation annoyed the religious leaders who were present. "Why doth this man speak blasphemies?" they responded. "Who can forgive sins but God only?"[512] There was nothing wrong with their view that God is the only One who can forgive sin. They were completely right about God. Yet, they were still WRONG. They were wrong about Jesus and who He was!

---

510   Mark 2:3.

511   Mark 2:5.

512   Mark 2:7.

Chapter 9

It's a Matter Of Trust

In our concluding thoughts, two questions must be answered: First, how can Lewis' works be trusted? Secondly, how can we willingly expose ourselves and those we love to the works of a writer who subtly conveyed some very dangerous teachings?

Lewis professed to be a Christian yet he used myths that are clearly pagan in origin. He concocted a hybrid religion acceptable to almost every religion in the world.

The Bible is not silent on these matters. In order to truly worship God, the truth must be of paramount importance. Jesus pointed out that the truth divides the true worshipers of God from those who simply mouth their devotion and obedience toward Him.

> But the hour cometh, and now is, when the true worshippers shall worship the Father in spirit and in truth: for the Father seeketh such to worship him. God is a spirit: and they that worship him must worship him in spirit and in truth.[513]

We may agree morally and even politically with many of those who do not proclaim salvation by grace, or the other essential elements of the truth of Scripture; however, we must constantly stand firm regarding our theological differences. We do not have permission from God to minimize doctrine, change the Bible, soften its message, or compromise on any of its wonderful

---

513   John 4:23–24.

truths. Since Lewis' messages are equally acceptable to cultists, Romanists, and liberals, are we rash in saying that C. S. Lewis is bad for your spiritual health?

As always, we must turn to the Scriptures both for insight and guidance. The Bible tells Christians not to be yoked up or connected with those who fail to proclaim the truth concerning these matters.

> Be ye not unequally yoked together with unbelievers: for what fellowship hath righteousness with unrighteousness? And what communion hath light with darkness? And what concord hath Christ with Belial? Or what part hath he that believeth with an infidel? And what agreement hath the temple of God with idols? . . .[514]

A person's answer to the previous five questions posed by the apostle Paul reveals the spiritual condition of that individual's heart. *Belial* is the personification of wickedness and ungodliness. A *concord* means to be in agreement and harmony. The Christian is to have no fellowship, communion, concord, part, or agreement with those things that are anti-Christian. The passage continues by explaining why this spiritual separation is so necessary and concludes by insisting that we are to "come out from among them" and, in fact, separate ourselves from them!

> . . . for ye are the temple of the living God; as God hath said, I will dwell in them, and walk in them; and I will be their God, and they shall be my people. **Wherefore, come out from among them, and be ye separate,** saith the Lord, and touch not the unclean thing; and I will receive you. . . .[515]

The *Passion* movie had Christians flocking to the theaters in droves. Now, C. S. Lewis has them there again, and, as of late, a supposedly truly Christian film is bringing them back once again. The film is *The End of the Spear*. Of

---

514   2 Corinthians 6:14–16.

515   2 Corinthians 6:16–17.

course, the majority of pastors are probably ignorant of the fact that the star
of the movie, Chad Allen, is a homosexual activist.[516]

How far will these evil associations take us? Should the children of light
and the children of darkness be gathering together so that each can get his
own message from these movies? How can both groups be equally satisfied?
Here's how one writer explained the Narnian phenomenon:

> The professing children of light, sitting next to the children of darkness,
> watching the movie together, and both leaving the movie theatre satis-
> fied, the one group convinced they have just seen a wonderful "Christian
> allegory," the other group knowing that they have just seen an occult
> fantasy![517]

How has this mixing come about? What strange germ has possessed believers and non-believers alike so that they now watch the same movies and
laugh at the same jokes? Is this something commendable or is it something
lamentable?

> I have given them thy word; and the world hath hated them, because **they
> are not of the world,** even as I am not of the world. I pray not that thou
> shouldest take them out of the world, but that thou shouldest **keep them
> from the evil.** They are not of the world, even as I am not of the world.
> Sanctify them through thy truth: thy word is truth. As thou hast sent me
> into the world, even so have I also sent them into the world.[518]

> Love not the world, neither the things that are in the world. If any man
> love the world, the love of the Father is not in him. For all that is in the

---

516 Jenni Parker, "Saint Defends Casting of Homosexual Actor in Christian Missionary's Story
     (1/19/06).
     www.headlines.apaepress.org/crchive/1/192006.asp

517 Shaun Wilcock, "'The Chronicles of Narnia': Occult Fantasy of a Close Roman Catholic."
     www.biblebasedministries.co.uk/indexRomeUpdate.htm

518 John 17:14–18.

world, the lust of the flesh, and the lust of the eyes, and the pride of life, is not of the Father, but is of the world. [519]

There is a story of a man who raised dogs to fight. He had two very large dogs; one was light in color, the other rather dark. He told everyone that the dark dog would beat the light dog in the next fight. The two angry dogs were put in the pit, and after about an hour of fighting, the dark dog killed the light-colored dog. People were amazed that the man knew how the fight would turn out.

"How did you now that the dark dog would beat the light dog?" someone asked.

The man said, "I fed the dark-colored dog and starved the other."

Should Christians be feeding their old nature by reading, and viewing, questionable material and starving the new man? Why not strengthen the new nature with wholesome spiritual food? We are commanded to: "... put ye on the Lord Jesus Christ, and make not provision for the flesh, to fulfill the lusts thereof."[520]

Modern Christianity is trying to be as much like the world as possible—with its music, dress and activities. Our desire to be accepted by the world has an inverse relationship to our level of spirituality. As we try harder and harder to be accepted by a world that hates our Lord, we draw closer to them and further from Christ. The apostle tells us that we are to depart from iniquity.

Nevertheless the foundation of God standeth sure, having this seal, the Lord knoweth them that are his. And, let every one that nameth the name of Christ depart form iniquity.[521]

For such an high priest became us, who is holy, harmless, undefiled, separate from sinners, and made higher than the heavens. . . . [522]

---

519   1 John 2:15–16.

520   Romans 13:14.

521   2 Timothy 2:19.

522   Hebrews 7:26.

Ye are of your father the devil, and the lusts of your father ye will do. He was a murderer from the beginning, and abode not in the truth, because there is not truth in him. When he speaketh a lie, he speaketh of his own: for he is a liar, and the father of it.[523]

There is much that is erroneous in *The Lion, the Witch and the Wardrobe*. Lewis supporters argue that there are many similarities between the suffering, death, and resurrection of Aslan the lion, and that of Jesus. Here are some of the similarities:

- Both lay down their lives to save others. By Aslan's sacrifice Edmund is spared and Narnia restored;
- Both know that their deaths are necessary, and both know of their sufferings and agony;
- Both are treated cruelly by their tormentors, but neither of them complain, protest or resist;
- Both make sure that their friends are safe and the blow falls on them alone;
- Both endure their sufferings in the sight of their friends. Mary and Mary Magdalene witness the sufferings of Christ; Susan and Lucy watch Aslan suffering helplessly.[524]

But is it biblically accurate, and theologically correct to have Aslan, a lion—an animal—represent Jesus Christ?

The answer is an emphatic "No!" Jesus became like those for whom He came to die: "Wherefore in all things it behooved him to be made like unto his **brethren**. . . ."[525] The humanity of Christ (not "the animal nature of Christ") is clearly taught in Scripture. "For unto us a child [not a "lion cub"] is born."[526]

---

523 John 8:44.

524 "Is Aslan Jesus?", www.beliefnet.com/story/180/story_18010_1.html, pp. 1–2.

525 Hebrews 2:17.

526 Isaiah 9:6.

"His visage was so marred more than any man, and his form more than the sons of men."[527] It is one thing to use allegory, but the allegory must never obscure, or distort, the truth. Aslan the lion distorts a precious biblical truth of the full deity and full humanity of Jesus Christ. The distortions will cause further confusion.

But, does the Bible ever use allegory? It sure does, but such an admission is not an endorsement of C. S. Lewis. In Galatians, Paul is speaking about the Christian's relationship to the law. He explains:

> Tell me, yet that desire to be under the law, do ye not hear the law? For it is written, that Abraham had two sons, the one by a bondmaid, the other by a freewoman. But he who was of the bondwoman was born after the flesh; but he of the freewoman was by promise. **Which things are an allegory**: for these are two covenants; the one from mount Sinai, which gendereth to bondage, which is Agar. For this Agar is mount Sinai in Arabia, and answered to Jerusalem which now is, and is in bondage with her children.[528]

In his allegory Paul does not create a make-believe world that does not exist (as in the case with Narnia), nor does he allegorize the Old Testament and deny that there ever was a man by the name of Abraham who had sons (as in the case of Replacement Theology). Paul doesn't allegorize the Old Testament at all. Rather, he uses an historical account allegorically and gives real people and events another meaning.

Lewis' Own Words on the State of Truth in the World

Lewis' final book, *The Discarded Image: An Introduction to Medieval and Renaissance Literature*, reveals his views on the inevitability that people will discard long-held beliefs, including the discarding of a biblical worldview. He concluded that when people no longer favorably view the old paradigm or

---

527   Isaiah 52:14.

528   Galatians 4:21-25.

cultural model with its beliefs and values, they simply discard it for another. Lewis wrote:

> When changes in the human mind produce a sufficient disrelish of the old Model and a sufficient hankering for some new one, phenomena to support that new one will obediently turn up. . . . Each reflects the prevalent psychology of an age almost as much as it reflects the state of that age's knowledge.[529]

Lewis' unwise declaration disregards the sobering admonition from the book of Isaiah where we are told that our thoughts and ways are not God's thoughts, nor His ways.[530] In the epilogue to *The Discarded Image* Lewis makes a rather profound prediction:

> It is not impossible that our own Model will die a violent death, ruthlessly smashed by an unprovoked assault of new facts—unprovoked as the *nova* of 1572. But I think it is more likely to change when, and because, far-reaching changes in **the mental temper of our descendants** demand that it should. The new Model will not be set up without evidence, but **the evidence will turn up when the inner need for it becomes sufficiently great**. It will be true evidence.[531]

In a sense Lewis is very prophetic. He may indeed be offering "the evidence"—in view of the warnings of Scripture—which indicate that men gravitate toward darkness rather than light. Jesus said, "And this is the condemnation, that light is come into the world, and men loved darkness rather than light, because their deeds were evil."[532] Men will naturally gravitate toward darkness.

---

529   Lewis, *Discarded Image,* pp. 221–222.

530   Isaiah 55:8–9.

531   Lewis, *Discarded Image,* pp. 222–223.

532   John 3:19.

As we come to a close, we cannot escape the haunting image of Aslan the lion, representing Jesus Christ, being sacrificed on a stone altar. Is all of this just innocent Christian entertainment, or is it something far more sinister? C. S. Lewis was a literary scholar in his own right. Yet, the uncritical acceptance of his writings and views by the vast majority of evangelicals is clearly unwarranted. When truth is mixed with error, the resulting falsehood is unacceptable to those who value truth.

Bibliography

"A Gallery: Family and Friends of C. S. Lewis," *Christian History*, Issue 7, 1997 | www.ctlibrary.com/3365

Abel, Ernest L., "Marijuana" | www.hoboes.com/html/Politics/Prohibition/Notes/Marijuana12000.html

Amazon.com reader comments for *Mere Christianity* | www.amazon.co.uk/exec/obidos/tg/stores/detail/-/books/0006280544/customer-reviews/203-0755764-5551136

American Heritage® Dictionary of the English Language, Fourth Edition (Houghton Mifflin Co., 2000)

Armstrong, Dave, "C. S. Lewis's Views on Christian Unity and Ecumenism" | http://ic.net/~erasmus/RAZ339.HTM

"Aslan Is Still on the Move," *Christianity Today*, August 6, 2001, Vol. 45, No. 10, p. 32 | www.christianitytoday.com/ct/2001/010/22.32.html

Baehr, Ted and James, *Narnia Beckons: C. S. Lewis's The Lion, the Witch, and the Wardrobe and Beyond* (Nashville: Broadman & Holman, 2005)

Baehr, Ted, "Redemptive Rendition of Narnia," December 26, 2005 | www.thenewamerican.com/artman/publish/article_2818.shtml

Ballor, Jordan, "Would C. S. Lewis Have Risked a Disney 'Nightmare'?" Acton Institute for the Study of Religion and Liberty, December 14, 2005 | www.acton.org/ppolicy/comment/article.php?article=300

Barfield, Owen, *Unancestral Voice* (Hanover: Wesleyan University Press), as quoted on website | www.owenbarfield.com/Encyclopedia_Barfieldiana/Ideas_Concepts/Reincarnation.html

"Beyond the Double Bolted Door," *Christian History*, Issue 7, 1997 | www.ctlibrary.com/3359

Biema, David Van, "How to Tell If the Lion, the Witch, and the Wardrobe Is a Christian Film," *Time*, October 3, 2005 | www.time.com/time/arts/article/0,8599,1113226,00.html

Brown, Sarah Price, "Narnia Fuels Public Fascination with Christian author C. S. Lewis" | www.ucc.org/ucnews/jan06/narnia.htm

Carey, John, "A Bully Bewitched," *The London Times*, February 11, 1990

Carter, Humphrey, ed., *The Letters of J. R. R. Tolkien* (Boston: Houghton Mifflin Co., 1981)

Chattaway, Peter T., "Comment: The Paganism of *Narnia*" | www.canadianchristianity.com/cgi-bin/na.cgi?nationalupdates/051124narnia

Chesterton, G. K., *The Everlasting Man* (San Francisco: Ignatius Press, 1993)

Christensen, Michael J., *C. S. Lewis on Scripture* (Abingdon, 1989), Appendix A

Christianity Today, October 25, 1993, as quoted in www.rapidnet.com/~jbeard/bdm/exposes/lewis/general.htm

Cloud, David, "C. S. Lewis and Evangelicals Today" | www.wayoflife.org/fbns/cslewisand.htm

Colson, Charles, "C. S. Lewis and God's Surprises," from *We Remember C. S. Lewis: Essays and Memoirs*, David Graham, ed., (Nashville: Broadman & Holman, 2001)

--- "Discerning the Trends: The Prophecy of C. S. Lewis," Breakpoint broadcast, November 29, 2004

--- *Evangelicals and Catholics Working Together: Working Towards a Common Mission* (Nelson Reference, 1995)

--- "Three Died That Day," November 21, 2003 | www.townhall.com/opinion/columns/chuckcolson/2003/11/21/170460.html

Connolly, Sean, "Animals and the Kingdom of Heaven," priest of the Diocese of East Anglia, doctoral work at the University of Oxford | www.all-creatures.org/ca/ark-194-animals.html

Coren, Michael, "The Subtle Magic of C. S. Lewis' Narnia," December 8, 2005 | www.catholic.org/featured/headline.php?ID=2827

Coulombe, Charles A., "Hermetic Imagination: The Effects of the Golden Dawn on Fantasy Literature" | www.cheetah.net/~ccoulomb/hermeticimagination.html

"C. S. Lewis (1898–1963): General Teachings/Activities" | www.rapidnet.com/~jbeard/bdm/exposes/lewis/general.htm

"C. S. Lewis on Evolution" | www.ldolphin.org/cslevol.html

Cutrer, Corrier, "Mere Marketing," *Christianity Today,* July 31, 2001 | www.christianityto-day.com/ct/2001/010/8.19.html

"Dionysus" | www.answers.com/dionysus

"Dionysus" | http://en.wikipedia.org/wiki/Dionysus

Dorsett, Lyle W., "Helen Joy Davidman (Mrs. C. S. Lewis) *1915–1960: A Portrait*" | www.cslewisinstitute.org/pages/resources/cslewis/JDavidmanProfile.php

Dulles, Cardinal Avery, "Mere Apologetics," *First Things,* June/July 2005, pp. 15–20 | www.firstthings.com/ftissues/ft0506/articles/dulles.html

Dutka, Elaine, "'The Lion, The Witch,' and the Faithful," *Los Angeles Times,* October 5, 2005 | http://pewforum.org/news/display.php?NewsID=5458

Eldred, Jody, *Changed Lives: Miracles of the Passion* (Harvest House Publishers, 2004), back cover

Encyclopedia Barfieldiana, "Anthroposophy" | www.owenbarfield.com/Encyclopedia_Barfieldiana/Ideas_Concepts/Anthroposophy.html

--- "C. S. Lewis" | www.owenbarfield.com/Encyclopedia_Barfieldiana/People/Lewis.html

--- "Reincarnation" | www.owenbarfield.com/Encyclopedia_Barfieldiana/Ideas_Concepts/Reincarnation.html

--- "Rudolph Steiner" | www.owenbarfield.com/Encyclopedia_Barfieldiana/People/Steiner.html

Fannin, Kerby F., *While Men Slept: A Biblical and Historical Account of the New Universal Christianity* (Addison, MI: Life's Resources, Inc., 2002)

Foster, Phoebe Kate, "When We're Old Enough to Read Fairy Tales Again," Part 2 of 3, December 9, 2005 | www.popmatters.com/books/features/051209-narnia-2.shtml

--- "When We're Old Enough to Read Fairy Tales Again," Part 3 of 3, December 9, 2005 | www.popmatters.com/books/features/051209-narnia-3.shtml

Giles, Jeff, "Next Stop: Narnia," *Newsweek,* November 7, 2005 | msnbc.msn.com/id/9863780/site/newsweek/

"Good Luck Pieces," California Astrology Association | www.calastrology.com/goodluck-pieces.html

Gopnik, Adam, "Prisoner of Narnia," *New Yorker,* November 21, 2005 | www.newyorker.com/critics/content/articles/051121crat_atlarge

Graham, David, "Shadowlands," from *We Remember C. S. Lewis: Essays and Memoirs,* David Graham, ed. (Nashville: Broadman & Holman, 2001).

Greeley, Andrew, "Relax, It's Only a Fairy Tale," *Chicago Sun–Times,* December 9, 2005 | www.findarticles.com/p/articles/mi_qn4155/is_20051209/ai_n15922263

Green, Roger Lancelyn, *C. S. Lewis: A Biography,* Revised Edition (Harvest Books, 1994)

Griffin, Emilie, "Lewis and Me: Through the Years with C. S. Lewis" | www.explorefaith.org/lewis/influence.html

--- "Who Is C. S. Lewis" | www.explorefaith.org/lewis/bio.html

Griffin, William, "Recommended Resources: C. S. Lewis," *Christianity History & Biography,* Issue 7, 1997 | www.ctlibrary.com/3373

--- "The Whos and Whats of *Mere Christianity*" | www.explorefaith.org/lewis/mere.html

Groen, Rick, "Weaving a Magic World of Wonder," December 9, 2005 | www.theglobeandmail.com/servlet/story/RTGAM.20051208.wxnarnia1209/BNStory/Entertainment/?query=narnia

Groothuis, Douglas, book review of *C. S. Lewis and Francic Schaeffer: Lessons for a New Century from the Most Influential Apologists of Our Time* | www.ransomfellowship.org/R_Burson.html

Houpt, Simon, "God's Blockbuster," March 12, 2005 | http://www.theglobeandmail.com/servlet/ArticleNews/TPStory/LAC/20051203/WALDEN03/TPEntertainment/Film

Houston, James, "Reminiscences of the Oxford Lewis" from *We Remember C. S. Lewis: Essays and Memoirs,* David Graham, ed. (Broadman & Holman, 2001)

Hurst, Josh, "Into the Wardrobe and Straight to Hollywood," December 5, 2005 | www.christianitytoday.com/movies/special/narnia-news.html

"The Inklings," *Christian History & Biography,* Issue 7, 1997 | www.ctlibrary.com/3364

"Is Islan Jesus?", December 16, 2005, reprinted from *101 Questions About the Chronicles of Narnia* | www.beliefnet.com/story/180/story_18010_1.html

"Is the film The Lion, the Witch and the Wardrobe faithful to C.S. Lewis' book?" | http://preview.gospelcom.net/interviews/narnia.html

Jacobs, Alan, *The Narnian: The Life and Imagination of C. S. Lewis* (New York, NY: HarperCollins, 2005)

Jasper, William F., "Discovering the World of Narnia," *The New American*, December 12, 2005

Kennedy, John W., "Southern Baptists Take Up the Mormon Challenge," *Christianity Today*, June 15, 1998

Kjos, Berit, "Narnia—Part 1: Dialectic Synthesis: Myth+Truth=Deception," December 2005 | www.cuttingedge.org/articles/db059.htm

--- "Narnia—Part 2: A Four-legged Creator of Many Worlds," December 2005 | www.cuttingedge.org/articles/db060.htm

Land, Richard, "Looking Back on the Disney Boycott," *Faith and Family Values*, July–August 2005

Lenaire, Gary, "The Other Side of Narnia: Why Many Fundamentalists Hate C. S. Lewis" | www.realityspoken.com/cslewis.htm

Lewis, C. S., *The Abolition of Man* (New York, NY: HarperCollins, 1971)

--- *The Chronicles of Narnia*, Book 1: *The Magician's Nephew* (New York, NY: HarperCollins, 1984), originally published 1956

--- *The Chronicles of Narnia*, Book 2: *The Lion, the Witch, and the Wardrobe* (New York, NY: HarperCollins, 1984), originally published 1956

--- *The Chronicles of Narnia*, Book 4: *Prince Caspian* (New York, NY: HarperCollins, 1984), originally published 1956

--- *The Chronicles of Narnia*, Book 5: *Voyage of the Dawn Trader* (New York, NY: HarperCollins, 1984), originally published 1956

--- *The Chronicles of Narnia*, Book 6: *The Silver Chair* (New York, NY: HarperCollins, 1984), originally published 1956

--- *The Chronicles of Narnia*, Book 7: *The Last Battle* (New York, NY: HarperCollins, 1984), originally published 1956

--- *The Collected Letters of C. S. Lewis*, Vol. 2 (New York, NY: HarperCollins, 2004)

--- *God in the Dock: Essays on Theology and Ethics*, Walter Hooper, ed., Trustees of the Estate of C. S. Lewis, 1970

--- *The Great Divorce* (HarperSanFrancisco, 2001)

--- *Letters to Malcom: Chiefly on Prayer* (Orlando, FL: Harcourt, 1992)

--- *Mere Christianity* (HarperSanFrancisco, 1952)

--- *Of Other Worlds: Essays and Stories* (Orlando, FL: Harcourt, 1994)

--- *The Pilgrim's Regress: An Allegorical Apology for Christianity, Reason and Romanticism* (London: Geoffrey Bless Ltd., 1992)

--- *The Problem of Pain* (New York: Harper Collins, 1996)

--- *Reflections on the Psalms* (Orlando, FL: Harcourt, 1986)

--- *Surprised by Joy: The Shape of My Early Life*, Revised Edition (Orlando, FL: Harcourt Brace & Co., 1995), front flap

--- *Till We Have Faces: A Myth Retold* (Orlando, FL: Harcourt, 1984)

--- *The World' Last Night and Other Essays* (Orlando, FL: Harcourt, 1987)

Lindskoog, Kathryn, *Journey Into Narnia* (Pasadena, CA: Hope Publishing, 1998)

Long, Karen R., "With 'Narnia,' C. S. Lewis becomes part of the culture wars," *Times–Picayune*, December 9, 2005 | www.nola.com/movies/t-p/index.ssf?/base/entertainment-0/1134109941218830.xml

Lutzer, Erwin W. and John F. DeVries, *Satan's Evangelistic Strategy for the New Age* (Wheaton, IL: SP Publications, 1989)

MacDonald, G. Jeffrey, "Christians battle over 'Narnia,'" *The Christian Science Monitor*, December 8, 2005 | www.csmonitor.com/2005/1208/p14s03-lire.html

Machen, J. Gresham, *The Christian View of Man*, (London: Banner of Truth Trust, 1965, originally published in 1937)

Markos, Louis A., "Myth Matters," *Christianity Today*, April 23, 2001, Vol. 45, No. 6, p. 32 | www.christianitytoday.com/ct/2001/006/1.32.html

Meyers, Jim, "Disney's 'Narnia': Christ Need Not Apply," December 9, 2005 | www.newsmax.com/archives/articles/2005/12/8/204407.shtml

Miller, Lisa, "A Man and His Myths: The Creator of Narnia Was a Scholar, a Drinker—and a Believer, *Newsweek*, November 7, 2005 | www.msnbc.msn.com/id/9863783/site/newsweek/

Mikita, Carole, "Faiths Come Together for Premier of 'Chronicles of Narnia,'" November 29, 2005 | www.ksl.com/?nid=148&sid=133602

Moll, Rob, "C. S. Lewis, the Sneaky Pagan," June 28, 2004 | www.christianitytoday.com/ct/2004/126/12.0.html

Morgan, Christopher, "Narnia's Lion Really Is Jesus," December 4, 2005 | www.timesonline.co.uk/article/0,,2087-1903338,00.html

Moring, Mark, "Narnia Comes to Life," *Christianity Today,* November 1, 2005 | www.christianitytoday.com/movies/interviews/douglasgresham2.html

--- "The Man Behind the Wardrobe," October 31, 2005 | www.christianitytoday.com/movies/interviews/douglasgresham.html

Mueller, Steven P., "Beyond Mere Christianity: An Assessment of C. S. Lewis," Christian Research Institute, December 20, 2005 | www.equip.org/free/JAL400.htm

Murty, Govindini and Jason Apuzzo, "'Narnia' a Classic Tale of the Ages," *Newsmax,* December 9, 2005 | www.newsmax.com/archives/articles/2005/12/8/230129.shtml

Nelson, Dale, "Barfield Scholarship: Legacy of the Second Friend" | www.owenbarfield.com/Barfield_Scholarship/Nelson.htm

--- "The Inklings: Lewis, Tolkien, Williams and Barfield Explore Theosophy and Reincarnation" | www.crossroad.to/Quotes/spirituality/tolkien-lewis.htm

Nesbit, E., *The Story of the Amulet* (New York, NY: Penguin Books, 1996)

Neven, Tom, "The Passion of the Christ," *Focus on the Family* | www.family.org/fofmag/cl/a0029428.cfm

Olasky, Marvin, "Off With His Head," *World Magazine,* June 16, 2001, Vol. 16, No. 2 | www.worldmag.com/articles/5075

Olsen, Ted, "Apologetics: C. S. Lewis," *Christianity Today,* January 1, 2000

Overstreet, Jeffrey, "The Chronicles of Narnia: The Lion, the Witch, and the Wardrobe," *Christianity Today,* December 8, 2005 | www.christianitytoday.com/movies/reviews/lionwitchwardrobe.html

Passantino, Gretchen, "Are We Destined To Be Gods and Goddesses? Does C. S. Lewis Defend Mormonism's 'Progression to Godhood'?" *Cornerstone Magazine,* Issue 119 | www.cornerstonemag.com/pages/show_page.asp?423

Packer, J. I., "Still Surprised by Lewis: Why this nonevangelical Oxford don has become our patron saint," *Christianity Today,* September 7, 1998 | www.ctlibrary.com/ct/1998/september7/8ta054.html

"Queen of Heaven: The Life and Times of Mary Magdalene," Vol. 3 | www.marymagdalene.ca/03_0150.htm

"Rick Warren Brings New Dimension to C. S. Lewis Summer Institute," June 24, 2005 | http://biz.yahoo.com/pz/050624/80515.html

Riss, Richard M., "Is Christianity the Only True Religion?" | www.grmi.org/renewal/Richard_Riss/evidences2/26onl.html

Robbins, John W., "Did C. S. Lewis Go to Heaven?", www.trinityfoundation.org/journal/php?id=103

Sandor, Richard, M.D., "C.S. Lewis: The Life, Love, and Influence of the Man Behind the Wardrobe" | www.explorefaith.org/lewis/screwtape.html

Sayer, George, "C. S. Lewis and Adultery" from *We Remember C. S. Lewis: Essays and Memoirs*, David Graham, ed., (Nashville: Broadman & Holman, 2001)

Sheske, Eric, "C. S. Lewis and the Tao," March 2, 2005 | www.catholicexchange.com/vm/index.asp?vm_id=1&art_id=27704

Sienkiewicz, Henryk, translated by W. S. Kuniczak, *Quo Vadis* (New York, NY: Hippocrene, 2002)

"Silenus" | http://en.wikipedia.org/wiki/Silenus

Skinner, Andrew C. and Robert L. Millet, book review of *C. S. Lewis: The Man and His Message*, December 26, 2005 | http://deseretbook.com/store/reviews?sku=3826168

Smietana, Bob, "C. S. Lewis Superstar," *Christianity Today*, December 2005, Vol. 49, No. 12, p. 28 | www.christianitytoday.com/ct/2005/012/9.28.html

Smithouser, Bob and Steven Isaac with Tom Neven, "The Passion of the Christ" | www.pluggedinonline.com/movies/movies/a0001657.cfm

"Sojourners" | www.answers.com/Sojourners

Sprague, Duncan, "The Unfundamental C. S. Lewis: Key Components of Lewis's View of Scripture," *Mars Hill Review*, May 2, 1995, Vol. 2, pp. 53–63 | www.leaderu.com/marshill/mhr02/lewis1.html

Starhawk, "How Narnia Made Me a Witch," December 16, 2006 | www.beliefnet.com/story/179/story_17993_1.html

Stauffer, Douglas D., *Harry Potter: Innocent Entertainment or Darkness Disguised* (Millbrook: AL: McCowen Mills Publishers, 2001), DVD

Steuver, Hank, "Unmentionable No Longer: What Do Mormons Wear? A Polite Smile, if Asked About 'the Garment,'" *Washington Post*, February 26, 2000 | www.hankstuever.com/mormon.html

Thomas, Damian, *At Home in Narnia*, December 4, 2005 | www.theage.com.au/news/books/at-home-in-narnia/2005/12/03/1133422143366.html

Tolson, Jay, "God's Storyteller: The curious life and prodigious influence of C. S. Lewis, the man behind 'The Chronicles of Narnia,'" *U.S. News & World Report*, December 12, 2005

Townsend, James, "C. S. Lewis's Theology: Somewhere Between Ransom and Reepicheep" | www.faithalone.org/journal/2000i/townsend2000e.htm

Trexler, Robert and Jennifer Trafton "Did You Know? Interesting and Unusual Facts About C. S. Lewis," *Christian History & Biography,* Issue 88, Summer 2005, Vol. XXIV, No. 4, p. 2 | /www.ctlibrary.com/33346

"Turkish Delight" | www.tulumba.com

Vanauken, Sheldon, *A Severe Mercy* (New York, NY: HarperCollins, 1987)

Walvoord, John F., *Armageddon: Oil and the Middle East Crisis* (Grand Rapids: Zondervan, 1974)

Willcock, Shaun, "The Chronicles of Narnia: Occult Fantasy of a Closet Roman Catholic" | www.biblebasedministries.co.uk/indexRomeUpdate.htm

Wooding, Dan, ASSIST Ministries, "Absolutely Thrilling! Disney's Chronicles of Narnia", November 15, 2005 | www.assistnews.net/STORIES/2005/s05110091.htm

Woodward, Joe, "De-Fanging C. S. Lewis: Will New Narnia Books Lose the Religion?" | www.catholiceducation.org/articles/arts/al0103.html

Wright, Greg and Jenn, "Christians and Mormons Together," November 29, 2005 | www.hollywoodjesus.com/comments/narnianews/2005/11/christians-and-mormons-together.html

Yungen, Ray, *A Time of Departing: How a universal spirituality is changing the face of Christianity* (Silverton, OR: Lighthouse Trails Publishing, 2002)

Stephanie Zacharek, "The Chronicles of Narnia: The Lion, the Witch, and the Wardrobe" | http://dir.salon.com/story/ent/movies/review/2005/12/09/narnia/index_np.html

Zakula, Jeff, "C. S. Lewis Errata?" | www.keepersofthefaith.com/BookReviews/comment-display.asp?key=46

--- "C. S. Lewis—Who He Was & What He Wrote" | www.keepersofthefaith.com/BookReviews/BookReviewDisplay.asp?key=4

Author Bio

Douglas Stauffer

Author Bio

Larry Spargimino